JAPAN

The Blighted Blossom

Also by the author:

CHINA: THE AWAKENING GIANT *(McGraw-Hill)*

ROY THOMAS

Japan

THE BLIGHTED BLOSSOM

New Star Books
Vancouver, Canada

First printing May 1989
1   2   3   4   5   93   92   91   90   89

Canadian Cataloguing in Publication Data

Thomas, Roy, 1922–
Japan, the blighted blossom

Includes bibliographical references and index.
ISBN 0-919573-86-X
1. Japan – Social conditions – 1945–
2. Japan – Politics and government – 1945–
3. Japan – Economic conditions – 1945–
I. Title.
HN723.5.T48 1989   952.04   C89-091126-6

This book is published with assistance from the Canada Council.

Printed and bound in Canada
by Gagné Printing Ltd., Louiseville, Québec

New Star Books Ltd.
2504 York Avenue
Vancouver, B.C.
Canada   V6K 1E3

For Keiko

CONTENTS

The cherry is a king among flowers, as the samurai *is a king among men. But the blossom's life is short, as is the* samurai's.

So goes the Japanese folk saying. Brief, too, may be the lifespan of Japan's democracy.

PREFACE

*In terms of communication, Japan is like
the black hole of the universe. It receives signals
but does not emit them.*
TADAO UMASEO, Japanese intellectual, 1986[1]

Japan is at a crucial turning point in its history. Will it make progress toward greater democracy, or will it return to authoritarianism or even militarism? Many Japanese, whose voices we do not hear in the West, have a deep concern about the current course of Japan. We too should be concerned.

When they first arrive in Japan, foreigners are often sufficiently naive to believe in the conventional and rather idealistic image of the nation. The Japanese ruling elites go to considerable lengths to perpetuate the picture of Japanese life by ignoring many of its unpleasant aspects.

Some Japanese admit to this subterfuge. One observer has said of his fellow countrymen that they are among the easiest people to get along with when it doesn't matter whether you understand them; the most difficult when it really matters.[2] It is a paradox which extends to Japan as a country as well.

This reserve is particularly true of the upper echelons of Japanese society. The Japanese elites are uncomfortable with the idea that they might actually be understood by outsiders. Yet the argument they use to rationalize their isolation is that the uniqueness of being Japanese cannot, by definition, be grasped by foreigners. Thus, when the elites speak of "mutual understanding," they refer to outsiders' accepting the picture of Japan as presented by the Japanese.[3]

Myth-making is neither new, nor peculiar to Japan. In the modern era, rulers of many rising and expanding states have invented traditions to unite their people and to create an image for the outside world. In the case of Japan, however, outsiders have also fostered the myths. The West admired Japan during its war with Russia in 1905, and praised the Japanese for their pluck, heroism and unquenchable patriotism, not to mention their amiable dispositions. But only three decades later, during the 1930s, the West made an abrupt about-face, condemning the imperialist power. The judgment had reversed; only the simplification remained.

Even in the 1980s, "Japan-watching" rarely looks behind a few widely held myths. The Japanese are usually depicted as stoic workaholics, products of a rigid, ordered society which has made them, depending on your viewpoint, superhuman or monstrous. Their society is viewed as a unified, compact and homogenous whole, built on values of group loyalty, consensus and service to country. But Japan is actually a nation where strong elites and a rigid categorization of social classes is imposed upon a vibrant, diverse people.

The modern Japanese state grew out of military defeat and the collapse of the authoritarian regime. The old state was swept aside, and the new Japanese democracy was laid over the old social and class structure. Within this contradiction – the new style democracy and the old ways – Japanese authoritarianism still resides.

Rapid economic growth and the ideology of social harmony have allowed Japanese democracy to survive, if not thrive, against ultraconservative, nationalist and militarist factions. Between these forces remains the dilemma of Japanese democracy.

The book grows out of the author's first-hand knowledge of Japan, spanning 25 years. I first visited the country in 1962, and lived with a Japanese family in an isolated village on the island of Honshu. I returned numerous times since and have lived on all four major islands of the archipelago. I also attended one of Japan's greatest universities, Waseda, and have had ample time to study the people and their culture. Among my friends, two, in particular, should be mentioned, Keiko Higuchi and Yukiji Hachisuka. They did much to make my life in Japan so enjoyable. Through them I met and lived with their families and met their friends – many of whom became my friends too.

Many scholars gave me encouragement. Professor John F. Howes of the University of British Columbia read and discussed my manuscript and opened doors for me in Japan. In preparation of the manuscript I also owe thanks to a Japanese friend, Dr. Yoshifuso Ito of Nagoya University, as well as to Professor T.E. Vadney of the University of Manitoba, and to Dr. Ian McClymont. Further, Hiroaki Kato, now of the Osaka University of Economics, assisted in the early stages of the manuscript. And Keiko Sueuchi helped solve some of the subtleties of the Japanese tongue.

The final responsibility for the book is mine alone. Indeed, the interpretation of views expressed may be at variance with some of those whose help I acknowledge.

Lastly, I would like to thank those without whom the book might not have been completed: Carolyn Brown, David Leadbeater, Mary Powell, Greg Albo, Pam Mitchell and John and Ann Jackson. As well, I would like to thank Lanny Beckman of New Star and Iradj Bagherzade of I.B. Tauris for their editorial support in seeing the book through to print. Not least are those on the staff of the National Library of Canada whose help made my research on this side of the Pacific a pleasure.

1
RULE BY THE FEW

*The binding of the people's freedom was
exactly like being entangled in a spider's web.
In general, the people had to be savaged and stultified
to live under such a system.*
COUNT SHIGENOBU OKUMA, 1895[1]

*This clannish and clandestine combination of bosses,
hoodlums and racketeers is the greatest threat to
American democratic aims in Japan.*
COLONEL CHARLES L. KADES, a member of the Allied Headquarters
in Japan, 1947[2]

Government by Corrupt Bargain

Of all feudal states which survived into the nineteenth century,
Japan was the harshest. Crucifixion, dismemberment and boiling
alive all remained in the criminal code until 1867 and the Meiji
Restoration.

The Tokugawa Shoguns, the feudal lords, controlled Japan for
over two centuries, from 1603 until 1867. For much of this time,
1640 to 1858, all Westerners save a handful of Dutch merchants
were ousted. The issue revolved around the struggle of Western
missionaries to Christianize Japan, and came to a head with the
arrival of the Dutch in 1609. The Dutch were soon in conflict
with the Portuguese Catholics who had set up missions a century
earlier. The Shogun, Ieyasu Tokugawa, resolved the issue by
expelling all foreigners, except for the merchants of the Dutch
East India Company, who were confined to the artificial islet of
Deshima in the Nagasaki harbour. The subsequent two centuries

1

of isolation from the West became known as the Seclusion. Its great achievements were the enforcement of peace and the spread of literacy, but it had little else to commend it. The four major classes, the lords or *daimyo*, the warriors or *samurai*, the peasants, and the merchants each had distinctive laws. There was no escape, no city state where the peasants could hide and gain freedom as in Europe. Dissension was rife, but not strong enough to overthrow the old order. It was left to foreign imperialism to hasten its collapse.

Feudalism had outlived its usefulness in Japan. By the late feudal period, the warrior class had lost much of its reason for being: the country was at peace, and had been safe from foreign invasion for nearly 200 years. The warriors' disillusionment was fuelled by the Shoguns' failure to deal with foreign imperialism. Ironically, peace and superior education had turned the *samurai* into willing and able rebels.

The civil war between the feudal lords and the rebels in 1867 lasted only a few months. The new *samurai* leaders soon had to face the problem of national unity. They sought a figurehead around which the country could unite, and found it in the form of the emperor, a position which had existed but had played little part within the Shogunate.

After the defeat of feudalism, much remained the same. The emperor system and the traditional family and social institutions were carried on, although the formal class system was abolished. The emperor was proclaimed a deity; his reign was called Meiji or "Enlightenment," although the enlightenment was short-lived. Apart from a period of worshipping things Western, there was little intellectual ferment and life quickly returned to feudal patterns. The term Restoration was used by the new rulers to represent the return of the emperor to his proper place. In reality, the term was used to give the regime a sense of historical continuity and lend legitimacy to the new rulers.

However, these oligarchs proved as reactionary as their feudal predecessors. In fact, the aristocratic and paternalistic style of governing was strengthened by the belief that autocracy was necessary to strengthen Japan and to keep it from sinking to the ranks of a colonial country.[3]

The story of the United States' Commodore Perry, who first successfully landed in Japan in July 1853, is fairly well known. Perry was but one foreigner to land during this period, but his actions launched the first of many unequal economic treaties. Formal diplomatic relations were soon established, and two ports "opened up" for trade. The Europeans quickly followed suit. In turn, Holland, Russia, Britain and France forced harsh terms on Japan. That the nation was able to escape the fate of China was due to the unity and strength of the rebel leadership. The threat of foreign imperialism – always near – accelerated the transformation of Japan into an industrial state.

The new oligarchy understood the need for foreign technology and administrative skills, and officials were sent abroad to gain this knowledge. Because of the speed with which Japan had to build an up-to-date defence force, to create industry, and to fashion a suitable educational system, these important changes were accomplished by a small group of autocrats.

Hirobumi Ito was typical of these new men. One of his first tasks was to create a government bureaucracy from his own *samurai* class. In 1871, 87 per cent of the officials in the nine ministries of the central government were *samurai*; in 1880, they constituted 80 per cent of all officialdom.[4] All of the new recruits were sent to Tokyo Imperial University's Faculty of Law, training which ensured the perpetuation of a particular elite. These men came to be regarded as the cream of society – not because of their academic excellence alone, but because they were considered servants of the emperor rather than employees of the people. Thus was born one of the most powerful bureaucracies in the modern world.

Ito, apart from presiding over its birth, also "authored" Japan's charter. The Meiji Constitution of 1889 was a carefully formulated justification for a government in which the ruling clique had only minimal responsibility to the people. As befitted an authoritarian state, Japan's Constitution was based on the Prussian model. It was not designed with political parties in mind. Ito regarded them as dangerous.

The charter incorporated a "Diet," or parliament, which was bicameral: the House of Representatives was intended to speak for the interests of the propertied class, as was the practice at the time, and was given further qualified powers which it shared equally with an aristocratic House of Peers. The latter House was not elected, nor could it be dissolved; the cabinet, or Privy Council, was made up of imperial appointees, and the premier was chosen by the emperor on the advice of the *Genro*, or elder statesmen. Thus cabinets had little power: even with large majorities, they could be easily controlled. In fact, the distribution of political powers formed a hierarchy with no top.

Forty-one cabinets were formed during the life of the Constitution. Because members were appointed and responsible to the emperor, collective responsibility in the British sense did not exist. The prime minister lacked control, for each cabinet member was under pressure from a wide array of forces, which included the Privy Council, the House of Peers, the military commands, powerful bureaucrats and ultranationalists. Thus, from the outset, modern Japan was ruled by a series of overlapping hierarchies unaccountable to the Japanese population.

Although Ito had not foreseen political parties when he designed the Constitution, a few oligarchs favoured the formation of parties. In 1890 they founded two conservative groups which were briefly united only to split again. This quasi-party system became the pattern until the Pacific War. The two parties, the *Seiyukai* and *Minseito*, were to become little more than corrupt interest groups.

Like partyism elsewhere, the party was of first importance, and principles were secondary. Patronage and private financial contributions were the means most used to achieve office. Big business continued to enjoy the closest of relations with government, as it had since the Restoration. Mitsui selected and supported one party, Mitsubishi the other. The *Japanese Advertiser* commented in 1930, "Fifteen years have passed since the *Minseito* fought an election as a government party. The system . . . almost ensures a government victory . . . by a corrupt bargain."[5] Another critic, the radical writer Sakuozo Yoshino, added:

> The party politicians work under the orders of their paymasters, the plutocrats, and these orders are obviously to serve

the interests of big business, while the little man, and particularly the farmer, is progressively impoverished.[6]

The truth of these charges during the early 1930s was recognized by the military radicals, many of peasant origin, who vented their frustrations by assassinating party and business leaders alike, starting with Prime Minister Osachi Hamaguchi on 14 November 1930.

New Entrepreneurs

Japan's "economic miracle" began even before the turn of the century, and by the mid-1930s Japanese exports in manufactured goods constituted nearly 6 per cent of the world total.[7]

The commercial community played an instrumental role in the Restoration. The government, in its haste to industrialize, built its own factories and, as soon as they became profitable, sold them to the family firms. The *zaibatsu*, as these companies were called, were thus bound to the government by obligation, an intimacy which grew closer as the *samurai* began to enter business. Some *zaibatsu* married into *samurai* families, thereby achieving the respectability denied them under feudalism. In the process, they adopted *samurai* values, which leave little room for the economic individualism and obsession with self so basic to business people elsewhere.[8]

With the beginning of the Russo-Japanese War in 1904, Japan embarked on its imperialist ventures, annexing Korea in 1910. Industrial expansion was accelerated, and huge factories arose, each serviced by a myriad of small plants and home industries. It was during this period that the foundations of the management-labour structure that survives today were well and truly laid.

The work force was divided between full-time and temporary workers, the former becoming a labour aristocracy operating within a paternalistic family atmosphere. This division undermined the rise of a labour movement. Only a handful of workers became unionized and factory legislation promising minor protection to employees was rarely enforced. In any case, it did not apply to the vast majority in the smallest shops.

Out of this regimented system grew the myth of the loyalty of Japanese workers to their employers. An American magazine editor, turned Japanologist, wrote, "Japanese workers expect their employers to be as fathers to them, and they consider it only fair to give back a child's loyalty in return."[9] In fact, Japanese management ensured its workers' loyalty by requiring them to sign loyalty oaths. One such pledge stated

I shall obey shop rules as to hours of work and wages . . . You may discharge me at any time at your convenience, or in case of improper conduct on my part.[10]

When considering job applicants, one worker complained, his company was mainly interested in whether he had any political ideas: "But if you come in and bow your head low and work like a slave they'll gladly take you."[11]

Authoritarianism

The 1930s was the decade of the military, although before that time the armed forces had never been far from centre stage. In 1910, the army had founded the Imperial Military Reserve Association with the aim of turning every male citizen into a soldier and spreading the gospel of martial values. Nationalist, imperialist and reactionary, it made common cause with the conservative peasant leaders who preached hatred of the politicians and big businessmen.[12] Its policies were much like the Nazis' before Hitler came to power. By 1936 it had three million members.

Peasant discontent was long standing in pre-war Japan, where farm families were often forced to sell their daughters to textile mills, cafes or brothels, where they became virtual slaves. If a girl attempted to escape, her father's goods were confiscated. Hate, therefore, came easily to the peasants, and the army turned this to their advantage. Politicians and their big business patrons – portrayed as glutted with profit, fed by corruption – were easy targets. But discontent had to be carefully channelled: the nationalists had a deep fear of the spread of socialist thought.

The nationalists, of course, claimed to be super-patriots and wrapped themselves in the flag. They pictured the emperor as a prisoner of the ruling classes, and the call went out for a new restoration, so that, once again, the emperor could play his proper role and guard the welfare of the peasantry.

In 1931, during the depths of the Depression and agrarian distress, the people were hurting badly. Unemployment soared. Japan was also dealt a heavy economic blow by the introduction of the Smoot-Hawley Tariff in June 1930 which raised the import duty on Japanese goods entering the United States by an average of 23 per cent. It was not entirely coincidental that the Japanese military decided to resume its war against China in September 1931. Nationalism was used to get people's minds off their economic troubles; fanatical patriotism and emperor-worship was fostered. Some men were willing to engage in political murder for the sake of the greater glory of Japan, claiming their deeds were a response to the starvation in the countryside, and corruption in the cities.

The first of these "patriotic" acts was the shooting of Finance Minister Jonnosuke Inouye, on 9 February 1932. Then, on 5 March, Takuma Dan, the Chief Director of the Mitsui firm, was murdered. The two men had very different economic policies but, to their assassins, it was sufficient that they both wielded power. The niceties of policy were of no great concern. These two attacks were climaxed by the assassination of Prime Minister Takeshi Inukai on 15 May 1932.

According to their perpetrators, the object of these murders was to "save Japan from collapse by striking at the *zaibatsu*, political parties and men around the throne." The radicals failed to seize control of the state, but succeeded in destroying whatever hope there might have been to hold back authoritarianism. A leading journal of the time noted: "As far as outward formalities are concerned, parliamentary government is still in existence in Japan, but during the past three years its prestige has dwindled considerably." It added that with Inukai's assassination "the party cabinet system was suddenly and unexpectedly suspended."[13]

In reality, it was not suspended, it had expired. The principal cause may be found in the reactionary tendency which became pronounced after the outbreak of the Manchurian incident. Despite this collapse of democratic rights, newspapers still remained free to document the rise of police control, unlike newspapers in Nazi Germany. Indeed they boasted of it. A publicly announced meeting of police superintendents, held in the autumn of 1935 in Tokyo, included a discussion of the best type of torture instruments for Japanese prisoners. A new instrument, undescribed, was also said to be under contemplation for use on women prisoners. The press printed a government release announcing that more than 59,000 prisoners had been arrested for various "dangerous thoughts" offenses during the preceding three years.[14]

Democracy

Allied wartime propaganda painted Tojo, Hitler and Mussolini with the same brush, yet the leadership principle of fascist Italy and Nazi Germany did not take root in Japan, not even in wartime. General Hideki Tojo, the most powerful figure in the army, never succeeded in controlling the navy, the bureaucracy or the Imperial Court. Tojo never became a dictator. After becoming prime minister on the eve of the Pacific war, things continued much as before. Cabinets came and went, and ministers were replaced. Many pre-war aspects of Japanese democracy survived: the cabinet remained a federation of ministries and groups, each guarding its own privileges and autonomy.[15] In many respects, the Japanese prime minister was less powerful than a Churchill or a Roosevelt because he was merely a coordinator, not a chief executive. Decisions were made only after debates among the General Staffs of the Army and Navy, cabinet ministers and palace officials. The emperor, for his part, did little more than sanction the decisions of his cabinet, as his father and grandfather had done before him. Meanwhile, the bureaucracy, as the body which carried out many of the decisions, saw its power strengthened. But even bureaucratic power was never concentrated in the hands of any one person or group. The strong loyalty of the Japanese to local leaders did not allow for unity on a large scale, so no single disciplined party was ever created. The result was a nation ruled by a coalition of military officers and bureaucrats, none of whom attained total power.

The Diet continued to sit regularly during the war and its composition remained much the same as it had been. After the dissolution of the political parties in 1940, all the members retained their seats. What emerged was a national organization called the Imperial Rule Assistance Association. It was essentially an instrument of the bureaucracy with little power of its own. On 30 April 1942 Japan became the only major belligerent, save the United States, to hold an election during the war. Admittedly, it was "supervised," but there were choices, and while opposition to Tojo was forbidden, newspapers occasionally published small criticisms.

After the fall of Saipan in July 1944, General Tojo was forced to resign. He retired to become an elder statesman, offering advice when asked, but otherwise refraining from interference. Japan remained what it had been for some years – a society which was restricted, often brutal and authoritarian, though not totalitarian.

When Japan surrendered on 14 August 1945, the Allies, or in particular, the United States, immediately advanced a plan for democratic change. Ironically, the most important decision was to use those Japanese who had opposed democracy to carry out the reforms. One such man, Shigeru Yoshida, who became prime minister, was honest enough to declare that, as far as he was concerned, reforms would either be stifled or would be overturned after the Occupation.[16]

Some days before the official surrender, leading politicians and bureaucrats, unsure of their fate, met to discuss tactics for political survival after the impending surrender. These Japanese had, throughout the war, co-operated with their own military. Now they sought ways to co-operate with the victor's forces. Their policy was to place all the blame for the war on their own armed forces – a tactic which proved so successful that only one civilian was executed as a leading war criminal.

Once the pre-war politicians had assured their physical survival, they turned to the difficult goal of achieving power. For that they needed money, so they sought out the criminal gangs, known as the *yakuza*, who had been closely allied with nationalist policies for over 50 years. The mobsters had played an active role in the anti-union activities of the 1920s, the assassinations of the '30s, and had proved their patriotism during the war by attacking pacifists and liberals.

Many gangster-nationalists had prospered during the war, including Yoshio Kodama. A pro-militarist, Kodama had served jail terms during the 1930s, including one for political assassination. He had gone to China and, under the cover of the army, had confiscated diamonds, platinum, rubies, jade and other valuables. On returning home, he used part of his fortune to finance the post-war conservative parties. As a reward, Kodama, then only 35 years old, was appointed "adviser" to Japan's first post-war cabinet under the arch-conservative Prime Minister Prince Higashikuni, whom even the emperor's advisers regarded as "too reactionary." Thus began a long and congenial relationship with the conservative leadership which lasted until Kodama's death on 17 January 1984. During this time he was to serve as a link between the *yakuza* and the interests of the Japanese and the United States.[17]

But the huge sums necessary to reorganize the conservative parties could not be raised by war profiteers alone. In this respect, Japan's economic collapse and near mass starvation of 1945 proved a blessing in disguise. The government diverted huge quantities of war surplus and U.S. aid onto an active black market, and the profits helped keep the conservatives in power.[18]

Yet all the money in the world could not have guaranteed the continuity of conservative rule if the Occupation forces had not wanted it. Fortunately for the Japanese elite, the Occupation headquarters, named SCAP (Supreme Commander for the Allied Powers), included people of varying views. They ranged from left-leaning New Dealers to extreme right wingers, the whole lot presided over by General MacArthur, a man of undoubted gifts: aloof, unapproachable and possessed of a monumental ego.

MacArthur appeared to have a romantic notion of the nation he ruled. The Japanese, in his view, had evolved a feudalistic system of totalitarianism right out of mythology – but one which produced results.[19]

The new Japanese Constitution, signed in 1947, was the embodiment of his vision, and its democratic values can be measured by the intensity of the opposition to it. But the opposition was soon quieted by MacArthur's tough stand. He stunned the old guard by asserting that the Constitution was the only opportunity for the conservative group to retain power.

> I cannot emphasize too strongly that the acceptance of the draft constitution is your only hope for survival.[20]

Under the 1947 Constitution, the Diet is the highest organ of state power and the cabinet should, as is the British custom, be responsible to it. Because a modified role for the emperor was ensured in the new Constitution, its definition of people's fundamental rights was grudgingly accepted by the conservatives.

The most controversial part of the Constitution is the anti-war clause, Article IX. Its inclusion was not, as has sometimes been supposed, originally MacArthur's idea. The ban on war and arms had been suggested to the general by Prime Minister Kijoro Shidehara on 24 January 1946 in exchange for keeping the emperor system.[21] The clause specifies that the Japanese people forever renounce war as a sovereign right of the nation and the threat or use of force as a means of settling international disputes. To accomplish this aim, land, sea and air forces, and all other war potential, are never to be maintained, and the right of belligerency of the state is not to be recognized. With the Korean War, this clause soon became a dead letter, the United States being the first to insist on Japanese limited rearmament. All the Article really achieved was to give the right wing a basis on which to attack the whole Constitution.

Political Sabotage

We commonly equate democracy with the health of a multi-party system, yet partyism is a relatively recent phenomenon arising from the conflict among differing Western political theories. Its life has often been tenuous and not a little hazardous. The United States, and indeed most other Western democracies, still look benignly upon Japan's post-war virtually one-party rule, secure in the knowledge that the ruling group is of conservative persuasion.

During the Occupation, the Liberal and Progressive Parties were resurrected, the latter being the most conservative. During the belated purge of war criminals, the small number of wartime politicians who lost their jobs (about 16.5 per cent) included most of the Progressive Party leadership.

The political purges were a passing phase. Within three years, the "war criminals" had been re-elected to the Diet. In the meantime, their parties had regained vigour. The pre-war agricultural organizations were revived, and were used to dispense patronage to the farmers, who were grossly overrepresented in the Diet due to the pattern of electoral districts. Simultaneously, the Occupation joined the conservatives in perhaps the greatest political covert operation ever staged; its goal was to divide and discredit the left-wing opposition.[22] Among the targets were the social democrats, who had served the militarists within the Imperial Rule Assistance Association and later found their way into the Japan Socialist Party. Steps were taken to ensure that militants and communists who were already in jail would be kept there; some, indeed, died in prison after the war.

Kiyoshi Miki, an eminent philosopher, had been imprisoned during the 1930s, but was later released. He was rearrested in 1944 for harbouring an alleged communist, and died in prison in September 1945, more than one month after the end of the war.

In the wake of the Miki case, a Reuters wire service correspondent sought an interview with the home affairs minister, Iwao Yamazaki, who defended his actions:

All persons advocating ... abandonment of the imperial system will be regarded as communists and arrested under the Public Peace Preservation Law.

The interview was published on 4 October 1945 in the *Stars and Stripes*.

Personal hatreds among progressive leaders were nurtured,

and, through an adroit mixture of violence and bribery, factions were pitted against each other. The *yakuza*, who were to be so effective in later "union bashing," infiltrated the opposition and disrupted their meetings.

While the Left was subverted, the Japanese pre-war nobility continued to prosper with the support of some top American military personnel. In response to a SCAP ordinance cutting off the flow of public funds to the imperial princes, one general exclaimed:

> What do you mean by this outrageous business? Do you realize that it will compel the princes to go to work? . . . You can't do that! They're royalty.[23]

On the surface, the authorities had much to worry about. The people were hurting because of the economic slump, and black marketeering and corruption were rampant. Worst of all, elements of the working class were coming to believe they could change society. Nothing frightened the hierarchies more than the move toward worker control of factories.

In this case again, conservatives turned the protests of their opposition to their favour. Worker radicalism played into the hands of Prime Minister Shigeru Yoshida, who found sympathetic ears within SCAP when he denounced attacks on private property as virtual treason.[24] He and his circle persuaded General MacArthur to bring forward the date of the impending election. Their object was to spring a quick vote before the divided opposition could organize. The verdict was as expected. In April 1946, Shigeru Yoshida, president of the conservative Liberal Party, was returned as prime minister.

Yoshida was no democrat, but he certainly had style. He was known as "One Man," a nickname he facetiously explained as arising from his habit of barking like a dog (*wan-wan*, or "one-one") at others. Cocking a snoot at the Occupation, he continued to patronize Shinto shrines, and with a final flash of flair, he was baptized on his death-bed as "Joseph Thomas More," and buried with a Catholic service. This prompted one cartoonist to picture him ascending to heaven, wearing a kimono, with halo and wings attached, and smoking a cigar.[25]

Yoshida was to the Occupation's liking because, in 1945, he had counselled ending the war and was briefly jailed for this view. Based on that episode, SCAP portrayed Yoshida as a democrat. His earlier career, however, belied this picture. When he had served as ambassador to Italy, he had obtained its recognition of Manchuria (*Manchukuo*) as a sovereign state. In 1936, he and Nazi foreign minister von Ribbentrop signed the anti-Comintern pact allying Japan with Germany. While he was naturally reticent about the mention of such pre-war activities, he openly admitted his plan to block post-war reforms.

He called MacArthur's proposed Constitution, which deprived the emperor of formal authority, "revolutionary" and "outrageous."[26]

'Gyakkosu': The Reverse Course

General MacArthur was one of the most vocal advocates of breaking up Japan's industrial monopolies. In this, his view was more populist than conservative. He said of the *zaibatsu* that they had "so complete a monopoly as to be, in effect, a form of Socialism in private hands."[27] MacArthur's intentions caused criticism, but before this criticism would make itself felt, 28 holding companies with family control had been dissolved, and the assets of 56 individual owners of the ten leading *zaibatsu* were frozen, and their holdings and securities unloaded.

Despite this partial dissolution, Japanese industrialists were optimistic, and with reason. Indeed, the dismantling of Japan's corporate society had barely begun when American interests, organized in the so-called "Japan Lobby," used their considerable influence to oppose it. One of the key figures in the formation of this lobby was Joseph Clark Grew, who had been the United States ambassador to Japan from 1932 to 1941. Another bulwark of the lobby was General George C. Marshall, who later became the U.S. Secretary of State.[28]

In the magazine *Newsweek*, the lobby found a willing propaganda organ. Lobbyists asserted in print that the major mistake was the purge of the militarists and ultranationalists. Harry F. Kern, *Newsweek*'s foreign editor, concluded:

There is also a curious leftist and anti-capitalist tinge in the way the purge is conducted. A great many Americans in Tokyo feel that fellow travellers – or worse – in the government section have been able to infuse their ideology into the purge.[29]

Fortune magazine went further: "... the prime oddity is that General MacArthur has become the strong right arm of the leftists."

The lobby had a two-fold reason for wanting to keep things as they were. Philosophically, it favoured big business; pragmatically, it wanted a strong Japan as a bulwark against China and the USSR. Fearing to attack MacArthur directly, the lobby, through its voice in *Newsweek*, asserted that dissolution had been forced on MacArthur against military advice.[30] This misinformation was eventually exposed, but not before the group had gained its end.

General MacArthur was virtually impregnable to the Red Smear. The right wing in the United States had to be cautious when criticizing him. They joined the pre-war Japanese politicians in attacking the liberals within SCAP who, in the view of the *Mainichi Shimbun*, were "being duped by a hard core of 'Red' Americans, as well as by advice tended to them by communistic elements within the Japanese scene."[31]

SCAP's abandonment of its plan to dissolve the *zaibatsu* was but one measure signalling the end of the reformist era. Already political rights were in jeopardy and free trade unionism threatened. The press was beginning to wonder when its turn would come. The mass circulation *Asahi Shimbun* ruefully questioned,

> Is it not likely that the movement of democracy, which has seemed terrific, is nothing more than the movement of the waves on the surface of the water, and beneath the outer aspects no motion at all has been displayed?[32]

This is no overstatement, for the United States never intended to allow a social revolution. The reversal of post-war reforms had already started when MacArthur prohibited the general strike planned for 1 February 1947. The reaction of the workers can, in retrospect, be seen as political innocence, but many progressives in Japan at that time really believed the Americans were intent on promoting social democracy. Their disillusionment was total, as is evident in the observation of one socialist:

> If the strike of February 1 had been held, whatever the final outcome may have been, there is no question that the Yoshida cabinet and the forces of conservatism generally would have been seriously disturbed. The strike would also have disturbed the unconscious tendency of the people toward conservatism, and it would have shattered a wall that has not been breached since the Meiji Restoration, from the point of view both of popular psychology and history. If the strike had taken place, we would have discovered in no uncertain terms what a priceless thing is politics based on democracy.[33]

SCAP, relying perhaps on the disillusionment of the workers, recommended to Yoshida that he call another election. It was held on 25 April 1947 and its result was an unexpected and unpleasant surprise for all the authorities concerned. The Socialist Party won a plurality, gaining 26.2 per cent of the total number of seats in the Diet. Its leadership made the disastrous decision to form a government.

Tetsu Katayama became prime minister. A Christian who believed in gradual reform, he headed a coalition with the right-of-centre Democratic Party. The price for the coalition was stiff: the Democratic Party would accept only a cabinet in which the socialists were a minority. Furthermore, Katayama could include only those from the right wing of his own party in the cabinet. It was this weak government that faced a House of Representatives controlled by the conservatives, at a time when the economy was in a shambles and the workers disillusioned.

The United States then imposed measures that virtually destroyed the regime's electoral support. It forced the coalition to balance the budget, at a time of mass unemployment. It also compelled the coalition to assist business by fixing a flat base monthly wage in manufacturing. This "horribly low-wage policy," as it was called by the New York *Times*, sacrificed the working class in its eagerness to aid big business. In addition,

SCAP insisted on last-minute changes in the planned tax reform, changes which the New York *Times* claimed were "designed to place the bulk of the burden on the poor."[34] The administration was thus doomed from the start, almost as if the scenario had been written by the rightists.

The dissension which existed within Katayama's coalition came to a head. The idealists criticized the cabinet for its lack of radicalism. On 5 February 1949, when the cabinet presented a supplementary budget bill to the Diet, left-wing critics within the Socialist party made a motion to withdraw the bill. The motion was approved and Katayama had no choice: he resigned in February 1948, and a new coalition cabinet, including some Social Democrats, was formed under Hitoshi Ashida, leader of the Democratic Party. A more moderate liberal government it would be hard to imagine, yet it too ran afoul of Occupation politics.

The more liberal wing of SCAP had encouraged the social democrats in their moderate reforms, but the right wing was determined to return Japan to Yoshida-style conservatism. It had the backing of General Charles Willoughby, MacArthur's chief of military intelligence, referred to by MacArthur as "my lovable fascist."[35] This was not a mere slip of the tongue: a long-time admirer of Mussolini, Willoughby became upon retirement an adviser to Spain's fascist dictator, Franco.[36] Once posted to Japan, Willoughby recruited agents from the ultranationalist right and spent millions of yen in covert action against the centre and Left.

Willoughby's agents included men who in the normal course of events would be tried as war criminals. Just as the Americans recruited SS torturers as their agents in post-war Europe, Japanese militarists became key members of U.S. counter-intelligence. Prominent among them was Lt. General Seizo Arisue, wartime chief of Japanese military intelligence.

In September 1946, Willoughby made a speech to pre-war members of Japan's elite in which his bias became clear.

> The Japanese army has been a first rate army . . . It is accused of committing atrocities. But this is understandable when an army has its back to the wall.
>
> I know many of you are worried over the possibility of

new conflicts flaring up on Japanese soil. I want you to know that when such a conflict comes, we shall be shoulder to shoulder with you. I also want you to know that you have many friends in Headquarters.[37]

Willoughby also fiercely opposed the disarmament of Japan. His agency, working under a top secret order from the Pentagon, maintained the nucleus of the Japanese General Staff and the records of the Japanese Army and Navy, contrary to direct orders from Washington to SCAP.[38]

United States intelligence is credited with exposing the scandals within the Ashida administration that were to lead to its fall. That the Ashida scandals were exposed at all is interesting. At the time, there was a great deal of bribery, both of government and Occupation officials, although little of this was revealed. A Japanese historian accuses the rightists within SCAP of having selectively leaked the material. He claims that "if a showdown between the liberal and conservative factions within SCAP had not occurred the episode would have remained hidden."[39] What *is* known is that Willoughby used the counter-intelligence corps to infiltrate the Democratic and Socialist Parties.

Investigations showed that government officials had received bribes in return for government loans from the Showa Denko Company, a chemical manufacturer. The resulting scandals proved the last straw. The Socialist Party, which only a year and a half before had such high hopes, lay weakened and the chances of Japan developing an effective two-party system were severely curtailed.

Shigeru Yoshida returned as prime minister in 1948, and faced the electorate in January 1949. Every effort was made to ensure a conservative majority. The government pushed through a series of highly controversial election laws: one prohibited canvassing for votes, another placed severe restrictions on election meetings. SCAP issued supplementary directives aimed at limiting worker participation. The opposition's only hope lay in holding large rallies and in getting out the vote. Denied these opportunities, the decision was hardly in doubt. With Yoshida elected once more, the way was clear for continuous conservative rule.

And only a year later there occurred an event which was to further strengthen Japan's right wing – the Korean War, heralded by Yoshida as "a gift of the gods."

The war, which began in 1950, was the excuse Yoshida needed to get tough with his opponents. He hastily formed an "Un-Japanese Activities Committee" modelled on Senator Joseph McCarthy's committee in the United States. As with the congressional committee, proof of "loyalty" came to be defined in terms of political conformity. A new era of authoritarianism had fallen on Japan.

The war ended all remaining plans to break up the *zaibatsu*. Companies that had been partly disbanded were now encouraged to unite and expand. Supplying the United States military establishment became the top priority. With industrial expansion, ambitious and able men now replaced the aging pre-war *bantos* as managers. Collectively, the new business hierarchy became known as the *zaikai*. However, the revival failed to win universal approval among the Allies. Britain's representative on the Allied Control Commission observed that "A new monopoly has risen in Japanese banking," whereby "eight banks control 80 per cent of the industrial, financial and economic life of Japan."[40] The United States representative had this observation deleted from the minutes.

Criticism of the renaissance of the *zaibatsu* spread abroad. *The Times* of London noted

> that greater and greater power, economic as well as political, however, is now being made over to the Japanese, and the men who wield it show little sign that they have broken with the traditions of the commercial and militarist oligarchy, who [sic] originally committed Japan to her disastrous course of aggression.[41]

But such accusations had no effect on those who saw China as a dangerous enemy.

Following the signing of the Peace Treaty at San Francisco in 1951, the ultranationalist cause was strengthened. One of the most important developments saw the return to public life of the pre-war and wartime leaders who had been barred from public office by the Purge Program. Between October 1950 and April 1952, 210,282 mainly political leaders were freed from restrictions. Some re-entered active party politics and ran for the House of Representatives in the election of October 1952. This election was ironically characterized by bitter competition between the depurged pre-war politicians and bureaucrats, and the incumbent post-war politicians, some of whom had been colleagues in earlier years.

Yoshida called the election quickly in order to deny these recent compatriots time to organize their campaigns. In fact, the prime minister was concerned about losing his job, in view of the resurgence of the old leaders. But the conflict between Yoshida and the newly released prisoners was over power, not ideology. He did not hesitate to use militarists who were willing to serve him. A case in point was Tokutaro Kimura, who became Yoshida's powerful minister of justice. SCAP had written of Kimura in 1948, "He is undesirable for any position of power and influence over the people of Japan." In 1954, Yoshida appointed him to head the National Defence Agency, where he became known as "Japan's Joe McCarthy."[42] Kimura showed why he earned that title in a speech delivered to assorted rightists in 1952.

> There is information that the police are infiltrated by the reds, and there are many Communist Party members among the high ranking officers of the Reserve Corps ... If so, we cannot depend on the police, and there is a strong possibility the Reserve Force will become our foe.[43]

Kimura was by no means the only important old ultra-nationalist resurrected by Yoshida, but he was typical.

Yoshida's most lasting image is that of the Red Smear. He despised "liberal men of culture" (*Bunkajin*), dismissing many as anachronisms or Marxists, or both. Yet his vitriolic anti-leftist invective was more imaginative than that of the vast majority of ultrarightists. He coined a metaphor for perceived radicals.

> [They] may be likened to mermaids. Their faces suggest that they are beautiful maidens, but their bodies are like fish. Yes, they smell of fish.[44]

Yoshida won the 1952 election, but it was to be his last. By nature a dictatorial man, he had no wish to share power. It was this trait, shown in his opposition to unifying the two conservative parties, that spelled his end. Now considered expendable by the reinvigorated Right, he was gradually eased out, retiring in 1954. He had been elected five times since 1945. Now the way was clear to form a new alliance between the two conservative parties – the Liberals and the Democrats. The Liberal Democratic Party (LDP) was founded on 15 November 1955. A strong conservative coalition devoted to building a business democracy had finally been created.

The Yoshida Legacy

Political factions are peculiar to post-war Japanese politics. There were political party factions before the war, but they were mostly groups gathered for political discussion. Only after the formation of the Liberal Democratic Party in 1955 did the factions become important. Japan's conservatives encourage factionalism, and for good reason. The group concept comes easily to them, and the electoral system encourages it. Each Lower House district has from three to five seats, so a party can win a majority only if it puts up more than one candidate. When members of the same party are in political conflict, it can be difficult to work together afterwards. But the LDP, being a coalition of interests, can allow for competition, yet retain a semblance of unity.

The Liberal Democratic Party lacks a positive program; rather, it sees itself as a coalition against change and the forces of the Left. The party constitution is quite explicit. It states: "the LDP is . . . a party which is striving strictly for the elimination of pro-communist forces."[45] The LDP has no party organization as such. Local organizations take the form of *Koenkai*, individual Dietmen's support groups, loyal only to their boss.

The strength of these "parties within a party" depends primarily on the ability of each faction leader to raise money and provide services to his own supporters. As the head of each group hopes to become prime minister, the wheeling and dealing can become intense. But inasmuch as the factional chieftains become prime ministers in rotation, more or less, it is a case of "you scratch my back and I'll scratch yours."

The first priority of a Japanese politician, therefore, is to get votes away from other candidates of his own party. "The system guarantees a party split into contending factions, with no secure central authority, and [assures] conservative [results] in that radical reform is all but impossible."[46] The result is "money politics," the term the Japanese have given to the bribery and corruption that is part and parcel of the Liberal Democratic Party.

It is somewhat ironic that all of this manoeuvring is conducted to achieve the position of prime minister, which is, in fact, a weak one. The conservative prime minister of Japan is less powerful than any of his Western counterparts. He is limited in his selection of cabinet ministers and cannot dismiss them at will. He has to select his cabinet from a broad spectrum favouring those factions that supply the most money. Prime ministers also require the wholehearted backing of the other hierarchies, particularly the bureaucracy and big business. The head of government, then, is never his own man. He exercises little power, being beholden to others.

The Liberal Democratic Party is, in an important sense, a bureaucratic creation, as were its pre-war counterparts. Most prime ministers, most of the time, do as they are told. The reasons behind this rule by bureaucracy are clear. Since the LDP emerged as the virtually permanent "ruling" party in 1955, the links with the conservative civil service have grown ever closer. Control has rested, largely, with top civil servants brought in by earlier conservative parties, and with subsequent newcomers. Because there is a constant flow of bureaucrats into political leadership positions, close relations inevitably develop between leaders and their civil service deputies.

In recent years, about 25 per cent of the Liberal Democratic members of the House of Representatives have been former bureaucrats, and in the House of Councillors, the proportion is between 35 and 40 per cent. The result is a closed political-bureaucratic elite which has been called "two peas in a conservative pod."

It is hardly surprising, then, that six of the post-war prime ministers were former career civil servants, while other retired officials hold elected offices at the prefectural and national level. The Liberal Democratic Party is thus faced with pressure from bureaucrats within the civil service, and from former bureaucrats within its own inner circles. The bureaucrats can have a decisive influence because of their close ties to the corporate sector as well as to the party – prodding or cajoling one, or keeping tight rein on the other.

Japan's Think Tank

"Americans, it is said, found Japan occupied by the Japanese army, and left it occupied by the bureaucracy."[47]

As we have seen, it was a bureaucracy that had survived the war almost intact, losing only 0.9 per cent of its leadership. This compares with the purging of 70.6 per cent of the military elite, and 16.5 per cent of the politicians.[48] Thus, the civil service was in the best position to preserve the pre-war way of doing things.

Japanese bureaucrats can exert considerable pressure on politicians, because these latter depend largely on pork barrel politics to get elected. A Diet member must see that his constituency gets its full share of government funds and capital works, a largesse which is dispensed at the discretion of bureaucrats. Thus, civil servants can punish members who oppose their views by withholding or diverting funds. It has been said that cabinet ministers, more often than not, are the bureaucracy's instruments for control of the bureaucracy.

Such criticisms have been levelled at the bureaucracies in many Western countries. It is not surprising then that attacks on civil servants should be levelled by Japanese critics. One writes:

> This writer has always insisted that Japan is a democratic nation in name only, that it is actually a bureaucratic state, and that if politicians who represent the people, are ineffectual, then the roots of bureaucraticism will sink only deeper.[49]

But a civil servant's life is short. By the age of 50, a man who has reached the top echelons in a senior ministry is facing retirement. With a decade or more of a useful working life ahead, such men have experience to sell, and there are many willing buyers. These ex-bureaucrats' knowledge of government, and the prestige of their former ministries, count strongly with the electorate, making them excellent candidates for political office.

Many civil servants find congenial jobs in business. Those in the economic ministries, such as the Ministry of International Trade and Industry (MITI) and the Ministry of Finance, are tempted through promises of sinecures or of jobs upon retirement, gifts of stock, lavish entertainment and outright bribes. Over the years, the situation has so deteriorated that the Board of Audit's reports show that several billion yen, tens of millions of U.S. dollars, are misappropriated annually. Much of this missing money goes into the pockets of middle-echelon civil servants.

But the civil service is by no means in the pocket of the corporations. Some agencies, such as the Environmental Agency, are often in conflict with industry. Even the economic ministries have been known to be at variance with big business, although agreement is the norm. However, an amicable consensus is often impossible in times of economic recession. Whenever conflict arises, the ministry involved attempts to enforce its policies. Even an influential ministry such as MITI is sometimes forced to impose its will through legal channels. Occasionally, when the agency's legal authority to act is doubtful, this tactic can backfire. Even the conspiracy theorists have to admit that MITI is not omnipotent.

Early in the "Economic Miracle" era, MITI pressured Honda not to produce cars because the bureaucracy believed added competition would hurt the industry. This advice was ignored, much to the advantage of Japan's export industry. Usually, however, persuasion is successful. In response to the oil crisis of 1973-74, MITI requested all large consumers of electricity, and eleven major oil-consuming industries, to reduce consumption by 10 per cent across the board. Industry complied voluntarily with these measures despite the absence of any clear statutory authority for them. But, even after the government passed legislation, MITI continued to rely primarily upon persuasion to achieve price cuts in oil and other areas.

It is not, however, all a one-way street. On occasion, the *zaikai* make their wishes known to MITI. In 1982, it was informed by business leaders of their hope for a new law to aid industries in economic trouble. After some consultation, MITI complied.

It is true that MITI has tended to play into the hands of the mythmakers abroad by publishing propaganda that fails to show the whole picture. In May 1983, it tried to downplay its close relationship with big business in a publication entitled *Background Information on Japan's Industrial Policy*. In it, the ministry claimed that the government offered fewer subsidies and imposed milder regulations on businesses than those offered and imposed by governments of Western countries. In reality, the Japanese market is far from transparent. Agricultural production, in particular, remains a special preserve. Overall subsidies have amounted to at least 400 billion yen, or about two billion U.S. dollars, between 1976 and 1980.*

This complex web of government and corporate influence begs the question: What is the role of government in an advanced industrial society, and what changes in the role are desirable and feasible in Japan? Although Japan's government is small, it has more power in economic planning and business control than do the governments of other free enterprise countries. While its economic planning is applauded by many Western businessmen, its control over business is condemned. For example, MITI's influence over industry – far greater than the power of any ministry in the United States or Western Europe – goes against the *laissez faire* principle that less government interference in business is better. The Japanese government's role has thus fuelled the conspiracy theorists abroad, leading to the "new" image of Japan as

---

* The Japanese exchange rate was fixed at 360 yen to the U.S. dollar from 1949 to December 1971. With the arrival of flexible exchange rates in the 1970s, the yen strengthened relative to the U.S. dollar. Its value was 250 yen in early 1979, and it continued to strengthen until it reached 180 yen by the end of the year. In early 1989, the exchange rate hovered around 127 yen to the American dollar.

an "economic totalitarian society." Yet such a view ignores the conflicts within the bureaucracy, and fails to take into account the powers of other hierarchies, most particularly those of big business.

Big Business and Power

Industrialists have come to an accommodation with the ultra right wing in a number of countries. It was so in both the Germany and the Japan of the 1930s. True Japanese nationalists attacked big business to court popularity, but when the need arose they co-operated to their mutual advantage. After World War II and a short period of enforced corporate penance, the close association between the Right and the economic ruling class resumed and has remained to the present day.

A new breed of business tycoon has emerged in Japan since the war. Collectively known as the *zaikai*, it is comprised of the presidents and chairmen of the very biggest companies. The income of these men is tiny by the standards of Japan's current entrepreneurs, some of whom, like Kenji Osano, are a throwback to the robber barons whose sole interest was the pursuit of money.

Of the *zaikai*, Hideo Edo is a prototype. For nineteen years he was president of Mitsui Real Estate Company, whose development empire includes Japan's first skyscraper. Edo lives in a modest home, rises before dawn to till his garden patches, one on the roof of his garage. He does this from 5 to 7 a.m., and is at his downtown office by 8:30. He works an eleven-hour day.[50]

Edo's code of ethics is steeped in the values of big business. For example, he condemns a company official who offers false testimony in the Diet to protect himself, but he judges lying solely in the interests of his company in a different light. For him, maintaining the company's best interest is everything.[51]

The conservative politicians, while relying on the bureaucracy, are beholden to the business managers. Essentially, the politicians are the *zaikai*'s representatives in power. The selection of a prime minister is influenced by the opinions of the corporate leadership. It is no coincidence that three prime ministers were former high-level officers from the economic ministries, and that, among them, they were in office for fifteen of the LDP's first twenty years in office.

Business makes its views known through five organizations: Keidanren, Nissho, Doyukai, Nikkeiren and Sanken. Keidanren, the Federation of Economic Organizations, is the public representative of big business. It was founded in 1946 to unite management in a forum which could co-ordinate employers' interests and bring their influence to bear on policy and other important matters. Keidanren first established a close relationship with Prime Minister Yoshida, who was told, in effect, that as long as he favoured business his party would not want for money. While the big corporations have rarely had a problem making their voices heard, medium and small enterprises find the going more difficult. In response to this problem they formed Nissho, the Chambers of Commerce and Industry (C.C.I.). There are approximately 450 local chambers in Japan, which keep in close contact with local governments, city or prefectural, and lobby for business interests. The Tokyo C.C.I. acts as co-ordinator for all, and its spokesman is a powerful *zaikai* leader.

A third organization is noteworthy because it represents a post-war conscience on the part of Japanese private enterprise. The Doyukai, or the Committee for Economic Development, was established in the immediate post-war years by a handful of idealistic business people who were concerned lest Japan slip back into its former pattern of *zaibatsu* capitalism. It advocates labour representation in management and a system of co-operative administration, but its influence to date has been minimal.

A fourth group, Nikkeiren, the Japan Federation of Employers' Associations, deals with labour problems. It is so reactionary that SCAP vetoed its formation in 1946 on the grounds that it would thwart the development of free trade unions. However, SCAP had a change of heart after the Occupation clampdown on unions in 1948. At this point, SCAP found Nikkeiren could prove useful in controlling workers, so its formation was encouraged and welcomed. Nikkeiren justified this trust by demanding its members impose strict discipline on their employees.

Sanken, the Industrial Relations Study Council, is believed to be the most influential of all, although it maintains a low public profile. We do know that all of its members hold senior positions in Keidanren and Nissho. According to its founders, Sanken was established as an action committee. It is a compact council of some twenty like-minded power brokers who have the influence and the position to act quickly. It is viewed by at least one of its members as having a monopoly on political power. Some of the press agree. Founded in March 1966, it did not receive public attention until late 1970, when the *Japan Stock Journal* described it as the "Big Business GHQ," or, in the words of the *Mainichi Daily News*, as the Supreme Command of *zaikai*, ". . . a super powerful organization that 'can even buy Japan.'" The only authorities influential enough to stand up to it are the Ministries of International Trade and Industry, and of Finance.

It is clear that big business in Japan exercises greater political influence – both overt and covert – than do even the powerful industrial lobbies in the West. A senior Japanese executive put it in this way: "We do not present a petition to the party . . . we make demands on it."[52]

But Japanese employers are sometimes at odds, and rifts do appear. One clash was exposed in the *Oriental Economist* of August 1985. The problem concerned voluntary export controls, supported by the chairman of Keidanren, and opposed by executives in the export field, as well as in the automobile, communications and electronics industries. This conflict is typical; for, while the ruling elites are united in maintaining power, they are occasionally divided on important issues. Their divisions arise partly as the result of a new breed of post-war politicians and businessmen. The managing director of Keidanren, Keijiro Koyama, puts it this way:

> Big figures were once able to strike deals with political leaders on their own and make others follow, but today's leaders hear various opinions first.[53]

Certainly, the elites are very far from being the monolithic powers some fearful foreigners would have us believe them to be. However, the business community, always close to the levers of political power, has been nestling even closer to government with the 1987 election of Noboru Takeshita as party leader and prime minister. A new business support organization, inaugurated on 25 November 1987, is called *Chikuesei-Kai* – literally, a "world around Takeshita" forum.

It is shrewdly taking advantage of Takeshita's need for support, for, as Koyama admits:

> When a person becomes prime minister, he naturally needs closer ties with influential businessmen, and business leaders need to know him better. So, our mutual needs are matched.[54]

2

MONEY POLITICS

What controls politics is power,
and power lies in money.
PRIME MINISTER NOBOSUKI KISHI, c. 1956[1]

"Entertainment," gift-giving and bribery play a greater
part in business and politics in Japan than in any other
country in the world. This is a way of life which people
who want to deal with or to understand the Japanese
should keep well in mind.
KIMPEI SHIBA, "Japanese Journalist of the Year (1977)," 1979[2]

The Black Mist

Japan is one of the few nations where one is openly encouraged
to give gifts to or to entertain powerful individuals in order to
curry favour. When the bill for a few drinks and the company of
hostesses for associates can easily exceed US$2,000 an evening,
obligations mount up. However, according to the National Tax
Administration regulations, the entertainment receipts of private
companies are tax deductible, an exemption vigorously claimed
to the tune of a staggering one trillion yen, or eight billion U.S.
dollars a year.

The line between generous Japanese hospitality and outright
bribery is a fine one. It is a recognized truth that the Liberal
Democratic Party's successful reign is aided by corruption and
abetted by patronage. While we should keep in mind that political corruption is not unique to Japan, the Japanese have, perhaps, taken it furthest.

Certainly the lack of effective political opposition invites corruption. Any hope for an effective party system was destroyed during the early post-war years, when the U.S. intelligence agencies, and their Japanese agents, sought to subvert socialist opposition organizations. No fewer than ten United States intelligence agencies, military and civilian, were operating in Japan. Since 1945 they had infiltrated virtually every organization of any possible potential significance.[3] One historian has commented that this joint effort of intelligence agencies, using Japanese agents, was "perhaps the most massive and certainly the most sophisticated machine for political sabotage ever put in motion."[4] Despite its implication for Japanese democracy it was "fervently welcomed by its beneficiaries – *zaikai* potentates and their right-wing political establishment."[5]

An LDP caucus member was even more critical of the country's entrenched oligarchy:

> The worst thing possible about Japanese politics today is the fact that the same class of people who led and guided mistaken war policies of Japan from the start of the Showa period (1926 on) still continue in positions of power – overbearing in their arrogance and stubborn in their refusal to reflect upon their past. Like the suppurating roots of carious teeth, these people exude an offensive stench.[6]

Typical of this continuity is the career of Nobosuki Kishi, which demonstrates how a rightist could prosper with American blessing. A former economic czar of Manchuria, and architect of Japan's wartime economy, he joined Tojo's cabinet in October 1941, and was a co-signer of the declaration of war against the United States. He served as Industry Minister and, following Tojo's resignation in 1944, as Vice Minister of Munitions.

After the surrender, Kishi was held for three and a half years at Sugamo Prison as a Class "A" war criminal. But in 1952 he was released under a general amnesty and began a new political career during which he showed that he had lost none of his old style. It took him but five years to become prime minister, so that in thirteen short years he had moved from Tojo's war cabinet to become head of the U.S.'s most trusted ally in the Pacific.

Kishi owed his success to a coalition of ultranationalists, *yakuza*, and (indirectly) the U.S. Central Intelligence Agency. Yoshio Kodama, a fellow prisoner at Sugamo, was instrumental in Kishi's rise to power. Backed by Kodama's money and influence, he became unstoppable. Kodama had been released at the end of 1948 and had been employed by the Americans, first in military intelligence and subsquently as an agent of the CIA.[7] The extent to which Kishi was beholden to Kodama was made clear when he appointed one of Kodama's proteges, Yasuhiro Nakasone, to his cabinet. Kishi also brought into the mainstream of Japanese politics other pre-war nationalists with *yakuza* connections, including Ichiro Kono and Bamboku Ohno. Kono was a member of the Diet, a member of the LDP's inner circle, Minister of Agriculture, and supporter of the notorious Yamaguchi-gumi underworld empire.[8] Ohno, later the LDP's secretary-general, was also identified with the gangs.

Kishi was above all a survivor. He was able to stay in power for nearly eight years, one of the longest incumbencies in the nation's parliamentary history. It was a distinction he achieved by putting his administration fully in the service of business. Big business, in turn, footed the party's bills. Donations to the Liberal Democratic Party rose from 432 million yen in 1956 to almost 705 million yen in 1959. It was no wonder that the *Asahi Evening News* noted:

> It is a fact that financial circles are forced to moan. It has come to cost them huge sums of money ever since Kishi became Prime Minister. It is not difficult to presume that a considerable sum was secretly donated by individual businessmen ... It is a fact ... that the business circles strongly desire the overwhelming victory of the Liberal Democratic Party.[9]

To keep power, Kishi, like all Japanese prime ministers, needed not only money but support from all the faction leaders – enemies and allies. Kishi's third cabinet was typical. Its members were chosen, not necessarily on the basis of their allegiance to the prime minister, but of their strategic necessity. The following description of the taking of the official cabinet photograph, reveals much about the personal conflicts within the Japanese cabinet. (The names are spelled in the Japanese fashion, family names first.)

> It was midnight of 12 June, 1958 – no, it was the early morning of the 13th. In the lobby of the main entrance to the prime minister's residence, seventeen ministers, bathed in the brilliance of floodlights and dappled with flash bulbs, stood arrayed. They all wore different expressions. Among the flushed faces, the brothers Kishi Nobusuki, the prime minister, and Sato Eisaku, the finance minister, showed white teeth in irrepressible grins. But Ikeda Hayato, a minister without portfolio, Miki Takeo, the head of the Economic Planning Agency, and Nadao Hirokichi, the education minister, looked as if they had bitten into a worm and stood impatiently waiting for the ranks of photographers to break. It was a study in contrasts.
>
> That night, the brothers Kishi and Sato could not hide the smiling faces of victors. Ikeda, Miki, and Nadao were in the position of defeated generals suing for peace.[10]

The industrialists were willing to pay, just as long as Kishi was able to keep a tight rein on the factions and keep out of trouble in his handling of foreign affairs. However, things came to a head in May 1960 when the prime minister aroused wide-scale public resentment by introducing a revision of the Japan-U.S. Security Treaty.

The pact was controversial because it allowed U.S. forces to retain bases and harbour nuclear weapons in Japan. In the face of massive opposition from all those on the left, approval of the pact in the upper houses was bypassed by taking advantage of a constitutional technicality and by introducing the bill late in the session. At the same time, Kishi rammed the legislation through the lower house. He had the socialists physically thrown out of the Diet by the police, then the rump Parliament passed the revision. This savage behaviour added fuel to an already explosive situation.

On 26 May 1960, in the wake of the parliamentary fiasco, an editorial in *Asahi Shimbun* called for the resignation of Prime Minister Kishi.[11] The next day, the *Mainichi Shimbun* followed suit. To make matters worse, the government had invited U.S. President Eisenhower to Japan, a visit that was to coincide with the successful revision of the treaty. Eisenhower's visit was the final straw. Many Japanese saw it as a symbol of Japan's subservience to the United States.

In response, the public took to the streets. A series of demonstrations swept Tokyo throughout the month of June, attracting at their height more than 300,000 people from all walks of life.

On 11 June, after James C. Hagerty, the president's press secretary, had arrived to make preparations for the visit, 200,000 people took part in demonstrations in Tokyo. Fearful of the possibility of revolution, the government turned to the gangsters and the ultrarightists for help in quelling the anger of the crowds.[12] The LDP sent the head of its "Welcome Ike" committee, Tomisaburo Hashimoto, to meet the godfathers of Japan's underworld. Yoshio Kodama, the link with the mob leaders, proposed "an army" to protect the U.S. president. The plan called for the deployment of 18,000 yakuza, the common name for mobsters, supported by 20,000 rightists, to supplement the army and police.[13] As it turned out, these forces were not called upon, but the coalition remains. Units of yakuza are regularly used to harass militant workers, students, teachers and environmentalists – anybody, in fact, seen as a threat to law and order.[14]

Ultimately the public demonstrations caused Kishi to cancel Eisenhower's visit, and the resulting humiliation persuaded the bureaucracy and zaikai that it was time for Kishi to go.

But an episode about Kishi is worth recounting before his successor, Hayato Ikeda, appears on the scene. Told by one of Japan's leading journalists, Kimpei Shiba, this story gives us a peep behind the Japanese political scene at the highest level, a view rarely brought out in the open.[15] In December 1956, when Kishi announced his intention to run for president of the party, and thus become prime minister, he phoned Raita Fujiyama, one of Japan's most influential business leaders, but a very independent man of private wealth and not beholden to the zaikai. Kishi invited him to an exclusive geisha house in Akasaka, Tokyo, of the type where members of the hierarchy often meet,

and where many national decisions are made. As they dined on
sushi and other delicacies, Kishi informed the astonished
Fujiyama that his guest would ultimately become prime minister.
Kishi said he looked forward to grooming Fujiyama as his
successor as prime minister. The business leader succumbed to
the tempting offer, entered politics and set about establishing a
faction.

As Fujiyama recalls it, he received a phone call from Kishi on
1 July 1960 following the Security Treaty affair, asking him to
come to the premier's official residence. The meeting was brief.
Kishi explained that he was resigning and asked Fujiyama to run
in the election for president of the Liberal Democratic Party. He
promised him the full support of his faction.

However, at midnight two days later, Kishi phoned Fujiyama
and asked him to hurry over to his residence once more, where-
upon he asked Fujiyama to drop out because it had become necessary for him to back Finance Minister Hayato Ikeda.

The astounded and furious Fujiyama, who had already announced his candidacy, said he would be a laughing stock if he
pulled out. Kishi never explained why he had to ignore his
promise, but the reason was obvious. Fujiyama had financed
himself; he was not obligated to anyone for his political future.

With the benefit of hindsight, Fujiyama later said that not asking the *zaikai* for financial help was one of his biggest mistakes.
"An election is like a horse race," he explained. "If you have
money on a particular horse, you'd root for it to win. If *zaikai*
money was riding on me, they would have done all they could to
see that I came out the winner."

As for approaching the industrialists after he had exhausted his
own election coffers, he observed: "They never put their money
on a dead horse"[16] – a lesson Kishi had learned long before.

Kishi's successor, Hayato Ikeda, owed everything to the business aristocracy. On 23 January 1949, after only three months in
the Diet, he had been appointed Finance Minister of the third
Yoshida government, and in June 1959 the *zaikai* again saw to it
that he was promoted. This time he gained the all-important post
of Minister of International Trade and Industry (MITI) and was
subsequently elected on 14 July 1960 president of the Liberal

Democratic Party – a post that automatically led to the prime ministership.

Ikeda's attitude to the people's welfare was well known. It was while he was Finance Minister that he made his celebrated remark, "If the poor cannot eat rice, let them eat barley." This comment is matched by one he made in cabinet:

> If people stopped eating expensive fish like tuna and ate more common fare like mackerel, pike or sardines, they could cut down their living costs.[17]

All in all, Ikeda was a man who could be counted on by the Japanese authorities to pursue Japan's economic miracle with the necessary ruthlessness.

At the instigation of the business community, Ikeda put forward a program of accelerated economic expansion, a plan which was later to earn the two quite opposite foreign labels of "Creative Conservatism" from right wingers in Britain and the U.S., and "Economic Totalitarianism," particularly from the American business sector. In the plan, he promised a consumer society with a growth rate of 9 per cent starting in 1961.

Despite the program's appeal, the LDP was taking no election chances. Bamboku Ohno, then party vice president, proclaimed, "We'll win, by fair means or foul,"[18] an honest if indiscreet remark. In any case, the LDP won in 1960 and again in 1963, exercising a careful balancing of both means. It made a popular promise of stable government. This promise was kept, but not others.

A columnist remarked of Ikeda's government that it "continually reneged on its promises. Housing was a case in point. The Prime Minister was quoted as stating 'the housing problem will be solved'. But the government does nothing." The paper concluded that Ikeda would be known in later years as "the liar who said he never lied."[19]

When Ikeda was ultimately forced to resign because of illness in 1964, he was succeeded by Eisaku Sato, another ex-bureaucrat, whose power was based on the support of some 50 corporate presidents, vice presidents and board chairmen. During his term of office, the words "Black Mist" – meaning the aura of corruption – became a part of the Japanese vocabulary.

Eisaku Sato was a master manipulator. His political opponents claimed he kept a mental dossier on his fellow politicians so that he was aware of the family background and personal weaknesses of nearly every member of the Diet. This characteristic led his critics to dub him "Sato Quick Ears."

His family life was that of his generation. He married his first cousin, to whom he was engaged in high school. According to her, he treated her with "some severity." In his early years she claimed he was a "playboy."

His rise to the top was eventful. In 1954 he was accused of receiving about $56,000 in political bribes from shipbuilding executives, but was saved from prosecution by his patron, former premier Yoshida.

For nearly two years Sato's regime had fair sailing. It was only then that a major scandal rocked business, the bureaucracy and the party. In September 1966, a ranking official of the Agriculture-Forestry Ministry admitted to the House of Councillors Audit Committee that the Kyowa Seito Group – a sugar refining company – had used false receipts to get a loan from a government banking institution. High government officials were incriminated in the scandal, which involved loans amounting to seven billion yen. The forged receipts gave the impression that much smaller amounts were involved. In the Diet, the opposition peppered the LDP with other alleged cases of political corruption. As a result, the former chairman of the House Audit Committee was arrested on extortion and tax evasion charges.

One of Japan's largest dailies noted:

> The second Sato Cabinet is really a "scandal cabinet" . . .
> Many people were astonished at the decision by vice-ministers to sell state-owned land to former landowners for almost nothing . . . In fact the Sato Cabinet looks like an assembly of masters of mixing public and private affairs.[20]

Scandals became such a way of life in Sato's government that the LDP had no alternative but to admit them and go through the exercise of seeking their cause. At an extraordinary national convention of the LDP held in December 1966, then LDP Secretary-General Kakuei Tanaka concluded that the party's misfortunes were due to having been in power for twenty years

and "taking the easy way out." Many thought this comment galling, coming, as it did, from a politician who was not known as a
paragon of purity. One opposition member analysed Tanaka as
"probably a cross between the old-fashioned boss-type and the
big time gangster and racketeer type. Neither of these types has
an independent political spirit, and both are directly involved in
special interest."[21]

Both views have their truths, but to give the conservative
politicians the benefit of the doubt, most of the proceeds from
their financial dealings go back into the LDP's faction system to
make it work. Even their conspicuous spending is aimed toward
that end.

During this period, the newspapers began to print an increasing number of letters to the editor violently attacking the LDP.
The tone of the prose was direct: "The Conservative party is
rotten and full of pus."[22] Abroad, there was equal concern, although the language was less colourful. *The Times* of London, in
an article entitled "Roots of Democracy Still Weak," concluded
"that democracy in Japan is still too tentative a growth for one to
be sure it will survive this soiling ground."[23]

Sato ultimately quit in 1972 in an atmosphere of mistrust and
dissatisfaction. The leaders of two LDP factions, Takeo Fukuda
and Kakuei Tanaka, each sought to become his successor. Both
had been Sato supporters but Tanaka had carefully cultivated an
image independent from the old school politicians. His slogan,
"Let's turn the flow of the tide," was widely touted as a contributing factor to his victory. But the real reason he won was bribery. The *Sankei Shimbun*, a paper which supported the Liberal
Democratic Party, claimed that the candidates were buying votes
at 30 million yen each. As Tanaka's faction had the most money,
the outcome was never in doubt.

After fifteen years of unbroken corruption under three
successive ex-bureaucrat prime ministers – Kishi, Ikeda, and
Sato – the press portrayed Tanaka as "a youthful breath of fresh
air, a man of youth and action."

Tanaka: A Breath of Fresh Air

The youngest prime minister since the end of World War II was something of a folk hero. He was a self-made man who had never gone to any university. In the words of one Japanese observer, "This is the image which appealed to the people of Japan, trapped in the web of administered society, alienated from each other and filled with frustrations. They greeted Tanaka with a rousing cheer."[24] But Tanaka had no illusions; he once said: "I have nothing to be proud of. I have neither educational background nor authoritative post. The only thing I can rely on is money."[25]

Tanaka always had an eye for money. In 1942 he married a divorcee, Sakamoto Hana, seven years his elder and the daughter of a well-to-do construction company owner. At the time of his marriage, his 30-year-old wife extracted several promises from him. Foremost, that he was never to throw her out, and second never to kick her.[26] As far as is known he has lived up to both promises. Some years after his marriage Tanaka inherited his father-in-law's business and renamed it Tanaka Construction. He was soon well established with many helpful connections.

Tanaka's financial success story began, however, in 1945, when he was sent to relocate a major machinery factory in Korea so that it would escape Allied bombing. When the war ended, he held large government deposits of money, which, in the post-war confusion, he never had to account for. In 1947, he ran for public office.

Above all, Tanaka saw that money was the key to politics. He promised the local farmers schools, highways, and reclamation projects in return for their votes, and then made good on these promises.[27] He continued to use wealth to buy the votes of his electors in Niigata Prefecture.

A year after his election to the Diet, Tanaka was arrested for bribery for the first time in connection with the social democratic government's scheme of 1948 to nationalize the coal mines. He was convicted of accepting one million yen from the mine owners to vote against the scheme.[28] Tanaka had to run his first re-election campaign from jail. It is fair to point out, however, that numerous contemporary Japanese politicians have had brushes with the bribery laws, including Eisaku Sato and Hayato Ikeda, both during the shipbuilding scandal of 1954. (Other Japanese leaders at the time were under indictment for having accepted bribes in the more important Showa Denko scandal, including Prime Minister Hitoshi Ashida and Budget Bureau director Takeo Fukuda, Tanaka's great rival in later years.)

Tanaka gained his reputation for competence and laid the foundation for his fortune as Minister of Finance during the early 1960s. His brilliant grasp of detail later earned him the nickname "computerized bulldozer." As Finance Minister, Tanaka was in charge of government subsidies to local governments, and of expenditures for virtually all public works throughout the nation.

In recognition of Tanaka's abilities, the party made him secretary-general from July 1965 to December 1966. The secretary-general is described as "the prime minister's boy." His recollections about the post, published in the *Sankei Shimbun* of 9 December 1966, tell us something of the man, and how he was able to gain influence on a wide scale.

> Looking back, I can best describe the post of secretary general as a traffic cop standing at a crossroad with no signal light trying to direct a flood of trucks and pedestrians. If the people and problems steadily pushing in on you are not taken care of with dispatch, everything soon comes to a standstill.
>
> I had to set a schedule. But politicians, scholars, labour leaders, company officials – every sort of person from every occupation and station – would appear without warning and lecture, argue, cajole, and demand.[29]

Tanaka became prime minister in 1972 partly because of his undoubted competence and partly because he had more money to buy votes than did his rivals. He was thus able to gain the support of the conservative faction led by Yasuhiro Nakasone, a young, able ex-naval officer and, then as later, a darling of the extreme Right. His faction, although small, held the balance of votes. Tanaka rewarded Nakasone with the plum Ministry of International Trade and Industry portfolio. It was the first step on the political ladder for this ambitious young star. A decade later it was to be Tanaka's support that would enable Nakasone to become prime minister. Thus the debt was repaid.

Tanaka's first act as prime minister was to present his grand design, entitled *Remodelling the Japanese Archipelago*, in which he aimed to spread industry throughout the major islands. It was a grandiose, far-reaching scheme, with Tanaka's stamp all over it, but the way that it was carried out benefited mainly the land speculators, corporations, politicians, and not least, Tanaka himself. Scandals and conflicts soon arose. An early one involved land sales around Shibushi Bay, at the southern tip of Kyushu, where the value of real estate increased ten-fold after the plan was unveiled.

Another case occurred in the village of Rokkasho in a sparsely populated section of northern Honshu. Tanaka cited the village as ideal for a giant, new industrial complex. As he forecast it, Rokkasho, with a population of 13,639, would become a "model city" of 150,000 by 1985. It would boast its own petrochemical complex, oil refineries, steel works, nuclear power station and harbour. Rokkasho's citizens were deluged by real estate speculators, and land values skyrocketed. The reaction was much the same as it would be anywhere. Villagers attacked each other; families became divided between those who sought a quick profit and others who wished to preserve their rural way of life.

Kokichi Kawamura, a journalist who knew the area well, pointed out, "These people have suffered so many hardships that they see this chance to make money as their first real break. They don't want to think about the long-term disadvantages."[30]

The resulting conflict was labelled the "Battle of Rokkasho Village," but its only winners were the big conglomerates and Tanaka and his friends, who knew which industries were to be located, and where.

The *zaikai*, with their widespread holdings in real estate, looked to make huge profits and were hardly in a position to complain at this stage. Tanaka, believing he had popular support for his ambitious plans, even demanded that corporations fund individual LDP candidates for the impending 1974 election campaign. Such actions lost him much support among the *zaikai*, who believed they were being made to look foolish. Mitsubishi was assigned a previous police official and Sumitomo, a former vice minister of finance who was son of the late ultrarightist Prime Minister Hatoyama. The makers of Mazda cars took on the campaign of former Prime Minister Eisaku Sato's son, while Hitachi backed a movie star. Toyota promoted a television personality, and Shiseido Cosmetics, an economist. With such a well-publicized campaign under way, the daily press had a field day, concluding that the Liberal Democratic Party and the big corporations were working together, essentially as one. It was a discovery which could hardly have surprised any readers.[31]

This time Tanaka had gone too far, not least because his campaign had made the collusion between the conservative unions and management so obvious. Union leaders were told to switch their support from the LDP to the Democratic Socialist Party (DSP). The DSP was an ideal vehicle, for if the political process had not invented it, business would have. The party is composed of former members of the Socialist Party who had found it too radical. In fact, the DSP takes a stance very close to that of the government; the Socialist Party considers it conservative – a view borne out by the fact that the party was praised by Kogoro Uemura, a vice president of the Federation of Economic Organizations, a powerful employers' group.[32]

The switch to the DSP was certainly no challenge to Tanaka. He had lots of money and he knew how to use it. One foreign observer said that "Corruption in Japan is legitimized,"[33] and so it is. Tanaka was playing the same game as all the others, but doing it better. Personal economic gain was not his prime motive; he used money to get things done. He spent freely, spreading his wealth to all who would accept it. During 1974, the press charged that Tanaka had handed out gifts of from three to five million yen to *every* Diet member and many bureau chiefs in the ministries.[34] In Japan, this places the recipients in obligation, a perfectly acceptable way of obtaining favours one hopes to obtain.

This is not to presume that Tanaka gave away all of his money and eschewed the good life. Today, his private estate in Tokyo's Mejirodai area – popularly known as Meijiro Palace – is awesome. Coloured carp worth 40 million yen are said to be stocked in his garden pond. Because of its grandeur and cypress construction, Tanaka's parents' home in Nishiyama, Niigata Prefecture, is also called a "Cypress Palace." It is now a tourist spot. In a plot adjacent to his parents' home, Tanaka had built a mausoleum patterned after those of ancient emperors.[35]

Shintaro Ishihara, a popular author and member of the LDP writing in the early 1970s, blamed many of the political and economic problems of Japan on what he described as "hunger mentality." He believed the goal of catching up with and surpassing the West was taking the place of national morality. During the early days of Tanaka's administration, Ishihara wrote an article in which he pictured Tanaka as a symbol of the ruin and confusion in Japanese affairs. "I know of no other example of a politician whose character so epitomizes the society or so affects it."[36] Coming from an LDP member this criticism is either evidence of a spiritual conversion or is simply laughable, but Tanaka was fast digging his political grave.

In fact, Tanaka's big business support was short-lived. This was probably inevitable, for the prime minister never really belonged. He was not part of the "old boy's" network, he had never been to university and he was never a member of a *gakubatsu* or school clique. It was, however, none of these failings that lost him support. Rather, it was an exposé published in the monthly magazine *Bungei Shunju* in November 1974. The 61-page account was something very rare in the Japanese media – an exercise in investigative reporting of Japan's leadership. The article was a carefully documented catalogue of a lifetime of wrongdoing. It detailed land speculation, secretive delivery of money to political allies, cases of stock manipulation and, in general, one of the greatest abuses of power by a party whose name, in the words of a Japanese writer, had become synonymous with corruption and graft.

Tanaka owned thirteen companies, five of which were "ghost firms," which did not do any business. Most of the businesses in the group had been involved in notorious bribery cases that had rocked Japan's political world over the previous decade.

A newspaper columnist was moved to write:

How much money does Tanaka have? Tanaka has four different "faces" – Tanaka the politician, Tanaka the businessman, Tanaka the property owner, and Tanaka the ghost businessman. He is a "ghost businessman" because he runs "ghost companies."

Each of his four "faces" shows up in the complicated connections that make up the Tanaka family.[37]

Tanaka's associates, Kenji Osano and Kinichi Irinashima, had started their careers at the same time. All were jailed in 1948, Tanaka and his friend Irinashima for bribery in the case concerning nationalization of the coal mines, and Osano for illegal handling of gasoline used by Occupation forces. Osano may well have been the brains behind the Tanaka empire. The newspapers had dubbed him with a host of titles: "The Takeover King," "Business Sphinx" and "Monster Osano."

When the exposé was first published, the daily newspapers imposed their own news blackout on the subject. This was one scandal the elites wanted hidden as long as possible. The cover-up was possible only because of the close relationship between newspaper editors and the hierarchies. As the editor of one Japanese journal wrote:

... an extremely large number of those newspapers who professed their opposition to Tanaka's "money politics" were cultivating good relations with politicians on the sly to allow themselves to buy up public land at cheap prices for the construction of magnificent new office buildings.[38]

But this is only part of the story. The publishers are part and parcel of the establishment. The news they get is, in most cases, carefully "vetted" before printing. In short, the daily press is thoroughly enmeshed with the establishment, to the point that it would not ordinarily publish a critical exposé.[39] If the *Bungei Shunju* had been affiliated with a national daily, the story would never have been printed in the first place. As it was, only a handful of opposition papers picked it up.

The bureaucracy's control over the press is aided and abetted by the *kisha* clubs, the journalists' clubs, whose membership is restricted to those from approved newspapers. Each ministry has its *kisha* clubs, which are provided with their own offices and facilities and from which other Japanese journalists and all foreigners are excluded. This exclusion extends to government press conferences. The result is, in effect, significant government control over news.

After the Tanaka exposé, the *kisha* were united in silence while the publishers showed their true colours by sitting on the story for two weeks. Only after Tanaka had faced intensive and prolonged questioning before the Foreign Correspondents' Club of Japan did the local press print the story.

Even then Tanaka held on to office until late November 1974, following U.S. President Ford's visit to Japan. Even after his resignation, he remained the most powerful politician in Japan, in control of the largest and wealthiest faction, and in possession of a seat in the Diet. He was subsequently re-elected in spite of another, later scandal, and it was not until his illness in February 1985 that his power diminished.

Tanaka's resignation put the political power brokers in a quandary. They faced the difficult task of finding a leader untainted by corruption. Given such a short list of candidates, it should have come as no surprise that Takeo Miki, as one of the few with a clean record, was sworn in as prime minister on 9 December 1974.

In placing Takeo Miki's name in nomination for leader of the party, the LDP was being purely opportunistic. Miki was never considered anything other than a stop-gap by his peers. The *Asahi Evening News* expressed it clearly: "Here was a case of the LDP changing its facade to match the prevailing popular mood – an ingenious device for survival."[40]

Miki liked to call himself a born parliamentarian. "I am a child of the parliament. I'm the only Diet member who has retained a seat since pre-war days."[41] He tackled unpopular issues such as political funding, pollution and foreign aid. His attempts to "modernize" the party having failed, he had resigned as Tanaka's deputy prime minister. Subsequently, he dared to criticize his leader, which, not surprisingly, invoked Tanaka's loathing. Despite his record, the public was skeptical of Miki. According to a poll taken by the *Asahi Shimbun*, support for the party rose only marginally, from 42 to 45 per cent, when he became leader. Miki was at least an improvement over Tanaka, who could muster only 12 per cent support from the public during his last weeks.[42]

The new prime minister hoped to improve his party's standing in the December 1974 elections. The press did its part – editorial writers maintained that genuine reform was on the way, although no one who knew anything of the workings of the faction system believed it for a moment.

Miki was an anomaly: he was honest. He was soon nicknamed "Mr. Clean" by the press, to separate him from the corruption of his predecessors. At the same time, the party tried to give the impression that "Money Politics" was a thing of the past. It formed the National Political Association (NPA), a new organization designed to distribute contributions on an equitable basis to all political parties, with the idea of de-politicizing contributions. Yasuhiro Nakasone was placed in charge of contributions. First, he ordered that all donations be directed, as before, to the LDP coffers only. Upon hearing what Nakasone had ordered, the association's newly appointed chairman quit in disgust.[43] Blatant though it was, Nakasone's act did not cause a stir. Affairs quickly and quietly returned to normal.

It was "business as usual" as well for the LDP and the corporations, which considered their public penance done. The party shelved its proposals for dissolving factions, and the *zaikai* agreed that big business would donate some 5.2 billion yen to the party. It was then that the Lockheed scandal erupted.

Baring the Lockheed Affair

The Lockheed scandal first came to public notice – and before the Japanese courts – as a result of testimony before a subcommittee of the United States Senate, not through any investigation in Japan. The upper echelons of the Japanese establishment and the *kisha* were aware of it, but, once more, the daily press kept silent. The first and most devastating of the Japanese court rulings was the acceptance of depositions of two U.S. Lockheed executives, neither of whom were granted immunity from prosecution in return for their co-operation.

The words of A. Carl Kotchian, former Lockheed president, must have rung hollow to many Japanese businessmen. Emblazoned on the cover of *Saturday Review* in July 1977 was the following: "My initiation into the chill realities of extortion, Japanese style, began in 1972."[44] Yet, in his testimony, the president showed little surprise about the methods of doing business.

All Nippon Airways (ANA) had decided to purchase DC10 aircraft from the Douglas Aircraft Company in 1970 but switched, without notice, to Lockheed TriStars in October 1972. Following this suspiciously swift change of mind, five top-ranking ANA officials were arrested on charges of bribery. It was subsequently revealed that Lockheed, to promote its sales, had concluded a contract with Marubeni Corporation, one of Japan's biggest trading companies. Toshiharu Okubo, Marubeni's representative, telephoned Kotchian: "If you do three things, Mr. Kotchian, you will definitely succeed in selling the TriStar." He followed this up by saying that $400,000 was necessary, "to give $300,000 to the president of All Nippon Airlines, and also to make payment to six politicians."[45] This was the start of extended negotiations.

In the process, Marubeni engaged Yoshio Kodama, the "political fixer" and friend of ex-Prime Minister Kishi, as its clandestine consultant. Kodama became the intermediary between Lockheed, the Japanese politicians, the bureaucracy and the corporations. When the president of ANA proved uncooperative, Kodama used the *yakuza* to threaten him.[46] The president resigned and was replaced by a more amenable man. For his troubles, Kodama's consulting fee jumped from $138,000 a year in 1969 to more than $2.2 million in 1972. In addition, he was guaranteed a commission of $4 million for an initial order of three to six TriStars.

Bribes were received not only by the prime minister and the ANA officials, but also by the secretary-general of the Liberal Democratic Party, the chief cabinet secretary, the Minister of Transportation, the chairman of the special committee on aviation, and two parliamentary vice ministers of transportation. Tanaka himself accepted bribes totaling 500 million yen on four occasions between 9 August 1973 and 28 February 1974 through the Marubeni Corporation.

When the scandal erupted, Prime Minister Miki had been deeply involved in pursuing the *Bungei Shunju* exposé. He now addressed the new scandal with equal vigour. Tanaka and other faction leaders panicked and, having failed to stall the probe of the scandal, laid a plan to overthrow the prime minister. The plan backfired when it was exposed by the *Yomiuri Shimbun* newspaper, a leak which could not have happened without the acquiescence of some members of the elites. The *kisha* would have seen to that. For a short time, Miki was a public hero, but his days as prime minister were numbered.

On 27 July 1976, Tanaka became the fifteenth person, but the first high-ranking government official, to be arrested in connection with the scandal. Ironically, by allowing justice to take its course, Miki sealed whatever hope remained of staying in office.

The effect of Tanaka's arrest on the Liberal Democratic Party was earthshaking. The conservative *Japan Times Weekly* admitted that "money power" was ingrained in LDP politics and added that Tanaka's arrest would reverberate throughout the party: "The Lockheed scandal will thus inexorably expose 'the conservative regime's whole dirty underbelly.'" Tanaka's activity, the paper observed, "was the most blatant version of the money power politics of the conservative forces."[47] It was obvious from the heated reaction of this normally forgiving newspaper that the business and bureaucratic elite considered the Lockheed affair the last straw. Many faction members were obviously fearful of public reaction. A survey by the *Asahi Shimbun*, published on 27 March 1976, showed that 73 per cent of the people regarded the Lockheed matter as "a scandal that was bound to occur as a result of Japan's political make-up" – a system that invites corruption.

Except for people in Tanaka's home prefecture of Niigata, the Japanese public welcomed the news of the ex-prime minister's arrest. Elements of the press reacted emotionally, as reflected in some of the imaginative reporting. One article describes the routine at the detention house and how the former prime minister responded to it:

> Morning comes early at the detention house. At 7 o'clock
> sharp when the summer morning sun began shining through
> the grills, the warden's morning call came ... Tanaka rose
> in the bed ... his eyes were bloodshot and his usual, healthy
> ruddy face looked pale and haggard.[48]

Such emotion-laden tones were simply figments of the reporter's imagination, similar to sensational accounts in Western
tabloids. The reporter could not have witnessed these scenes, but
one writer observed that Japanese people have an appetite for
stories: "It leads up to the pleasure people get out of lynching.
They enjoy bringing down those who have climbed too high."[49]

One of the most startling revelations in the Lockheed affair
concerned the role of Yoshio Kodama. It was well known that he
had been involved in Japan's selection of a fighter plane in 1959.
At the time of the earlier affair, a Socialist Committeeman,
Isamu Imaizumi, had asked the House of Representatives Budget
Committee, "Why is it that the Chief Cabinet Secretary, (LDP)
Secretary General, and others should have to meet with private
citizen Yoshio Kodama in deciding which plane to choose?"[50] Of
course, the question was never answered, nor was it during the
Lockheed scandal.

Speculation was rife that it was not entirely Lockheed's idea to
funnel millions of dollars to Kodama. The CIA has been accused
of using the corporation as a channel to move large sums his
way, a suspicion based on the fact that Kodama had worked for
the CIA and that Washington had, in the past, given financial
support to the more extreme national elements within the LDP.[51]
What we *do* know is that Secretary of State Henry Kissinger,
under U.S. President Gerald Ford, made a special visit to Japan
in 1976 during which he refused to recommend the release of
U.S. government records on the case. Also interesting is that
Yoshio Kodama, a key figure throughout, avoided arrest.

The scandal added fuel to the anti-Americanism never far below the surface in Japan's bureaucracy. The Japanese "conspiracy" theorists even go as far as holding that the Lockheed scandal
was unleashed by the U.S. to knock out Kakuei Tanaka, who, as
prime minister, had tried to secure Japan's oil resources through-

out the world in a clash with U.S. oil interests.[52] Exaggerated, perhaps. Whatever the truth, the United States certainly made an effort later to curry favour with Tanaka, as we will see.

Meanwhile, the LDP faction leaders were in deep trouble. They had continued to preach self-reform during the scandal but neither the public nor the judiciary believed them. The innocent as well as the guilty paid the price of the affair. Miki's popular support fell from 45 per cent in December 1974 to 26 per cent in March 1976, only one month after the Lockheed case became public. This was a low equalled only by Sato's cabinet four years earlier. More understandable than Miki's loss of popularity was the public's reaction to the entire LDP. The results of the elections of 5 December 1976 represented its political nadir. The LDP lost its majority for the first time in 21 years, and hung on only by persuading eight independents to join its ranks. Former Prime Minister Tanaka, meanwhile, had easily retained his Niigata seat despite his arrest. His electorate was far more interested in what he could do for them, than in the goings-on in Tokyo. He and four other re-elected leaders, all of whom were linked to alleged wrongdoings, united in overthrowing Miki.

The anti-Miki forces included virtually all the major faction leaders who wanted to get the party back on its congenial track. Miki had become a divisive force. Most members thought he was attempting to increase his public popularity by playing up his image of Mr.Clean. They called an extraordinary party convention on 31 October 1976, at which they recommended that Deputy Prime Minister Takeo Fukuda succeed Miki. Fukuda immediately proclaimed that each LDP member should take full responsibility for the scandal. He made a direct attack on Miki, saying that the problem would not resolve itself under the leadership of a man who "pretends that he alone is free from any blemish."

Fukuda's words were not lost on the English-language press, either in Japan or abroad. The *Japan Times Weekly* concluded that Fukuda was a hypocrite – he was the man who had thwarted reform and was now accusing Miki of having failed to cleanse the party.[53] The foreign press echoed this sentiment. *The Economist* observed that Fukuda had joined the anti-Miki forces to further his cherished ambition of becoming prime minister. It accused him of being arrogant and impertinent to suggest that he alone was qualified to clarify the case.[54]

But Fukuda had successfully rid the party of Miki, a coup he could not have accomplished without the consent of the hierarchies. The bureaucracy and big business had not trusted Mr. Clean since he submitted a bill to revise the anti-monopoly law – against the advice of senior bureaucrats and without discussing it with the *zaikai*. Business interests were particularly annoyed that he had placed the investigation of the scandal ahead of economic matters. Fukuda, therefore, was elected with business' blessing. In voting for him, the party had chosen a man whom the hierarchies could trust, who could be counted on not to embarrass its members by casting aspersions on their honesty.

But neither he, the party, nor the *zaikai* could dust the scandals of the previous 30 years under the rug. In the mind of the public, politics was a dirty word.

Fukuda: The Right Man

Takeo Fukuda is an ex-bureaucrat from the right family, the right university and the right ministry who had held all the right top jobs; politically, he is more conservative than most of his conservative compatriots. His rise to power was only slightly blemished, by LDP standards. In 1948, as director of the Finance Ministry's Budget Bureau, he was indicted for taking bribes. Nevertheless, after he left the government, the voters in Gumma Prefecture elected him to the Lower House, where he remains to this day. In the meantime, he was cleared of the bribery charge. Perhaps after reflecting on his own past, Fukuda formed the Moral Reform League, though its purpose had little to do with morality or reforms; it became his own lobbying group. Fukuda, therefore, was well placed in the mainstream of conservative politics when he became prime minister on 24 December 1976. His first pledge was to eliminate factionalism within one year, a promise which, like many others, he was never to keep.

A new bribery scandal broke shortly after his taking office. The Komeito, or "Clean Government Party," uncovered Korean payoffs to Japanese politicians and called for a full parliamentary investigation. Fukuda turned down the proposal. But exposés of bribery within the LDP continued to surface. One party leader observed, perhaps naively, "Outsiders would be shocked if they knew the extent to which bribery and even extortion are practised in political circles in Japan." He further claimed that secretaries of politicians were daily offered millions of yen by businessmen in return for a receipt of several million more.[55]

Payoffs to parliamentary secretaries were hardly news. Having no regular incomes, these aides often live off donations from members of the underworld.[56] None of this was a particular source of embarrassment to the new prime minister. Nor should a booklet produced by the bureaucracy have been cause for concern for Fukuda. Yet it proved to be the major scandal of his term.

In 1972 the Ministry of International Trade and Industry had published, in Japanese, a 70-page pamphlet entitled *Rebate Systems in Japan*. It was intended to be helpful and it caused no stir at the time. But during the Fukuda era, an English version was circulated. The document describes methods of payment, types of rebates and payments of rebates to customers. It contains virtually everything a prospective price-fixer might want to know and is essentially a guide to bribery, by Western standards, for foreign businessmen. What embarrassed the administration was the timing of its publication, which coincided with the Lockheed scandal.

The whole thing was blown out of all proportion, as a result. It became a bit of a farce. The document would never have been released if the Japanese bureaucracy felt there was anything wrong with it. After all, it only described long and well-tried practices.

It was in this climate that Prime Minister Fukuda sought re-election as party president, and election as prime minister, in August 1978. He had already promised another faction leader, Masayoshi Ohira, that he would not seek office again, but rather back him for the post. If true, Fukuda reneged. What resulted was headlined the "Dirty" LDP Election Campaign.

LDP presidential elections are not subject to the Public Offices Election Law, leaving campaigners free to violate all ethical standards with relative impunity. The usual rumours were circulated, including one that the Fukuda and Ohira factions had each given one million yen to their Diet members to solicit votes in their own constituencies. It was said that another sum was to be given to each successful candidate after the election was over. All of these acts demonstrated once again that money was spread lavishly by the wealthier factions. However, accusations of a different kind were levied from all sides. Nakasone accused his opponents of overall corruption while, in a counter-accusation, Ohira specifically claimed Nakasone had registered 300 false names, each giving Nakasone's office as his home address.

But it was left to Kakuei Tanaka to prove once more that it was he who really manipulated the LDP. Certain that he could control Ohira, Tanaka backed him, and he did so in a very typical manner. First, he obtained the membership lists, which were supposed to be secret, then demanded that influential LDP members who "owed" him allocate so many thousand votes for Ohira. The result of the mail ballot was a clear victory for Masayoshi Ohira. Fukuda was out.

The new pro-Ohira members, the losers claimed, had their membership fees, plus bonuses, provided for them.[57] This smacked of sour grapes, as there was nothing illegal about buying political advantage. However, such charges were particularly embarrassing because the party elections were being held under a new system with participation by 1.5 million party members and "friends." This system was heralded as an attempt to democratize the party and give it a new acceptable image. Instead, it became obvious to the nation that Tanaka, a man facing criminal charges, had manipulated the election. The whole affair became a public scandal.

It was perhaps just retribution for Fukuda. He had publicly committed himself to dissolving the factions, yet he had taken the lead in increasing factional activity. In the end, it was the faction system that beat him. On 7 December 1978, Ohira became the 68th prime minister of Japan.

'Arrogant Ohira'

As had become common among incoming LDP prime ministers,
Masayoshi Ohira tried to create new issues and hold out new
promises, a proposed "honeymoon" with the voters, familiar as
well to countries in the West. Specifically, he offered welfare
and peace. However, his "new broom sweeps clean" strategy did
not work. With notable indifference, the public continued to
view Ohira as Tanaka's puppet. The prime minister's selection
of his cabinet appeared to confirm this perception. He included
many members under suspicion of bribery, although he stopped
short of accepting Tanaka for Minister of Justice, a position crucial to the ex-prime minister's efforts to keep out of jail. Ohira
thus failed on two counts: he gained no popular support, nor did
he please his patron. But more difficulties were on the horizon.
The Ohira administration soon found itself embroiled in yet another aircraft scandal. This time it was 1979, and the manufacturers were McDonnell-Douglas and Grumman Aircraft Engineering Corporation. Once more, the original evidence came
from U.S. congressional investigations. Four senior LDP
members were implicated: former Prime Ministers Kishi and
Tanaka, and former Directors-General of the Defence Forces,
Matsuno and Nakasone. For Tanaka and Nakasone, this was the
second corporate aircraft scandal in which they had been named
under oath as guilty of bribery or extortion. Once more, the government was charged with hiding its involvement – which it did
with some success. None of its members went to jail.

The United States was again blamed for the scandal, as was
the case in the Lockheed affair, and people like Nakasone were
painted by many within the establishment as innocent victims.
Victims they weren't, but neither were the American corporations innocent. In fact, of course, Nakasone and friends appeared
innocent because their colleagues could be counted on to shield
them, even at the expense of some popularity. Ohira's refusal to
pursue the extortionists in this, the latest of a long line of Japan-
U.S. scandals, led to his nickname, "Arrogant Ohira."[58]

The affair did not help Ohira, although he was in no way responsible for it. He still expected to strengthen his standing in

the House of Representatives election of October 1979, when yet
another scandal shook the party and the whole establishment.
The Kokusai Denshin Denwa Company (KDD), a government-
controlled telephone company with a monopoly over all international calls, had amassed great wealth by over-charging its
customers.[59] With the monies gained, its executives organized a
smuggling ring to bring in quantities of goods from abroad.
Apart from direct payments to customs officials to bring in
smuggled merchandise, KDD's management instituted a system
of padded expense accounts to cover the costs of meals and sex.
The *Asahi Shimbun* revealed that KDD had used 2.4 billion yen
(US$200 million) for entertainment expenses in 1978, while
reporting only one million yen to the Postal Ministry.[60]

Unlike the aircraft scandals, the blame fell not on a few, but
on many. The case involved company and government officials
as well as Diet members from various parties. The latter were,
naturally, unwilling to investigate. It was not surprising that, despite its magnitude, the scandal long remained hidden. It broke
only when company employees were caught smuggling.

The Japanese have had to develop a sense of humour to cope
with the constant atmosphere of scandal. The *Shukan Asahi* held
a competition among its readers to parody the corruption
surrounding the KDD case. One winning poem was entitled
"Politicians' Alchemy" and referred to the former president of
the Kokusai Denshin Denwa Company, who tried to hide the
many gifts he had bought. What it loses in translation, it retains
in scorn.

> Scattering money right and left.
> Buying too much and now
> Trying hurriedly to hide
> The mountain of furniture.[61]

Unfortunately, this affair led to two suicides. The second left a
note when he died to say he had killed himself to protect his
superiors. Manabu Itano, the president and the man chiefly responsible, quickly resigned and so avoided being summoned as a
witness before the Diet. He had wisely decided his guilt was not
worth his life.

In the midst of the affair, elections were held on 7 October 1979, with results which were far from satisfactory for the LDP. Ohira managed to gain a slight majority but only by convincing ten independents to join the party. In return, he had to promise to tighten discipline among the civil servants.

Ohira was in an unenviable position. He faced difficulties not only because of the many Diet members involved in the KDD scandal, but because of the KDD's links with the bureaucracy. Whatever actions he took would make enemies, so he steered a middle course of inaction. Rival factions within his own party, still bitter over the bribery-ridden nomination meeting, became so angry about the lack of leadership that many abstained on a Socialist Party vote of non-confidence. What happened next was unforeseen. The vote toppled the government, to the great shock of Ohira and the bulk of the LDP. The prime minister was compelled to dissolve the Diet and call an election for 22 June 1980.

That campaign will be best remembered for the role played by the Japanese press. The opposition campaign was based on Ohira – it was clearly out to paint him as the personification of incompetence and corruption. But, as few outside the journalist clubs were aware, Ohira was dying of a heart ailment. He had been receiving treatment for twelve days when he succumbed to a stroke. The press portrayed his death as sudden and unexpected, prompting opposition accusations that the news of his illness had been kept under political wraps. With Ohira's "unexpected" death, the opposition lost the focus of its campaign and the government gained a sympathy vote to salvage a victory. All the politicians named as defendants in the Lockheed trials, save one, were returned. As the Japanese media smugly admitted, "the death of Prime Minister Ohira is presumed to have helped the LDP to win its comfortable majority."

The subsequent party nomination of Zenko Suzuki as the new prime minister offers a clue to how the party works, for although Suzuki had held no important cabinet or party position, he had been active behind the scenes. He was involved in putting Ikeda in power, in ousting Miki and in making Ohira prime minister. He had, in fact, a highly developed political instinct, and he was above all a "party man," a reliable stop-gap choice.

Smoke-filled back rooms are one of the traditional locales in which party bosses choose political leaders in some Western countries. In Japan, decisions are still made in those back rooms, or, more particularly, in the exclusive traditional geisha restaurants in Tokyo's Akasaka district. Kakuei Tanaka held the balance of power behind the scenes until his illness in 1985. Without the votes of his faction, it remained difficult for anyone to seize the leadership of the LDP. Yet, officially, Tanaka was no longer affiliated with any party and was a defendant in a criminal case. As his overriding concern was to be acquitted, he supported only those who, he believed, could help to extricate him from his legal predicament. That is why he backed Suzuki.

Suzuki repaid his patron by giving cabinet and party positions to members of the Tanaka faction and to others who, like the prime minister, were awaiting trial. In the long run it was to no avail. Tanaka was sentenced to a four-year prison term in 1983 – a sentence which still stands despite numerous appeals. Most recently, in August 1987, Tanaka's appeal to the Tokyo High Court was rejected and his attorneys filed an immediate appeal with Japan's Supreme Court. It represents the last possibility that Tanaka's conviction will be translated into punishment.

In 1980, Suzuki entrusted Tanaka's supporters with the management of party affairs and the running of the Diet. Yasuhiro Nakasone was placed in charge of the Administrative Management Agency, a move which led the managing editor of the *Asahi Shimbun*, a paper which guards its autonomy more than most, to say:

> No matter how much Suzuki may say his government is clean and just, there seems to be no assurance he will really clean up the cesspool of money politics . . . I feel that properly constitutional government will come about only in the distant future and after great efforts.[62]

For many Japanese, disillusionment is constant, and the promises of politicians are received apathetically, if not with downright distrust. Prime Minister Suzuki promised that his first action would be to establish an ethics committee, but when he resigned two years later, few were surprised that it still had not been done.

The LDP seems immune to criticism. Any attack from the

radical left is almost certainly considered a political bonus. It was understandable, then, that the government was unconcerned when the Japanese Communist Party, in early 1982, alleged that Prime Minister Suzuki and 45 other politicians, including cabinet ministers, had concealed illegal contributions on their tax returns. The shock came when these accusations were substantiated by the National Police Agency, which informed the JCP that, as of 7 July 1982, papers on nineteen politicians had been sent to the prosecutors. The prosecutors dismissed all cases, claiming they found too little to bring to court. Nobody believed the prosecutors but nothing more was heard of the matter.

If fault finding by communists can be casually disregarded, complaints by the "power brokers" within the LDP cannot. Two serious accusations were made during 1982 against the prime minister by his peers. The "hawks" accused him of being "dovish" on foreign policy, while the *zaikai* complained of his lack of decisiveness in economic affairs. The final blow came on 12 October 1982 when the Tanaka faction, bowing to pressure, withdrew its support from Suzuki. He had fulfilled his purpose and the party turned to search for a successor. The choice came at a critical time: the United States was in dire economic straits and was looking for a scapegoat. Congressmen and senators blamed Japan's protectionist practices for problems in the U.S. and mounted increasing allegations of a Japanese conspiracy and trade war.

The Japanese back room boys needed a man who could come to an accommodation with U.S. President Reagan. They sought a "hawk" and a strong conservative. Yasuhiro Nakasone filled the bill on both counts. An advocate of increasing military budgets and nuclearizing Japan, he had headed the Defence Agency and, as a protegé of Kodama, he had impeccable extreme right-wing credentials. With the support of Tanaka, his nomination was assured. The ties between Tanaka and Nakasone are close ones – both were affiliated with the *yakuza* and ultranationalist groups. Their careers had crossed a number of times – both were implicated in the Lockheed Affair. Most importantly, Tanaka was obligated to Nakasone, for Nakasone had put his faction behind the candidacy of the ex-prime minister and had made possible his original rise to power.

The Nakasone election in 1982 was vintage Tanaka. The cartoonists in the smaller papers had a field day. One, in the *Evening Fuji*, showed 10,000-yen notes being counted at the polls instead of ballots.

Nakasone paid a visit to Tanaka's faction immediately following his victory, and bowed deeply before its members in thanks for their help. The whole episode was broadcast over national television. One cannot imagine such a scene in any other of the world's democracies. So obvious was the power of Tanaka over Nakasone that the *Asahi Shimbun* called the new prime minister "Tanakasone."[63]

Nakasone: 'The Weather Vane'

A successful politician needs luck as well as skill. Nakasone has been blessed with both. He reached the political pinnacle at a time when Japan had established its economic miracle and was seeking new directions. This suited his character admirably as he had swayed in the political wind all his life, earning his nickname, "the weather vane." Once in office, however, he has more and more determined the policy. In the process, he has made many enemies, particularly within the bureaucracy. As an early advocate of a presidential-style leadership, he proved the strongest prime minister for decades, although he operated from a position that is weaker than his counterparts in the West.

Many Japanese politicians make a point of publicly distancing themselves from those with underworld connections. Nakasone has few such reservations, as his choice of cabinet colleagues demonstrated. His Construction Minister, Hideo Utsumi, was, according to one highly respected publication, "notorious for his corruption."[64] His Minister of Justice, Akira Hatano, a politician of the Tanaka-Nakasone school, summed up its moral principles by saying "that seeking morality from a politician is like asking for fish at a vegetable shop."[65] Akira Hatano's own questionable actions included being linked to an Osaka bribery case.[66] A third,

Labour Minister Akira Ohno, is the son of the lake Bamboku
Ohno, who was connected with Yoshio Kodama during the
Lockheed-Grumman aircraft procurement scandal. The younger
Ohno had raised about US$435,000 in campaign funds from a
group tied to the *Yamaguchi-gumi*, Japan's largest criminal
group.[67]

Criticisms of a different character were levelled at Nakasone's
choice for the Foreign and Defence Ministries – Shintaro Abe
and Kazuo Tanikawa. After their appointments, the *Tokyo
Shimbun* observed that the hopes of the LDP "hawks" and the
zaikai had not been misplaced – Nakasone's choices ensured that
the new government would prove a ready ally of the United
States.[68]

The opposition's immediate suspicion was that Nakasone's
administration, having inherited Tanaka's money and power
politics, planned to revise the peace clause of the Constitution in
preparation for full rearmament. The prime minister's trip to
Washington in January 1983 did nothing to dispel that fear. But
Nakasone, while a strong anti-communist, was above all a
nationalist. He played on Reagan's desire for a remilitarized Japan to protect his country from the Congress' threat of protectionism against Japanese products. Although he realized his
actions had political repercussions at home, he went some way in
assuring the president of his hawkish stance while appearing co-
operative on the matter of Japanese imports. Above all, he demonstrated an ability that was later to gain him national popularity:
he could talk to a foreign leader, man to man.

The Japanese Socialist Party called the Nakasone-Reagan
summit of January 1983 "a dangerous plot designed to remili-
tarize Japan," an accusation given credence by the introduction
of the defence budgets of July 1984 to 1987. These budgets include increases in military spending far surpassing other areas of
expenditure, despite an overall government austerity program.

The people's distrust of Nakasone during the early months of
1983 was deepened by the next act of the Tanaka drama. On 12
October 1983, the ex-prime minister was finally sentenced to
four years in prison and fined 500 million yen for taking bribes
from the Lockheed Corporation. His lawyers appealed and he

was released on a 300-million-yen bond. When the opposition demanded Tanaka's resignation from the House, Nakasone headed off a debate on his expulsion by calling a snap election.

This act was seen as such a blatant power play that, on 18 December 1983, the voters handed the LDP its greatest political defeat to that date.

The LDP lost 36 of its 286 seats up for re-election, leaving the party six seats short of a majority. It was a setback which once more forced the LDP to broaden its base. Nakasone was able to persuade nine independent conservatives to join the LDP and he also formed a coalition with the eight-member New Liberal Club (NLC), a group which tends to the far right. This coalition was the first since the Katayama and Ashida administrations of 1947-48.

But Nakasone's personal popularity quickly rose to its earlier level. The Japanese took a natural pride in Nakasone because he could hold his own with world politicians, yet also talk to the people in a plain and straightforward manner. Ironically, this very popularity had earned him the distrust of the power brokers. He had also gained the enmity of the bureaucrats because he reversed the custom of taking orders from them. The same authorities also considered him "too americanized." This is ironic, because it was his reference to the U.S. as a mongrel society which caused a diplomatic uproar resulting in his apology; not that this remark would lose him any votes at home.

Meanwhile, the position of Nakasone's patron, Kakuei Tanaka, was further weakened. He had succeeded in evading prison but, in February 1985, he suffered a severe stroke. Seriously divided after the illness of its leader, the Tanaka faction was badly in need of money. On 20 June 1985, it held a large fundraising party which included among the guests LDP faction leader, ex-prime minister and ex-Class "A" war criminal Nobosuki Kishi, as well as one foreigner, Mike Mansfield, the United States Ambassador to Japan.[69] It would be difficult to imagine a clearer message to the Japanese than Mansfield's presence to underscore U.S. government sympathies with Tanaka.

In the elections of 6 July 1986, the LDP regained its power with an unprecedented victory in both houses. It won 304 of the

512 seats in the House of Representatives and 72 of the 126 seats up for re-election in the House of Councillors. In the aftermath of this victory, strong opposition to Nakasone within the party, bureaucracy and business circles was, for the time being, stilled. The prime minister got a grudging vote of confidence from other faction leaders, and an extension to the party's normal two-term tenure for prime ministers. Nakasone's own political and religious traditionalism came to the fore when he credited his victory as "something beyond human accomplishment . . . a voice from heaven – the voice of God."

Nakasone's selection of his new cabinet reflected his new independence, and perhaps his obligation to God. He was no longer forced to rely so heavily on the factions of Tanaka, Suzuki and Fukuda;[70] he was now freer to choose men in his own mold. Kazuo Tamaki was one of those, and his background was typical of the new generation of the LDP politicians. Tamaki, like Nakasone and 230 other members of his party, were members of *Seicho-no-Iye*, a mammoth rightist religious organization which advocates a revision of the Constitution and a restoration of state Shintoism. Founded in military circles in 1930, *Seicho-no-Iye* counts among its advisers Takeo Fukuda as well as Yasuhiro Nakasone.

Tamaki's involvement in far-right religion was furthered when he organized an association called *Shukyo Seiji Kenkyukai*, or Study Group for Religion and Politics.[71] In this respect, too, he typifies the new "old type" politician who has gained power in the Nakasone era: ultranationalist and fanatically anti-communist. Such men maintain strong links with extremist Buddhist and Shintoist sects and Japan's underworld.

But Nakasone has succeeded not only by selecting the right men for the right jobs; rather, he has skilfully manipulated the bureaucrats and the *zaikai*. He took that most American of institutions, the "think tank," and adapted it to his purposes. Until the Nakasone era, the party in power decided policy by having the bureaucrats conduct a study and propose alternative plans, from which the politicians selected one. Nakasone, on the other hand, presented his own plan to the civil servants, and they were expected to turn it into legislation. In Japanese terms, this was revolutionary, for Nakasone had at least temporarily wrested from the civil servants the right to draft policy.

Tanaka claimed the credit. As early as the 1970s, he was quoted as saying that "Eighty per cent of the prime minister's job consists of getting the civil service to do what he wants." As recently as his interview in the July 1983 edition of the Japanese *Playboy*, he said he had advised Nakasone, then prime minister, "Stay on top of the bureaucrats."[72] By applying this approach first to the bureaucracy, and then to industrial organizations as well, Nakasone built up greater power than any of his predecessors. One is reminded of Prime Minister Kishi's words: "What controls politics is power, and power lies in money."

3

THE DEATH OF EDUCATIONAL DEMOCRACY

The Way here set forth is indeed the teaching bequeathed by Our Imperial Ancestors, to be observed by their descendants and the subjects, infallible for all ages and true in all places.

IMPERIAL RESCRIPT ON EDUCATION, 30 October 1890[1]

We hereby proclaim the Imperial Rescript on Education to be null and void.

HOUSE OF COUNCILLORS RESOLUTION, June 1948[2]

Much of it [the Imperial Rescript] *expresses universal moral principles. It has qualities that transcend its form, that speak to us today as then.*

PRIME MINISTER KAKUEI TANAKA, 1974[3]

The Early Years

Japanese feudalism was a type of government least likely to give rise to the form and substance of a free society. Feudal education was aimed at maintaining the class structure. Within it, the *samurai* were taught the code of the warrior; the peasants learned submissiveness. Oppressive as the system was, schooling was widespread, and most Japanese learned to read and write.

During the Seclusion, the Dutch remained, having persuaded the authorities that, unlike the Catholic Portuguese, they had no proselytizing intentions. The Japanese who translated their works became known as "Dutch scholars." These translators learned by rote, and taught in the same imitative manner. In fact, the first centres of advanced learning – including the predecessor of the Imperial University of Tokyo – started as translation schools. Thus Japanese universities inherited the custom of learning by recitation. Unlike the West, Japan had no higher schools that encouraged creative thought.

Education was to play a key role in the Restoration of 1868, as stated by Kohei Kanda, a member of the oligarchy: "If we desire unity to prevail throughout the land we must bring about universal obedience to the rule of the government."[4] It was this tradition which led to the present system of education in Japan – years of rote learning, punctuated by competitive exams based almost exclusively on memorized facts, and an uninspiring "four wasted years" in university. This system shaped the generation which, in the last quarter of the nineteenth century, overthrew feudalism. It survived as a means of political control in the face of vain struggles for intellectual freedom. The grim reality of today's education system will be explored further in the next chapter.

There was a time when it seemed education might take a different course. Japanese cultural historians usually designate the period from 1873-77 as the age of "civilization and enlightenment." Authorities at that time redesigned the school system on the model of French schools, with some reference to the American system. With this reform came liberal political ideas. But these experiments ended with the emergence of the Popular Rights Movement in the late 1870s.

Afraid of democracy, the hierarchy searched for an authoritarian model for education. Prussia appeared to offer the ideal. The transition was relatively easy, as Western liberalism, let alone radicalism, had never gained roots in Japan. Intellectuals, with their abstract and unrealistic thinking, were distrusted. As early as 1880, the government compiled a list of books – all favourable to Western liberal ideas – and proscribed their use as textbooks. It was the first official move against democratic ideas.

The Meiji enlightenment had still to run its course, and it was not until 24 years later that all texts were nationally regulated. By that time, the legal foundation of Japan's education system had been laid.

By the turn of the century, the sole directive for education was the Imperial Rescript on Education of 1890. This document was not really about education at all, but about obedience, loyalty and subservience. It was a composite of Confucianism, a set of values used to teach total submissiveness; Shintoism, Japan's ancient religion which emphasizes the mythological origins of Japan and the emperor; and Prussian autocracy, which glorifies the power of the state. The three combined to instil obedience within a state presided over by a sacred being, the emperor. It was an authoritarian blueprint of daunting proportions. Japan's leadership sought to build a disciplined nation capable of defending itself. By this standard, the Meiji leaders had every reason to be proud.

The Meiji government's imposition of controls on freedom of expression, which started in 1880, was partly an extension of the feudal practice of keeping the people ignorant. It started at the top: administration was centralized and controlled by the Ministry of Education. Teachers were treated as servants of the state, and forbidden to take part in political activities.

Lafcadio Hearn, a writer and teacher during the Restoration, wrote that the object of education was to train an individual to occupy an exact place in the mechanism of a rigid society, never to take independent action.[5]

Japan's victory over Russia in the Russo-Japanese War of 1904-05 strengthened militarism. The armed forces joined with the businessmen and bureaucrats to form Japan's ruling elite, the start of a congenial relationship which was to last until the end of the Second World War. Political parties were co-opted for a time, and even acquired a degree of influence, but essentially these bases of power remained the same. Imperial Decrees replaced legislation with increasing frequency. Textbooks of this period began to emphasize national morality and the ethics appropriate to a feudalistic imperial power. Students were taught:

> Our nation forms in its entirety one great family, based on the family system . . . we Japanese revere a line of emperors extending through ages eternal . . . The unity of loyalty and filial piety is indeed the distinguishing mark of our national polity.[6]

Loyalty and filial piety requred not only indoctrination but police oppression. Major riots in Tokyo in early September 1905 were quelled by the police, who exhibited shocking brutality. At least seventeen civilians were killed and perhaps 2,000 wounded, mostly by police swords.[7] Martial law was declared to enforce order.

During World War I, the era as well of the Russian and German revolutions, liberal, social democratic and Marxist ideas began to circulate. This was also the era of "Red scares" in Japan, as in the Western world. Freedom of thought was stifled through several measures, the most notable and reactionary being the Peace Preservation Bill. Under it, dissidents faced clandestine arrests and months of imprisonment, while stripped of basic human rights.

The Meiji leadership had early recognized the need to perpetuate itself. Toward this end, it turned to a well-established Western institution, the boarding school. These schools, such as the First Higher School in Tokyo, were to occupy a very special position in Imperial Japan. The students, like their fellows at Eton or Groton, were imbued with school and group loyalties. The schools' conservative, if not reactionary, outlook made them a force for political and social stability. They taught youth to abhor all forms of dissent, independent thought and social change.

This carefully educated elite was to be the core of Japan's political and business world. Its members were the ones ordained, by selection and training, to lead. The schools offered them a sense of belonging and identity which they would keep throughout their lives.

Women were excluded. There *was* a short period when a small number of women received higher education of good quality, but this period ended with the conclusion of the Enlightenment. Likewise, women had little access to the prestigious state universities. Their exclusion was based on the view that "It is better for women that they should not be educated, because their lot throughout life must be in perfect obedience." Middle class girls in the towns had facilities for dressmaking, flower arranging, the tea ceremony and home economics. For girls in the countryside, no facilities were provided.[8] Co-education existed only for the six years of elementary school – the extent of compulsory education. This system, which remained basically unchanged until 1945, created a sharp division between schooling for the masses and for the elite. Only 14.3 per cent of the population reached secondary and higher education in 1940.

The "liberal twenties" existed in Japan, but that decade could hardly be called liberal by any standard of Western democracy and, by the 1930s, any such pretense collapsed. The ethics textbooks issued in 1933 preached absolutism. In them, loyalty and patriotism were expounded under the name of "love for the fatherland." The emperor and the state, absolutism and nationalism, were completely fused.[9]

The police were one group which left nothing to chance. They viewed freedom of expression as an impertinence to be stifled and crushed. A critical editorial in the *Japan Advertiser*, dated 17 January 1930, was entitled "Students and Dangerous Thoughts":

> The police display a fear of labour oratory which is unnecessary, and quite unworthy of Japan. If their methods do not exactly encourage communism, they certainly prepare the ground in which communism grows ... ordinary electors who go to political meetings and find themselves spending the night in a cell are not likely to be friendly to the authorities afterwards. They are being prepared for "dangerous thoughts."[10]

"Dangerous thoughts" were to remain the main target of the traditionalists in modern Japan.

In 1936, lectures on Japanese culture were made compulsory at all government universities and colleges in Japan – the object, "to foster the national character and enhance the Japanese Spirit ..." To ensure that professors carried out this instruction to the letter, all shorthand notes of lectures were sent in advance to the Director of the Thought Bureau of the Department of Education.[11] A few courageous intellectuals braved prison or worse by refusing to be party to this blatant militaristic propaganda.

By the end of the war this system lay shattered. The bulk of the buildings had been destroyed, many male teachers had long since been conscripted for the armed forces, and, during the last months, most students reported to school only to receive job assignments. The education of sixteen million children and youth had virtually come to a standstill, leaving the U.S. victors to impose whatever educational system they thought best for Japan.

The New Start

That Japan's new post-war educational system should be praised by a number of foreigners is not surprising. After World War II, the United States set out with honest endeavour to establish a system that was fair, egalitarian and open to free speech and association. Unfortunately, there was much between the desire and the consummation. The system as it was conceived never came to pass. But recognition of this failure abroad was slow. While the *Japan Economic Journal* of September 1984 was sounding the alarm – "Nation attempts to save education in deep trouble" – influential Westerners were still ranking the Japanese system with the best in the world.

The failure of the U.S. to make it truly top-rank was due partly to the difficulty of imposing a foreign educational structure on an alien culture, and partly to the inability of SCAP to decide what it wanted. There were those within SCAP who believed that freedom of expression was dangerous. Nothing illustrates this better than the case of the Imperial Rescript on Education. It was not until June 1948, nearly two years after Japan's defeat, that the Rescript was modified. The failure to repeal it explicitly is one sign of the strength of the conservatives within Parliament and also within SCAP.

The Occupation's original objectives were clear: to stamp out militarist and nationalist sentiments and replace them with values of human rights, freedom of thought, and the promotion of peace. To these ends, SCAP made a good start. Militarist-minded educators were purged, the Shinto religion was separated from the state, and the teaching of pre-war ethics, history and geography courses was suspended. The next step was to provide equal educational opportunity for all.

The Special Education Law of 31 March 1947 did away with

the old streams and substituted a single structure which aimed to abolish the elitism of the pre-war era. This system comprised nine years of compulsory education, six at elementary school and three at middle school or lower secondary school. Students could continue a further three years at high school, followed by a four-year university course, or six years for medical or dental schools. There were three types of higher education: universities, junior colleges and technical colleges. An innovation incorporated into the high school curriculum was vocational courses, an area of training which had traditionally been undertaken by business.

From October through December 1945, the Occupation introduced reforms to end sex discrimination. Co-education was introduced into the middle or junior high schools in 1947 and into the public high schools in 1950. Standard university entrance was instituted in 1947 and universities were open for the first time to any candidate of either sex. Women were given another boost in 1949 when 211 colleges for women that had not been recognized under the old system were certified, giving them new status as legitimate institutions of higher learning. Genuinely equal opportunity for education seemed close to reality.

The next important step was to make education directly responsible to the people. To this end, elected boards of education were established in the 46 prefectures and five largest cities. Their duties were to prepare and administer the local programs. The Ministry of Education was limited to giving advice and guidance; it could no longer dictate curriculum. This reform was opposed by the more traditional elements, who bided their time and finally reversed the reforms in 1956. Meanwhile, many youth and intellectuals came to see education as virgin soil ready for Occupation reforms. Student movements arose; some students even sought voices in school administrations. Typical of such movements was the student body of the Ueno Girls' Middle School in Tokyo, which received public attention when it went on strike. As a result, it achieved a say in running the school, and also struck a blow for women's rights.

Such events alarmed the hierarchies, who blamed the teachers for their lack of control over the students. The gulf between the authorities and the teachers has been so great in post-war Japan that they have been said to belong to two different races.

The Red Threat

Japan's defeat left an ideological vacuum in the country. Teachers were among the most disillusioned, conscious that many considered them responsible for pre-war indoctrination. They turned against their own earlier teachings and, as communism was the bane of those who had oppressed them, some educators became sympathetic to its ideals.

It was during this intellectual ferment that the Japan Teachers' Union (JTU, known in Japanese as *Nikkyoso*) was founded by both secondary and elementary school teachers in Shimbashi, Tokyo, on 2 December 1945. It was affiliated with the Japan Socialist Party but remained open to all political persuasions.

One of the JTU's earliest tasks was to give teachers a sense of self-worth, which meant defending them against charges that they were responsible for the nationalist fervour of the war. The union took the view that teachers were as much the victims of the system as other Japanese. Hence, the union objected to teaching courses on morals, which had been nothing but propaganda for militarist and nationalist values and could become so again.

After the war, the welfare of the classroom teacher became a primary concern. The JTU's first act was to send a series of proposals to the Ministry of Education, requesting that those dismissed during the war be immediately reinstated, that administrators and school principals be democratically elected, and that each school be given autonomous rights. These stipulations reflected the radicalism of the period; teacher militancy was at an all-time high.

However, these proposals coincided with the early months of the Cold War. Chiang Kai-shek was facing expulsion from mainland China and anti-communist fervour in the United States was reaching a climax. In this tense political atmosphere, many Republicans and conservative Democrats came to look upon Japan as a bastion against the "Red Tide" of Chinese and Soviet communism. So, only months after releasing Japanese communists from the jails, SCAP set in motion its own Red Purge, and repealed many of the rights which it had only recently granted.

Enthusiastically abetted by the conservative government,

some Occupation "advisers" set out to reimpose restrictions on students and teachers as well. The growing militancy of teachers and students provided them with their excuse. A first measure was taken in 1948, when college students, including those old enough to vote and hold office, were prohibited from belonging to campus political organizations.

The following years of 1949 and 1950 were momentous ones. China was finally "lost" to the communists, and the Korean War broke out. Both were seen by the United States government as proof of communist designs in the region. In response, the Occupation authorities stopped and, in many cases, reversed the course of reform in Japan. After 1 June 1949, under a ruling of the government's National Personnel Office, teachers and other public employees were forbidden from engaging in virtually all political activity. SCAP backed the government ruling, stating that the national law was violated if a teacher should call on his pupil's parents and discuss politics during his visit, call attention to the political claims of any party, be an active party member, promote any political discussion in school hours, or even permit students to "sing any song connected with a political movement within the grounds of his school."[12]

In 1950, when the Korean War began, Japanese authorities took the opportunity to rid the education system of many teachers who opposed the government. Although it was legal to belong to the Communist Party, and no definition of communism was ever given, those with alleged communist connections lost their jobs.

The Americans, gripped by a fear of communism, soon talked of dismissing professors so labelled. Dr. Walter Eelles, SCAP's adviser on higher education, reflected this fear in a speech before a university audience on 19 July 1949, in which he declared:

> ... we dare not have known communists as university professors because they are then no longer really free to teach or carry on research ... they cannot be allowed to be university professors in a democracy.[13]

This demand set off a storm of protest from those Japanese who believed in free speech and who feared being dragged into the Cold War. Politicization of education once more became the major issue, and a deep division appeared. On one side were the conservatives, who preferred a return to the pre-war guidelines, on the other were those eager to build on early post-war reforms.

One result of this blacklisting was the founding of a student federation, *Zengakuren*, which soon found itself in conflict with the hierarchies. Its earliest confrontations concerned freedom of speech in the classroom.

It was, perhaps, ironic that the site of one of the first demonstrations against thought control was that most traditional and prestigious centre of advanced learning, Tokyo University. There, on 5 October 1950, police clashed with some 2,000 students. This demonstration was quickly followed by another at Waseda, a leading private university, and yet another at famed Kyoto.

Faced with such demonstrations, the government was forced to delay the purge of the faculties. It proved, however, to be but a temporary triumph for the students. The Japanese regime and the United States authorities persevered, freeing thousands of convicted "war criminals," many of whom took over jobs held by anti-militarists.

The timing of the "reverse course" caused many Japanese to believe that the U.S. Occupation was less concerned with democracy and more with turning Japan into a Cold War ally. As a result, the only real supporter of the American authorities in the early period, the teachers' union, became one of their greatest antagonists. The JTU, with the Public Employees' Union, continued the fight on two fronts: agitating for better working conditions and for the right of political dissent.

It was in this charged atmosphere, heightened by the Korean War, that the JTU proclaimed its code of ethics in 1952. The code was written by a group of fifteen scholars and comprises ten parts. Among the most controversial clauses are:

> Teachers shall seek proper government; Teachers shall fight
> side by side with parents against corruption in society and
> shall create a new culture; and Teachers are labourers.

The response of the hierarchies was predictable. The editor of one journal maintained that the leadership of the union "was largely in the hands of pro-communists." Along the same lines, a commentator on education contended that the views of the vast majority of teachers had been diverted from the ideals of democratic socialism into Marxist channels.[14] The teachers' reactions to the code were mixed. Some, remembering the Imperial Rescript, were against any form of charter; others, with good reason, feared political repercussions and loss of jobs. But most supported their union as the main hope for a better future.

After the Peace Treaty between Japan and the Western Allies was signed in 1951, the regression to pre-war educational practices accelerated. During 1952 and 1953, there were discussions in the Diet over whether to reinstitute training in ethics and patriotism. Eventually, on 3 June 1954, the Diet passed a law further curbing the political activities of educators. By then the idea of a free education by free educators had been officially attacked as "unsuited to conditions in Japan."[15]

When the Liberal Democratic Party was formed in the autumn of 1955, education was the number one issue on its agenda. It wasted no time. The government's first post-Occupation Minister of Education was a close associate of the LDP. During the Occupation, the position had always been held by academics. Since 1955, however, all Ministers of Education have been conservative politicians, save one under Prime Minister Miki. Such appointments are common in the West, but it was a new practice and it aroused fear in Japan. The distrust grew when Shigeo Odachi, who had a reputation for repression, was named to the post. Hearing of the appointment, MacMahon Ball, the British Commonwealth Representative on the Allied Council for Japan, voiced a feeling held by many scholars: "the appointment means a quick twilight and a long night of freedom of thought." Odachi, he noted, "had held office in two cabinets from 1939 to 1944 and was mayor of Singapore in 1942. He is used to authority."[16] Ball was a master of understatement.

'Teachers Become Bothersome'

Public misgivings about the Liberal Democratic Party's plans for education were magnified by the LDP's escalating feud with the teachers. The major controversy surrounded the Teacher Efficiency-Rating Plan, promoted by the government as a measure to improve the quality of teaching, but seen by teachers as part of a campaign to destroy the JTU. The struggle against the plan became one of the greatest anti-government movements in recent Japanese history.

Things came to a head on 23 April 1958 when 35,000 teachers walked out, closing 80 per cent of Tokyo's schools. A nationwide strike, called for 15 September, was supported not only by the JTU, but by many parent-teacher organizations as well. While parents took differing views, the struggle united the conservative politicians, ultranationalists and the mobsters. The latter have been (and continue to be) used to break up JTU meetings and assault union leaders. On one occasion, the JTU chairman was attacked and severely beaten. He and sixteen other union members required hospitalization. Fierce fighting between riot police and student sympathizers was constant. As anti-government demonstrations grew, the teachers' strike was declared illegal.

From 1956 to 1960, the period of the Efficiency Rating struggle, the ministry punished over 56,000 teachers: 112 were dismissed, 292 suspended, 1,018 demoted, 3,076 formally reprimanded, and 52,273 had their salaries reduced. In addition, 4,420 were accused of "criminal" activities.[17] The scale and severity of these actions, unprecedented within democratic countries, demonstrate the role of state coercion cutting across both private and public sectors of Japanese society.

The confrontation lessened somewhat in 1960 when the government faced a different challenge – the passage of the Japan-U.S. Security Treaty. It was not until the following year that the government was able to return its full attention to the JTU and the teachers.

Then Minister of Education Masuo Araki had given his word to break the union. He told educators to "shut out" the JTU from the nation's schools, and cited statistics obtained from Japan's secret police, the Public Safety Investigating Agency. These purportedly showed that the JTU had 3,000 Communist Party members on its rolls. Such rascals, Araki charged, could not be trusted to educate Japanese youth. The solution, he claimed, was to "... get rid of *Nikkyoso* in order to pass down to the generations to come our culture and virtues built up by the efforts of our forefathers." Araki branded the teachers as "thieves intent on robbing the youth of their spiritual health by 'brainwashing techniques'" and he attacked the union for "attempting to destroy the mandatory curriculum and turn children into tools of a communist revolution."[18] He restated his position that he would not meet with union leaders under any circumstances.

Some believed the pendulum had swung back to the nationalist era. Dr. Edwin O. Reischauer, former U.S. Ambassador to Japan, wrote in the late 1950s: "the Japanese education system has become in some ways more thoroughly dominated by the government today than it was before the war."[19] In fact, the LDP looked with fondness on pre-war education, as illustrated by remarks made in preparation for the celebration of the Meiji Centennial in 1967: "We recognize that the Meiji period was a splendid period worthy of nostalgia ... the decline of patriotic energy common among present day youth is an important and dangerous problem to state and society."[20] The LDP was doubtless pleased when a 1987 survey showed that only half of high school students support article 9, the "peace clause" of the Constitution.[21]

Since Araki's day, the press has done little to calm the waters, preferring to back the government position. One 1982 editorial surmised that many public school teachers must be communists at heart if not in public. The paranoia about communism led one foreign journalist to observe, "... one might think that Japan's schools were staffed by traitors or quislings."[22]

Propaganda, police suppression and the establishment of "cooperative" unions have succeeded in whittling away the strength of the Japan Teachers' Union. In 1986, the Ministry of Education announced with self-satisfaction that, as of 1 October 1985,

Nikkyoso represented less than half of the nation's teachers, and, in the same year, of the 43,795 new teachers, only 41.2 per cent joined any of the four teachers' unions.

More than statistics attest to the fact that the Japan Teachers' Union is waging a losing battle. Glorifying Japan's military past has once again become respectable in Japanese schools. Many teachers see these attempts to change the Occupation-inspired education system as an effort to put education back in militarist hands. As a result, the JTU is very vocal in confronting what it calls the "reactionary educational policies of the government and ruling Liberal Democratic Party."

The fear is not ill-founded. Under constant prodding by a series of U.S. administrations, and egged on by Japanese rightists, the hierarchies appear intent on molding young minds to accept the steady remilitarization of the country. It was, after all, only a few years earlier that a geography text told students:

> How appropriate our location is for fulfilling our mission, which is to extend over the continent and across the seas. And how symbolic the shape of our archipelago – as though stretching out its arms and legs in all directions![23]

Rewriting post-war textbooks is but one weapon in this process of turning back the clock. Social studies books which are critical of militarism and Japanese expansionism have been listed in a Ministry of Education booklet provocatively entitled *Textbooks That Cause Anxiety*.

'Textbooks That Cause Anxiety'

The concept of an objective approach to history is attractive, if unattainable. Yet most democratic societies at least go through the motions of attempting to achieve it. For some years, Japanese textbook authors were encouraged to strive for objectivity in their work. Up to the early 1950s, it had been possible for teachers at all levels to give lectures on such controversial events as pre-war peasant revolts, the fight for workers' rights, socialism, pacifism, the Korean annexation and the invasion of

China. This approach was remarkably progressive and self-critical – much moreso than contemporary histories of Japan by most foreign authors.

This era of educational freedom started in the autumn of 1946 with the publication of Japan's first history textbook written outside the ancient 1881 guidelines. Entitled *Kuni No Ayumi*, "The Course of Our Country," it began with a description of Stone Age Japan, not, as in previous works, with mythology. It was a precursor of the new thinking, published a year before the 1947 Fundamental Law of Education which set out the new aims of following the ideals of the Constitution as well as recognizing the sovereignty of the people and the basic rights of the individual.

Kuni No Ayumi was inaugurated in classrooms in September 1947. Instructions for teachers and parents accompanying it expressed a new philosophy of teaching as well: ". . . It [the book] is not meant to be systematically explained and committed to memory, nor should it be the only teaching material used."[24]

No other nation offered its students such an objective view of its past, a fact admitted by the very people who were fighting for a return to pre-war practices. To defend their point of view, conservative commentators pointed to foreign textbooks, saying that the French do not include accounts of the Algerian and Vietnam wars in primary and lower middle-school level texts. They further observed that British school textbooks, while listing the empire's colonial acquisitions over the years, do not elaborate on how they were acquired – through war and conquest.[25] Traditionalists offered such examples to justify the rewriting of their own school books. By 1986 Japanese history texts were once again becoming saturated with nationalist and militarist views.

A comparison of 1956 and 1986 history texts demonstrates the return to pre-war standards. In the earlier works, descriptions of the Sino-Japanese war included admissions that the Japanese army started the war. In 1986, texts ignore the question of responsibility, observing only that the Japanese army began fighting the Chinese due to Chinese provocation near Mukden, Manchuria. In another case, among the hundreds of changes ordered during the intervening years, the words in the 1956 book ("our country

... caused countless suffering and damage to the peoples of Asia") are deleted because, the ministry observes, there is also an opinion that the "Greater East Asian War afforded the opportunity of independence to the peoples of Asia."

Japan's rulers cannot be faulted if, as they claim, they wish to show only that they were no worse than other imperialist powers. But that is not what appears to have happened. Instead, the curriculum tends to whitewash the militaristic and nationalistic past for the purpose, critics fear, of resurrecting those values.

In present-day texts, authorities wish to paint Japan's entry into the Pacific War as the act of a vulnerable country forced into war out of economic necessity. Thus, the Pearl Harbor bombing is portrayed as a defensive reaction to an economic embargo applied by a powerful foreign state. This distortion is made to appear plausible by the omission of the other essential facts, such as Japan's aggression against China.

Omissions are common in the history books of all nations, but Japan differs from other democratic states in this respect at least quantitatively. There is, for example, virtually no account of the Allied Occupation in modern texts. Japan's leaders are reluctant to admit that the very structure of their nation is the result of remodelling by a foreign power. An exception to this rule is made when they wish to blame the United States for the faults of the Japanese system. To justify textbook censorship, conservatives paint the Americans in SCAP as left-wingers intent on promoting individual rights, rather than communal responsibilities. And how, they ask, can children respect a society if they are reminded about the atrocities and aggressions it committed in past wars? Their solution is to rewrite all the "left-wing" texts of the Occupation years.

Japanese censorship certainly does not lack precedents. The United States has been a poor role model. One of many notorious examples of U.S. censorship – well known to most Japanese, but not to Americans – involved the Japanese Ishii regiment, or Unit 731, which conducted ghastly experiments on live humans, including American prisoners of war.[26] Its biological research led to the inhumane deaths of thousands of Allied men, women and children. After the war, those responsible not only escaped Allied prosecution, but were employed by the U.S. military, and lived out their lives under its protection. According to long-secret documents, secured under the U.S. *Freedom of Information Act*, the American government participated in the cover-up to secure exclusive rights to Japan's expertise in germ warfare.[27] When a textbook writer included this episode, already exposed in a national bestseller, the Ministry of Education demanded it be excluded:

> Reliable academic studies, theses and books, as yet do not exist on this problem, and it is too early to treat this matter in text books. Please delete.[28]

Late in 1983, all reference to Unit 731 was deleted from Japanese school texts.

Perhaps the most famous and certainly the longest single censorship case involved Saburo Ienaga, a liberal professor of Japanese history. In 1963, he submitted for approval his popular textbook *A New History of Japan*, first published in 1947. The Ministry did not accept his revised book, objecting to some twenty passages.

Two of the government objections involved passages about the emperor. In one, the ministry took exception to the statement that "the date of the origin of the emperor is not an objective historical fact"; in a second, Ienaga discussed the Meiji Constitution and described it as "giving the emperor wide powers, while the rights of parliament were narrow." Both sentences were ordered deleted.[29]

When he failed to get approval following still further revisions, Ienaga brought suit for one million yen against the ministry, charging that the Textbook Authorization Procedure was unconstitutional because it infringed on freedom of expression. More than twenty years later, on 19 March 1986, the Tokyo High Court upheld the government's case that the state has the right to exercise control over textbook content. The judge decreed that the government could not be found guilty of censorship because books not authorized for school use are freely published and sold. Ienaga announced that he would appeal the ruling to the Supreme Court, where it is now being considered.

Sometimes censorship rulings can have international repercussions. One such case was the July 1982 decision of the Ministry of Education involving the use of the word *shinryaku*, meaning invasion or aggression. The government ruled that this word had no place on the school bookshelf when referring to Japanese actions, although the ministry had allowed publishers to say that Germany had "invaded" Poland in 1939.

The annual "Textbook Report 1982," published by the Japan Textbook Publishers' Union, offered examples of changes, which were then made public in the Japanese press. The national *Asahi Shimbun* observed that the use of the word "advance," in place of "invasion," brought back memories of a period when wartime governments called military retreats "strategic manoeuvres." The *Mainichi Shimbun* ran an entire series on the controversy, accusing the ministry of censorship. German textbooks, the paper claimed, accurately described Nazi atrocities.

It is important to consider the context in which this censorship was conducted. Japanese corporations were in the midst of negotiating economic deals with China. The Chinese were understandably thin-skinned when the topic of the Sino-Japanese War came up. The People's Republic, whose own rewriting of history is well known, reacted to descriptions of the war in Japanese books by withdrawing an invitation to Education Minister Heiji Ogawa to visit Beijing in September 1982. As a result, Prime Minister Suzuki decided, several days later, that Japanese history textbooks should be revised once again. This reversal came just after Ogawa had firmly stated that he would not make any changes under foreign pressure.

This controversy provoked a strong reaction from Japan's ascendant right wing. The right-of-centre journal *Sankei Shimbun* repeatedly appealed against succumbing to foreign pressure. Meanwhile, a new LDP group established on 31 July 1986 protested what they saw as persistent foreign interference in domestic affairs and the government's alleged "grovelling diplomacy."[30] The group consisted largely of young and ambitious Diet men from all factions, including the one headed by Nakasone. Although only eighteen in number, they represented what is called the "New Right," and had considerable support throughout the ruling party.

Government censorship has broadened since the founding of

the LDP. At first, the government was satisfied to delete unsavoury facts. By the 1980s, it has gained enough confidence to demand the reinsertion of mythology and the glorification of the military. A Japanese quarterly with Foreign Ministry connections piously defended the government by reprinting an article which concluded that "if Japan was to be accused of the invasion [of China], then Columbus' discovery of America should be renamed as the first step in the invasion of the New World."

Troubled Universities

Universities have been the birthplace of dissent, and hence the object of government control, in many countries. Japan is no exception. A year after the 1950 anti-purge confrontations at Tokyo, Waseda and Kyoto, two further episodes took place at Kyoto University. In the first, a Diet member, a supporter of the U.S.-Japan Security Treaty, was verbally taunted while giving a speech to students. The second, and better-known, episode has been dubbed the "Kyoto Emperor Incident." During a tour of the region, the emperor became the object of an unfriendly demonstration, viewed as treasonous by the authorities. Police were dispatched to seek out left-wing activists suspected of involvement and clashes resulted. In the Diet, Education Minister Teiyu Amano placed the blame squarely on the university professors for failing to teach their students "correct thoughts." At the same time, corporate business leaders made it clear that they would never hire graduates with a radical background, regardless of their university or department. The Ministry of Education, in turn, threatened both professors and students with disciplinary action before taking aim at the administrators.

The government was not long in exercising direct control over universities through its funding powers. In Japan, national universities are fully funded by the state under law, and are therefore ensured a degree of independence. Private universities, on the other hand, lack resources and have to rely on student fees and whatever they can beg from the government. Private funding of universities has never been a tradition in Japan. Being constantly in need of funds, they are most open to political interference. Feeling the pressure of an alarmed business sector, the ministry sought to control the university presidents, reasoning that if it could appoint administrators sympathetic to the government and give them powers over faculty and students, the problem of unrest would be solved. Educators and their supporters reacted vigorously. The Japan Teachers' Union, the Science Council and the *Zengakuren* all protested to the Ministry of Education. The government tried, in turn, to push through legislation intended to bring in controls over administrators. It bypassed the Diet by using ministerial directives or cabinet orders. This attempt to subvert standard parliamentary procedure backfired. The opposition was furious and engaged the government in violent debate which ended in political deadlock.

Control over the universities was becoming an increasingly urgent government priority, because of students' growing dissatisfaction with its foreign policy. The decision to renew the U.S.-Japan Security Treaty was, as we have seen, extremely unpopular and resulted in a great upsurge of student protest. Furious, and perhaps fearful, the bureaucracy took action. The Ministry of Education called on university presidents to discipline their students and expel those who were exerting a bad influence.

Liberal arts courses such as history, economics and political science were the main targets of government concern. The one-time LDP Vice President Bamboku Ohno said that the liberal arts simply served to support the *Zengakuren*. Addressing a gathering of Yamaguchi-gumi, Japan's largest mob, in Kobe, he observed that intellectuals are unlike politicians and the *yakuza*, who share devotion to honourable traditions.[31] Ohno subsequently announced that he intended to eliminate all government-supported humanities programs from national universities. In keeping with this sentiment, Education Minister Matsuda proposed to shift all liberal arts courses to private universities. This move was intended to control the content of the courses, as private universities depend, as we have seen, on the government for grants. The plan met with such academic opposition that it was dropped.

Prime Minister Ikeda saw in such resistance a communist threat, claiming that education was being used as a stepping stone to revolution. He directed the new hard-line Minister of Education, Masuo Araki, to assess once more the university system.

The ministry proposed a central governing body on each campus to be composed of educators and politicians. Its main job would be to rubber-stamp the decisions of the Minister of Education. Opposition to this new plan surprised even the LDP. The president of Osaka University put his views bluntly: "There is a danger of authoritative interference should the Ministry of Education ... come meddling in these matters, and they therefore must be restrained."[32] Other university presidents spoke in a similar vein.

Prime Minister Ikeda, clearly acting in anger, was forced to call together the heads of eight major national universities in an attempt to resolve differences. Even in such a discussion, where it would be possible to achieve a consensus, the presidents adamantly refused to approve the government's proposals, condemning them as political interference.

The old die-hards had tried to go too far, too fast, even for some members of their own party. The issue caused a split in the LDP – on the one hand were those like Ikeda and Araki who wished for a "modernized" Imperial Rescript; on the other, those willing to settle for a more moderate dismantling of the post-war system. Because of the disagreement, the cabinet postponed consideration of the bill.

Student Revolt

While some see education as a way to produce loyal and submissive citizens, authorities in the East and West have often discovered it doesn't work out that way. In the light of Japan's history of feudal education, one can understand the reaction of an already worried leadership when student demonstrations started once more in the 1960s.

The *Zengakuren* was better organized than it had been a decade earlier. It had established groups in all the nation's universities. Politically, too, it was more united. Communist Party members had ceased to play a leadership role and, in fact, following the Korean War, the party line had changed. It now opposed militancy, alienating the mainstream of the student movement as a result. Such a change, however, did not bother the hierarchies, which continued conveniently to label *Zengakuren* as a communist front.

Japanese student unrest reflected some of the same concerns common in many Western universities during the 1960s, among them peace and disarmament. Its platform was anti-nuclear, anti-war and anti-militarist, which inevitably brought it up against the LDP and U.S. military interests in Japan.

A turning point for the student movement came with the Sunagawa incident. In October 1956, the government tried to survey farm land around Sunagawa city in order to enlarge the mearby U.S. military base. When students sat down with the farmers on their land to prevent the survey, the expansion of the base became a national issue.

A leading newspaper headlined: "Sunagawa is Surveyed; Score Hurt – Police Resort to Violence."

> A score of persons were injured in Sunagawa Town – police clashed with many citizens and labour unionists as the first peg in the controversial U.S. air base expansion area was driven in by the Procurements Agency's seven man survey team.
> By 9:00 a.m. 2000 people opposed the survey, and 1000 police had gathered in the town.[33]

Protests against the move involved a broad cross section of Japanese society. Students played a leading role and saved from expropriation those farms whose owners objected. It was a victory not so much against the United States but against LDP policy.[34]

Sunagawa was followed by struggles aginst the U.S.-Japan Security Treaty in 1960. Demonstrations against the alliance, the first held on 19 May, grew in size and reached their peak on 15 June. On that day, unarmed demonstrators, mostly women, were attacked by male right-wing extremists backed up by gangsters and armed police detachments. Sixty protestors were injured. Shortly after this incident, a female student at Tokyo University,

Michiko Kanba, was killed outside the Diet, allegedly by the police, but probably by gangsters. When 4,000 students entered the Diet gates that same evening to protest her killing, the police attacked, injuring more than 1,000 students and other demonstrators, and arresting 182 students.

After June, the arena of discontent changed to the private universities.

Japan was in the midst of great economic expansion, and all available capital was being invested in industry. There was little left over for health, welfare or education. Private universities were particularly hard hit. Underfunded, ill-housed, and poorly equipped, they survived by imposing drastic increases in student fees. It should not have come as a surprise that conflicts arose. One of the first was at Keio, a status university, which, like the others, was in deep financial trouble.

Although Keio students have a reputation for apathy, they staged a strike in the fall of 1960 for reasons that were largely altruistic. They realized that the fee increase would limit entry to students from wealthier families. The strike put the authorities in a difficult situation. They had been fairly successful in painting protesting youth as a radical fringe, but now they faced students from the upper echelons of society demonstrating on the campus of a highly respected university. The usual accusation – that protests were run by a communist conspiracy – would not stick.

The Keio action was the first of many such revolts. Because the economic problems were not about to go away, the strike had a snowball effect. The next campus to react was Waseda. Like Keio, it was a prestigious school with high fees, overcrowding, and obsolete facilities. The Waseda strike of 18 January to 22 June 1966 became a milestone in student involvement, embracing the largest number of students to that date.

Turmoil at Waseda was predictable. A year before, university President Ohama had disclosed the problems facing private universities at a press conference. He proposed that the government act quickly to adopt the British-style "university grant committee" system to help lessen the financial burdens on private schools. Ohama maintained that all of the schools had requested such government aid, but had been ignored.[35] Following the latest refusal, the administration had increased fees and tuition. The student body learned of the increases after the fact.

The disturbance started peacefully enough, but the decorum soon deteriorated into an increasingly familiar confrontation, as reported by one journalist:

> The plunge of high-brow academic grievances into low-brow catcalls and snake dancing topped off with scuffles between the students and police shows up the sad state of private education in Japan.[36]

However, activities on the Waseda campus were soon to take an uglier turn.

By tradition, Japanese universities are reluctant to allow police on their grounds, so when Waseda students took over the campus and closed the undergraduate departments, the university authorities used the traditional method of control. Historically, an unofficial campus police force has been formed by student athletes, including baseball and volleyball players. They are organized into paramilitary clubs, living in off-campus dormitories. Politically, they tend to extreme conservatism, and are ready and willing tools of university administrations.

Waseda is well supplied with student clubs, which number more than 2,000. It has the reputation of being the "club capital" of Japan. Of course, only a very few of the clubs fall into the category of goon squads. In Waseda's case, they ultimately proved no match for the mass of demonstrating students. But in the process there developed the worst intramural clash between students in the history of Japanese higher education. One observer describes it:

> One morning last week representatives of the anti-strike athletic club member students stormed the sit-down demonstrators and injured scores of the strike leaders in a stick swinging melee while breaking through the barricade of chairs and desks in front of the main administration office.[37]

Riot police were called in. Heavily armed with batons, shields and water cannon, they finally broke the student barricades on 21 February 1966, and 203 students were arrested.[38]

In the weeks between this and the expulsion of the student body in March, student activists remained on campus, keeping warm at night by making bonfires of furniture as they planned their next day's strategy. All teaching and lectures had long since ceased, save for the graduate schools and the International Division. But on 6 March 1966, the police took the unprecedented step of occupying the campus, barring all students from the university.

Events at Waseda got mixed reviews. Hideji Kawasaki, a Liberal Democratic Party member of the House of Representatives who studied at Waseda until 1935 commented: "The Cabinet must always be prepared to extend helping hands to many of the outstanding private schools, now suffering from the heavy burden of high interest." Others took a different line. Typical was the novelist Itaru Kikimura, a graduate of Waseda's department of literature in 1948.

> To tell the truth, I was deeply disappointed. The eldest of
> my sons is still a primary school boy, but when he grows up
> I would not like to see him enter Waseda University.[39]

Although the undergraduates at Keio and Waseda were ultimately dispersed, their protests did bear some fruit. National attention was drawn to the plight of private universities and colleges, forcing the government to increase its financial aid programs. But the basic policy of "cheap" government remained unchanged. Twenty years later, in the university year ending March 1986, the Japan Association of Private Colleges and Universities recorded a record deficit. The Association cited restrictions on government subsidies and the growth of tuition and fees as major factors for the worsening finances.[40]

Two other struggles, each differently motivated, developed in 1968 at Tokyo and Nihon Universities. Both caused great distress to the hierarchies. The Tokyo and Nihon schools are quite distinct – the former is elitist, the latter a huge degree-producing machine catering to the lower-middle class. Because similar uprisings took place at such different institutions, it was no longer possible to claim the disturbances were caused by one group, or that student leaders were nothing more than radicals or malcontents. Nor indeed, after Nihon University, could the Liberal Democratic Party escape its direct responsibility.

The disturbance at Tokyo had a devastating effect on Japan. One might imagine the reaction in England or the United States if undergraduates closed Oxford or Harvard. When a society's chosen few rebel, it shakes the nation. Yet the spark that set off the demonstrations seemed small. Interns at the prestigious medical school, including the sons and daughters of some of Japan's wealthiest families, were complaining about their pay. Their dissatisfaction was enough to set off a far broader, and till then latent, disgust with the university. Two-thirds of the student body had spent one, two or three years after high school studying to pass Tokyo's entrance examinations. What they found as undergraduates they did not like. The facilites in most cases were poor, the classes overcrowded and the lectures boring and uninspiring.

After the interns' complaints had set off protest, events took a then familiar path: the students occupied the campus, the administration was unbending, and a resulting massive student movement paralysed the campus for a year. The impact of the uprising on the mass of Japanese students was the strongest and most direct in the history of Japan's student movement. The strike was finally broken, but not before over 8,500 riot police armed with duralumin shields, armoured vehicles, water cannon and a tear gas-spraying helicopter were called in. This finale lasted two days and the whole scene was witnessed by millions of amazed Japanese on national television.

The reason for the disturbance at Tokyo University had little to do with problems in the School of Medicine; it was motivated more by the gut reaction of many undergraduates who had sacrificed their youth to enter this, the greatest university in Japan, and had been gravely disillusioned by what it had to offer. For these privileged young men and women, it would probably be their only exercise in dissent on their rise to positions in the ministerial office or corporate boardroom.

Nihon University was a very different case. Its educational facilities and curricula were poor, and the administration repressive and corrupt. Bribery was, at that time, a common way of entering the school and passing its courses. Student ability is, to this day, much lower than in the University of Tokyo, and Nihon graduates rarely rise above the lower echelons of the white-collar class. Until 1968, the administration, with the aid of its athletic clubs, had little difficulty in keeping peace among the 100,000 students.

If the Liberal Democratic Party believed it had survived other student uprisings with its reputation intact, it could have no such illusion about Nihon. A leading Japanese journalist headed his column of 12 July, "Scholarly Tax Cheats." He wrote:

> Tax evasions by Nihon University reportedly have exceeded Y 800 million. It is said that three executives had received "tax free" wages totalling over Y 100 million each ... This situation makes us realize anew that a ... [university business] makes exorbitant profits.
> We can understand the feelings of the angry students.[41]

Two days later the same columnist observed: "Bloody clashes have finally occurred at Nihon University, which used to be called a university which had no strikes. The tax evasion incident served as the trigger."[42]

Events in 1968 at this huge diploma factory shattered the image of a government concerned with the welfare of its youth. The disclosure that university authorities had misappropriated many hundreds of millions of yen of university funds did not concern the Liberal Democratic Party, until it was discovered that much of the missing money had gone to the LDP electoral fund. This disclosure turned into a political embarrassment. The chancellor proved to be a friend of Prime Minister Sato, and, after donating to the party, he invested the rest in a large home for himself. The affair ended in humiliation for the administrators. Chancellor Furuta and five others were forced to bow low before the whole student body; a small payment, perhaps, for escaping prison.

If the disturbances at Tokyo and Nihon showed that the subservience of youth could not be taken for granted, the 1970 Takushoku University affair cast light on Japan's traditionalist morality.

Takushoku is the sort of university that Japanese traditionalists would like to see nationwide. The name means literally "colonization," a reflection of its military and imperialist past. In 1970, its president was a leader of the nationalist wing of the Liberal Democratic Party, one-time Minister of the Self-Defense Forces, and later prime minister – Yasuhiro Nakasone. Campus discipline was maintained by members of the "martial arts" student clubs, composed of youth recognizable by their close-cropped hair and high *geta*, or wooden clogs.[43] They formed a sort of police auxiliary, a vigilante force whose services were not limited to their own campus. They assaulted students at Nihon and other universities. As far as their administration was concerned, they did their job well; while there were a series of incidents at Takushoku, none of them escalated into mass demonstrations.

The 1970 affair began with a student wishing to quit one of the student clubs. As a result, he was violently assaulted and nearly killed. The barbarity was succinctly described in one news editorial:

> . . . there is a sadistic cruelty about the case . . . It recalls all the stories one has ever heard about the tortures of the ill-famed *Kempeitai* [the pre-Occupation military police] . . .[44]

A like revulsion was felt by most Japanese. President Nakasone resigned over the incident, but still maintains continual contact with the university. As a guest speaker, he neglects to mention university violence but frequently emphasizes the unique role of the Japanese race and the importance of traditional morality. He is not on record as criticizing its practice or lack of it at Takushoku.

It should be noted that in 1984, Nakasone, then prime minister, established a commission to seek ways of returning Japanese education to its traditional values, still exercised in the usual manner at Takushoku.

Once a Japanese student enters a university – any university – he is there until he graduates. It is very rare indeed for a Japanese undergraduate to change universities. If he is dissatisfied with his university and quits, he is regarded as a bad risk and is unwelcome at any other school. Partly because of this tradition, the violent rituals practised at Takushoku were rarely discussed off campus, even though the hazing of students had reached depths rarely experienced in the West.

In September 1986 a member of a karate club nearly died as a result of hazing and another was seriously injured. The university's sole response was to close the club. One academic observed: "For years the club had been brutalizing younger members," and concluded that traditional values encourage this sort of closed hierarchical feeling.[45]

Those who wish to see the reintroduction of pre-war morals in universities are found mainly among political and business leaders. It is revealing that only 20 per cent of scholars in the humanities agree with this movement, another instance of the gulf that separates the authorities and intellectuals in Japan.

By the late 1980s, campus militancy had all but vanished, due in part to escalating unemployment, and to the realization that government control continues to grow. Enrollment in the armed forces increases annually and militarist values continue to spread among the elites. The *Kidotai*, a 29,000-member elite police force, devotes its time to gathering intelligence on student organizations, while plainclothes police conduct round-the-clock surveillance of all student activists. Suppressing student groups, however, is recognized as merely a short-term method of control. The real solution, in the eyes of the conservatives, lies in turning back the clock on the teaching of morality in Japan.

4
MONEY FIRST, MERIT SECOND

We shall esteem individual dignity
and endeavour to bring up a people who love truth and
peace, while education, which aims at the creation of
culture that is both universal and rich in individuality,
shall be spread far and wide.
THE FUNDAMENTAL LAW OF EDUCATION, 1947[1]

The Japanese never challenge the unknown. There is
a lack of the spirit of exploration. Eventually you come
down to the lack of individualism.
LEO ESAKI, Japanese Nobel Prize Winner, 1982[2]

Examination Hell

In December every year, kindergartens in Tokyo begin accepting
applications for new pupils throughout the city. Competition
among parents to be among the first to apply to the school of
their choice is fierce. The same principles apply at every level of
Japanese education. These circumstances led one newspaper to
observe:

> The vision of parents lining up all night in the winter cold
> reminded us that this is a society in which everything is won
> only after fierce competition . . .
> Parents are aware that money comes first in Japanese ed-
> ucation. Merit helps to pass exams but in many cases even
> there the mediocre can achieve success through attending
> the right schools, supplemented by "crammers" and "tutor-
> ing."[3]

One manner of assessing an educational system is to examine its screening methods. In Japan today, students commonly call theirs the "examination hell." In it, memorization replaces understanding. There is no place for independent thought. Rote learning, of the kind required to master the difficult Japanese language, is also used to teach standard and simple answers to sometimes complex questions. The Ministry of Education decrees the "right" answer; the student's task is to find the solutions and interpretations which will agree with it. This rote learning is taken to ridiculous lengths in English-language exams, where students are forced to memorize pages of novels word for word.

Learning by memorization starts from the first days of school, proceeds through the period of compulsory education at junior high school, and even continues through university.

To assess their memorization skills, Japan's youth must pass tests of great difficulty for twelve years of their lives. There are examinations for entrance to kindergartens, private elementary schools, private lower secondary schools, upper secondary schools, undergraduate universities, and employment at all levels. The Japanese use these tests as virtually the sole mechanism for determining who will advance in society and who will not.[4]

The Japanese curriculum allows for no variance. Teachers are not free to engage in discussion or debate with their students, nor is there any opportunity for students to express original views. Despite this, some foreign observers see only the achievements, and working backward, believe the system must be producing a curious, sensitive and creative population. In fact, many Japanese happen to be curious, sensitive and concerned, but in spite of, not because of, their schooling.

Hideo Aizo, head of Keio University's Institute of Information Science, says:

> Japan seems to be a country which excels in making things, or which adapts existing technology to its own manufacturing, but which is exceptionally weak in terms of generating new concepts for its software.[5]

He blames education: "Training children how to construct concepts is not part of the Japanese system of education."[6]

A majority of students agree. According to a poll by the Prime Minister's Office, most say that creativity is *not* cultivated, and claim that in the eyes of employers, the status of one's school is more important than the calibre of one's ability. Nearly three-quarters of the students look upon their education as dehumanizing, while half believe schools exist only to fit students for accepted social molds.

It is current wisdom in the West that Japanese education is excellent at preparing youth for work; yet, even on this point, nearly half of Japanese students disagree. Faced with the negative reaction of Japanese students themselves, one may ask, who is to be believed? The foreign experts, who have never attended a Japanese school, or the students? Admittedly, young people often take a negative view of their own education, but one thing is certain: few of Japan's youth agree with the prevailing view of outsiders.

That the Japanese excel in teaching their own language is incontrovertible. Japan's illiteracy stands at only 0.7 per cent, the lowest rate of any major nation save the Soviet Union, and vastly lower than that of the United States.[7] It detracts little from this achievement to note that Japan, unlike the U.S. and some Western countries, has virtually no new citizens to socialize, no influx of peoples of other languages and culture to teach.

While the Japanese system encourages the absorption of "facts," and does so exceedingly well, one aspect of its success is often overlooked. Each year, Japanese students study 60 more days than those in North America. During the twelve years of elementary and secondary education, the Japanese student actually receives the equivalent of four more years of education than a comparable student in the United States. It would be difficult not to absorb more with that advantage, even allowing for the additional two years needed to learn to read and write Japanese. This advantage does not change the fact that students are required to work hard, in fact, much harder than many educators believe desirable.

The average Japanese student also puts in longer hours on

homework than his counterpart in other countries. A survey of youth aged ten to fifteen showed that over half of students study two hours or more each day outside school hours, as compared with one-fifth of students in the United States and France. Perhaps more indicative is the percentage of students whose daily study time exceeds three hours after school; it is nearly 20 per cent in Japan, 4.7 per cent in the U.S. and 3.5 per cent in France. Thus, for many students, home is little more than a place to study and sleep.[8]

With the heavy burden of homework come other, more concrete, costs of education. Over 60 per cent of children attend kindergarten, but state classes are in short supply. Thus, many are forced to enroll in privately run, highly priced schools. If the cost to parents is high, to children it is higher. They face entrance exams for the best kindergartens, and, as schools are often far from home, they must commute. For most, it can be a demanding and stressful introduction to childhood, incorporating many of the pressures and expectations imposed on adults in Japanese society.

The constant examinations faced by Japanese students are portrayed as a means of ensuring advancement based on ability, a view extolled mainly by parents who can afford the best schools. But in Japan, as elsewhere, exams actually work to maintain privilege. Real upward mobility is limited because the upper-middle class, secure in its wealth, has a great advantage over the masses of poorer Japanese. Like the well-to-do in other countries, the affluent in Japan are able to buy educational advantages for their children.

This state of affairs is not what the Occupation authorities had in mind when they laid the groundwork for the present system. They intended mass education to allow greater mixing of the classes; the opposite has occurred. In large measure, this continued division is caused by the difficulty of exams. To pass them, many young people have to attend cram schools, called *juku*, or have private tutorials, both of which are pricey routes to future success.

The last year in elementary school, which in Japan is the sixth grade, is the first stage of the really intensive training that is im-

posed on pupils. After six hours in school, they rush home with
work that requires about two hours of study. After gulping down
their dinners, they rush off to private school, which specializes
in preparing students for entrance examinations into junior high.
Here the pupils are given three hours of high pressure indoctrination seven days a week, yes, including Sunday. They study a total of eleven hours a day on weekdays. These boys and girls are
only eleven years old!

Juku are often patronized by parents who plan to send their
child to one of the well-known private middle or higher schools.
Some of these schools actually specialize in preparing students
for entrance to particular schools or universities. One unusual
example is a *juku* that specializes in preparing students to become doctors.[9]

Summer cram schools are a recent phenomenon born out of
this philosophy. They boast that they can train children to survive on only five hours sleep daily during the weeks prior to entrance examinations. To ensure they are awake, youngsters are
confined to the buildings, or in current Japanese jargon, are
"given no outdoor time." Most parents realize this is no life for
their child, but find themselves caught in a web. Philosophically,
they are opposed to the system, but, practically, they want to do
what is best for the child's future. Such boarding schools are
very expensive, so it is not surprising that opposition to these
practices is mounting.

Protest comes not only from the many parents concerned over
cost, but from those worried about the effects on their children.
Some parents complain that their children have no outside interests, and no time to cultivate them. One angry mother observed that:

> In the top of the class of the *juku* are the students who prob-
> ably have the best scholastic records but who are the worst
> of human beings.[10]

In a poll of parents, the results of which were printed in a national newspaper, only 4 per cent insisted on keeping the examination system as it is, while 45 per cent called for "changes" and
38 per cent for "abolition." It is interesting to note that, of those

parents in education or related fields, over 40 per cent explicitly demanded abolition of the examination system.[11] On the other side of the coin is the establishment view, expressed well and typically by Kinko Sato, councillor in the Prime Minister's Office. She believes that:

> If the proliferation of "*juku*" is to be called the ruin of education, I must point out that what really ravages education is the equalitarianism and standardization of an extreme kind . . .[12]

Elitism dies hard among the privileged of all countries.

In a system which determines success by tests, there is a great temptation to get around the rigid laws. "Boundary-jumping," an illegal but common practice, is one example. It means enrolling children outside the school district in a "better school" elsewhere, thus undermining the democratic and relatively equal school system envisaged by the Occupation.

Students cannot help but be aware of the vital relationship between money and status throughout the school system, but particularly in status schools. Students look down on and do not mix with those from lesser schools. Snobbism, class consciousness, in some respects a caste system, is as deeply ingrained in Japan's youth as among the elite private school children in the United States, or those in "major public" schools of Britain.

Ambitious parents are rarely satisfied, even when their children enter the school of their choice. It is common for parents to spend yet more time and money on improving the quality of elite schools.

> Thus, even though financed from tax funds and limited by a standard salary scale, such schools have better equipment than, and give financial incentives quite superior to those offered by, the average neighbourhood school.[13]

Teachers are attracted to particular schools by financial incentives. Extra gifts from parents and "fringe benefits" to principals combine to attract the most "gifted" teachers away from less fortunate schools. Usually, their gift is measured by the ability to drill memorization exercises into students. A teacher privately admits:

> I felt guilty at leaving our local state school, students wan-
> ted to learn and the staff was dedicated, but I was offered a
> house which my family could never hope for otherwise.[14]

Given this reality, better schools improve markedly and medio-
cre schools deteriorate or stagnate – as measured by the standards
of Japanese education. The best Japanese schools *do* produce
students who excel in mathematics, particularly at the elementary level. Sixth graders tested against students in five other
industrialized countries were ranked first, followed by those
from Sweden, Britain, Canada, France and the United States.
However, in the same test, Japanese students ranked second
from the last in science, beating only the U.S.

Such results belie claims of overall excellence. All the statistics *do* show is that Japan has been very successful in teaching
one subject, mathematics, by rote, in the sixth grade. In fact,
learning by rote is successful in a number of areas and grades,
but it is destructive at other levels and in most other subjects.
Perhaps most damning is that, in Japanese schools, the joy of
discovery, of debate, of being wrong for the right reasons, of research and investigation, do not exist.

Social Pressures

That the Japanese live in the most competitive of societies is
rarely questioned. The pressures on the young are intense, a fact
reflected in their attitudes toward their country, their parents and
teachers, as well as in their lack of self-confidence. Their views
on these subjects were surveyed in a poll of children from six
countries published by the Japanese Prime Minister's Office in
1965. Strong disillusionment on the part of Japanese youngsters
became immediately obvious.

When youngsters were asked in 1980 what gave them self-
confidence, 92.7 per cent of U.S. students cited their school
grades, against 36.6 per cent of Japanese. The feeling of worth is
reflected in a number of ways. Overall, more than 80 per cent of
the children believed their countries were good places in which
to live, but only 45.1 per cent of the Japanese believed so. The
Japanese children, surprisingly, rated lowest in obedience to

their parents – a mere 27.2 per cent admitted to being obedient – and also lowest in respect for their teachers, at 58.3 per cent.[15] These answers appear to contradict the image of a loyal, obedient, and respectful youth. While the obvious conclusion is that society as a whole, and repressive education in particular, shape these views, the traditionalists cite the same results to show the decline in moral values and the need to return to pre-war morality.

But statistics can distort reality. Rarely would one meet a youngster who wants to emigrate, or who considers himself disloyal. As for disobedience and lack of self-respect, most students make it clear that this reflects their place in the system at the time, a phase to be passed through, although for some the disobedience is real and lasting.

Parents are in a difficult situation: they wish to respect their children's discontent, yet see no alternative to their situation. Some mothers are forced to sacrifice their free time and find work to raise the monies to send their children to cram schools. This often produces a multiplier effect which causes them to pressure their child to work harder, which further increases alienation. As a result, a half of Japanese youngsters claim to dislike their own mothers at this stage of their lives.

As one student explained:

> We know our mothers have our best interest at heart. But in my case she is constantly nagging, constantly complaining. I don't think it is the best time for either of us. My sister has it much easier. As for my father, I rarely see him, often when he gets back home, I'm in bed.[16]

The root of the problem is that an individual's future is determined by the status of his school. The collegial network still exists to some extent in Britain and France, and less so in the United States, but in Japan it is a fact of life. Of Japan's 5,219 high schools, twenty account for 21 per cent of the successful candidates at the University of Tokyo. Acceptance to one of these high schools virtually guarantees the student success. In turn, a graduate of Tokyo is assured of a job in the bureaucracy or in a major company. His status is secured for life. It is no wonder that thousands who fail to enter a high school of their choice decide to take a year off for further preparation, rather than settle for a "second class" institution. This final year of cramming has earned the name of "The Japan Tournament."

While "Japan Tournament" is the ultimate plateau, there is an earlier tournament in junior high school, when students are divided into streams for achievers and non-achievers. These streams continue for the rest of the student's schooling, with no escape. The system thus closes off the path to high school status at a very early age. Those who fail to enter a route to college or university become disenchanted, one of the factors contributing to the high rate of juvenile delinquency.[17] Like some young people in Western countries, they see little future for themselves, and react against the society which has robbed them of it.

Junior high school teachers bear the brunt of juvenile hostility. Unlike their counterparts in senior high, the public junior teachers lack any form of in-school punishment. Corporal punishment, and expulsion from class and school, are banned in all state schools, and are not condoned in the others. But this does not deter all teachers. In Tokyo, teacher violence greatly exceeds student violence. Nearly all students who become "problem children" have experienced early beatings at the hands of their teachers.[18]

Seeking "vengeance" against teachers has become a tradition in some areas. In one instance, about 80 students subjected two teachers to a "kangaroo court," before assaulting them.[19] Understandably the issue is taken very seriously by the Japan Teachers' Union, which has called on its members to give top priority to finding a solution.[20]

Just over a year after such an appeal, high school students in Koshigaya, Saitama Prefecture, assaulted ten of their teachers and then damaged a patrol car called to the scene. The reason given for the violence was that a gym teacher had shoved one of their classmates.[21]

The image of obedient, well-behaved youth received a further setback when the prime minister admitted in 1983 that Japan had a student violence problem. Yasuhiro Nakasone made a rare television address in which he placed the primary blame for delinquency on the parents. Unfortunately for Nakasone, the National Police Agency chose that time to provide statistics which clearly related school violence to the testing system. It noted that 85 per cent of delinquents had done poorly in examinations, providing some support for those who condemned the "examination hell."

Student violence has also had an effect on society at large. Juvenile delinquency has been on the increase since 1973, although it remains less widespread than in some Western countries. During 1983, 197,000 adolescents were apprehended by the police, 4,000 more than in the previous year. Fifteen year olds registered the highest increase in crime at 9.0 per cent, which coincides with the fact that compulsory education ends at that age. Parents are worried. At one Japan Teachers' Union meeting in Hiroshima, a father pointed out that adults are carrying out patrols after school hours to prevent juvenile delinquency. He admitted he did not like the idea of parents keeping watch on their children, and saw distrust developing.

Scholastic pressures affect even the academically successful. In one case, a Tokyo senior high school boy killed his grandmother out of shame for her ignorance, and then committed suicide. He left a note stating that the elite are superior and the masses inferior, leaving no doubt about which category he belonged to.[22] In another instance, a father killed his son, a senior high school student, because he could no longer control the boy. His son had berated his parents for their inferior status, saying, "You don't have any education and social position . . ." The youngster had come to these views partly because his parents had made sacrifices to enroll him in one of the "superior" high schools.[23] Such acts are the exceptions in a reasonably ordered society, but they should pose questions to those who maintain that Japanese education does not breed elitism. In fact, it is elitism of perhaps the worst kind – not the privilege of birth or money which is so blatant in some Western countries, but privilege which seeks to impress that it is gained by merit *alone*, when, in fact, the true picture is quite different.

The government recognizes the need for reform. In 1984, Prime Minister Nakasone appointed a commission to scrutinize the examination method. It concluded that, "Despite its merit, the main thrust of this country's education has been to have students memorize information and facts. Too many stereotyped persons without marked individuality have been produced." A stronger condemnation could hardly be made. Yet the consensus in Japan is that the establishment will do little to change the system, despite the commission's findings, because the system is serving the hierarchies too well.

The real reason for the prime minister's concern turns out to be broader than reform of the exam system. He wishes to return education to Japan's aggressive past. His Education Minister claimed in 1983 that all problems of the youth are due to U.S. "leftist" Occupation policies that attempted to crush "Japan's pre-war morals, traditions and customs."[24] At the same time, the minister proposed a return to pre-war practices. This view was confirmed by the Prime Minister's Ad Hoc Advisory Council, which emphasized the need for "moral education," the usual euphemism for pre-war nationalism. With the most recent event at Takushoku University (see Chapter 3) still fresh in their minds, it is not surprising that this conclusion sent shivers down the spines of many Japanese.

Less Equal Than Others

High schools fall into different categories, but all are part of a hierarchical system from which there is virtually no way out. Once a student is in a lower status school, he has little chance of improving himself. Likewise, there is little prospect for late achievers. Those from wealthier families are luckier: they, at least, can take a year off to upgrade themselves.[25] Students with neither the time nor money lose out. Thus, the social inequalities persist with the complicity of the system.

High schools range from Nada High School in Kobe, an elitist private school, to private schools for the lowest academic level. Entrance to Nada is determined by wealth and exam scores. Attending Nada virtually guarantees a student entry to the university of his choice.

One student in such an elite high school explained that he was one of those from a family of moderate means. So he found himself working all the harder.

> I never ask questions, unless it is directly on the subject. It is a waste of time. Anyway it is impossible in class. The teacher lectures. He and your fellow students would be annoyed if you interrupted. It is not done.
>
> I do not mind. I know if I work very hard I will succeed and pass. Nothing else matters now. I am very lucky. I owe it to my parents.[26]

Elite private high schools are rare; most private institutions exist to educate those who have failed even to pass the entrance exams for the public vocational high school. Yet, even in these private schools, the poorer families often make great sacrifices just to enroll their children. That they do so is evidence of the tremendous pressure to achieve status through education.

Vocational schools, as in some Western countries, lack social standing. Entrance exams are not even available to students of these schools in Japan, a yearly reminder of their inferior position in society. Such youth are essentially second-class citizens. Most would choose the academic stream if it were available, but with that avenue closed they are stranded in vocational schools with little incentive. Sadly, they have little chance of getting a job with a reputable firm. They can only console themselves that school takes them out of their one-room homes for a day, and that there are others worse off than they.

At the very bottom of the high school ladder are night schools. This is difficult for Westerners to comprehend since there is little social stigma attached to night schools in Western countries. Indeed, there is a reverse snobbery on the part of those few students who graduate and eventually make it to the top. In Japan no such hope exists. Night schools are the last resort of those who fail to enter any day school. Students spend four years there, rather than the normal three, in order to make up for the fewer daily hours of instruction. At this level, motivation has been virtually destroyed.

The history of Japan's post-secondary education exemplifies what has happened to much of Japan's post-war democracy. When the Occupation exerted pressure on Japanese authorities to open up college education for all, the Japanese had little alternative but to agree. The number of universities increased, from the 44 before the war to over 400, a great step in extending Japanese education although one which, critics claim, has led to a dramatic fall in standards.

In the U.S. system on which Japan's was modelled, there are two somewhat contradictory goals – quality and quantity. The "Jeffersonian" aim would make higher education accessible to all but insist on standards, while the "Jacksonian" view treats every mind as equal and opens state universities to every high school graduate, regardless of capability. The real criticism of the latter is that educational standards suffer. By introducing the "examination hell," the Japanese system appears to have kept high standards but substituted the standard of money for merit.

Japanese universities and colleges are classified into three categories – national (set up by the national government), public (set up by local governments), and private. Budgets of the national and public institutions are mainly drawn from public funds, so university entrance fees are much lower than the fees for private universities. Private schools lack the endorsements given to some Western universities, and have to rely on government gifts. As a result, it costs nearly two and a half times as much to enter a private institution as it does to enter a national or a public one. Students from poorer families are therefore limited to state universities, which are the most difficult to enter. With far fewer institutions to choose from, students lacking money for cram schools or tutors must be exceptionally brilliant at passing exams. The situation is worsening, as an increasing proportion of those entering national universities are from the wealthiest 10 per cent of Japanese families.

Yet the myth still remains strong in Japan that universities are open to all with ability. Ironically, this belief is expressed mainly by those who sacrifice the most. The exceptional case of "rags to Tokyo University" is often trotted out to support the view. The establishment, of course, encourages this myth to preserve what is essentially a meritocracy for the wealthier families. As one scholar points out:

> Upper class families are able to send their children to private universities . . . lower class families do not have the financial ability to send their children to any university at all.[27]

The myth of equal opportunity is easily exploded. A survey of family budgets and education expenses conducted by the Tokyo Metropolitan Government concluded that the education costs for a middle class family represent up to a half of their budget. This example allows for a daughter in a private university, a son in a private senior high school, and another daughter in the fourth grade at a public primary school. For the average family with two children, one at kindergarten, the other at junior secondary school, education accounts for more than 20 per cent of the family's total spending.[28] Extra fees for crammers, private schools or tutors explain the hefty price tag. Such costs effectively exclude the children of poorer families from higher education.

As the status of a university is of such great importance, a student may sit for examinations for several private universities. Again, children from wealthier families have a great advantage, since the parents have to pay a fee in cash for each exam their youngster writes, and some take as many as ten. But the costs have barely begun. The average fee for a private university is high, in addition to which there is a large enrollment charge paid before acceptance, which is not refundable if the student withdraws for any reason. Quite often, the student will pay this fee to the first university that accepts him and will then continue writing entrance examinations in the hopes of being accepted by a "better" school. Thus, parents are saddled with costs ranging from many hundreds to thousands of yen.

Such fees are beyond the means of poor families. Not only can they ill afford multiple applications, but the tuition costs at private universities are far beyond their budgets. To pass the entrance exam for national universities, poorer students may work by day and enroll in a private night school for exam preparation. But, once more, they face the financial barrier. These schools require a high initial deposit for the first half year, and some even require parents to buy bonds or to make "donations" before acceptance. Such institutions know that many parents will seek out "loan sharks" and mortgage their future to give their children the best education that money can buy.

Poorer families are caught on a treadmill. Lack of money means students must take a part-time job, which means they are able to study less, which makes a university education unlikely. Lack of education forces young people into lower-income jobs, so that, in the next generation, their children will be unable to afford a university education.

One question remains: cannot brilliant but needy students win scholarships, as they do in all advanced Western countries? The Japanese government boasts of the millions it has awarded, but as one professor pointed out, these scholarships are only student loans, which the students have to pay back, with interest. The only students exempted from repaying are those entering the government or public sector. As well, loans or payments are so small that, while they may cover an entrance fee to a national university, they do not leave enough to live on. Certainly, they do not even make a dent in the cost of attending a good private institution.

Students who can afford higher education are confronted with another pecking order. National universities are accorded the highest status. Of these, perhaps three are of the first rank – Tokyo, Kyoto and Hitotsubashi. There are a good many of the second class, such as Osaka, Nagoya, Tohoku, Kyushu and Hokkaido.

All applicants have to pass a two-day standard exam for any of the nation's 83 state institutions. This innovation, which came into effect in 1979, was designed to lessen the pressure of the "examination hell" by cutting out the multiplicity of exams for each university. Private universities, on the other hand, have retained their own individual entrance exams. These too have their hierarchical structure, Keio and Waseda being given pride of place.

With so many students seeking entry into so few status universities, it is not surprising that there is an entire category of high school graduates who spend one, two, sometimes three years studying, attending cram schools, being tutored and taking the annual entrance exam.

Private preparatory schools exist to tutor such students, but getting into a good "prep" is almost as difficult as getting into a good university. The student has to face yet another entrance exam with the knowledge that only one in eight is admitted. These crammers exist solely to prepare students to pass entrance exams for particular universities. The additional studying and experience of such students, called *ronin*, give them a distinct advantage over those graduating straight from high school. There is even a popular belief nowadays that one cannot expect to get into a famous university without having failed the exam two or three times beforehand. Indeed, at the prestigious University of Tokyo, *ronin* comprises two-thirds of the student body.

Snobbism goes to the most extreme lengths. If a Japanese student living and studying abroad is a graduate of a lesser university, he will be ignored by his own embassy's personnel. But a graduate of a first rank university will have many doors open to him. It goes without saying that the Ministry of Foreign Affairs is staffed almost exclusively by graduates from status universities.

Women's Liberation in Reverse

The Constitution calls for equal educational opportunities, yet girls are discriminated against once their compulsory education is completed. As there are not enough public high schools in Japan to accommodate all the young people, private ones fill the gap. The majority of these, outside of Tokyo and Osaka, are segregated. Young women in such schools find themselves in a "female" stream that carries them through into universities that offer two-year courses of study. These are now very largely female institutions. Only 12 per cent of girls who graduate from high schools enter four-year universities, compared with 39 per cent of boys. Moreover, 90 per cent of junior university students are women and 40 per cent of these are streamed into "home making" courses. The government's claim that more women than men now proceed to higher education is true, but they do not benefit from the same quality of education as the men.[29]

In the junior universities, emphasis is placed on producing "good" wives and "wise" mothers and no more. Some bureaucrats demanded in the 1960s that the home economic courses, which boys and girls took together in the post-war democratic system of education, be limited to girls only. Since skilled jobs for women were then so scarce, it was argued, they really didn't need a college education.

The government quickly followed up on these demands. In the Curriculum Council Report of 1969, home economics was made compulsory for girls only. If Western preferences are any guide, this made a lot of boys happy. But it left girls with no freedom of choice. The director of the Elementary and Secondary Education Bureau defended the move as recently as 1982, insisting that:

> The goal in making home economics a compulsory course for high school girls is to recognize the special qualities of womanhood, helping them to become good future wives and mothers . . .[30]

But it is seen as part of a pattern which blocks social, sexual and political emancipation of women in Japan. It was no coincidence that the revised school curriculum of 1973 dealt with the "proper" education for each sex.

It is interesting to compare the preamble of the 1947 school curriculum with that of 1973. In May 1947, the Ministry of Education declared: "We do not believe that the position of women can be improved by emphasizing the differences in the sexes and giving different education to boys and girls." But in the 1973 curriculum, "General housekeeping becomes compulsory for every girl. The theory and practice of 'everyday manners' will be taught to make girls more genteel and to break the 'trend of argumentativeness.' The making of the *kimono* . . . will be a compulsory subject so that wives can at least make their husband's *yukata*. Gymnastics for boys are also to be increased by 22 per cent and *kendo* and *judo* are both to be made compulsory."[31]

It would be nice to believe that the majority of teenage girls are aware of, and fight against, such discrimination. But if many random conversations are any guide, the reverse is true, and polls of females in general appear to bear that out. It must be added, however, that Japan has its share of militant women dedicated to equal opportunity and treatment. It is startling for many Westerners of both sexes to realize that of the Japan Communist Party's membership, nearly 40 per cent are women. As the Hoover Institution informs us, there are some 470,000 party members in Japan, meaning that nearly 178,000 are women, a sizeable number by most European or American standards. And there are also many women in the Socialist Party, including its leader, who are actively involved in the feminist movement. So far, their total political impact has, however, been modest.

The compulsory teaching of domestic service for girl students only is one of the most overt reinforcements of the division of labour within society and must be seen as extreme within industrial societies: "The status of domestic science courses is a direct contravening of the United Nation's guidelines and yet there has been no move within the Education Department to alter the situation."[32]

The range of courses offered in all-girl high schools is limited. Science, mathematics and technical subjects are given little time in the schedule, thus encouraging students to take courses that qualify them only for a domestic role. It is significant that the only two aspects of education mentioned in LDP policy on the family are domestic education in schools and adult education for women.[33]

Few of the authors of the 1947 report foresaw that Japan's democratic trends would be curtailed before their effects could penetrate social and family life. The establishment is simultaneously attempting to block democratization while raising the family to the status of a cult, imbued with a patriotic and religious glow. On the one hand, it proposes the traditional view that a woman's place is in the home; at the same time it encourages women to enter the work place as "temporaries" at substandard wages. It is a hypocritical and exploitative view, but one which the political opposition and feminist groups have not yet been strong enough to mount effective opposition against.

Corrupt Practices

It is not surprising that near-bankrupt universities, ill-paid staff, absurdly difficult exams requiring short rote answers, and a society obsessed with status would conspire to make bribery and extortion a recurring fact of life in Japan's educational systems.

The Japanese people are as honest as any, but parents in dire straits are tempted to break the law, whether by "boundary jumping" or getting advance copies of their youngsters' exams.

At Waseda in 1980, the parents of about ten examinees paid a total of 46 million yen to obtain copies of the question and answer sheets from faculty members of the Commercial Department. This after the parents had spent substantial portions of their income over the years to get their children that far.

Educators, too, succumb to corruption. In one case, the chairman of a preparatory school swindled parents of 30 million yen each with a promise to get their youngsters into university.[34]

The form of entrance examinations seems tailored for wrongdoing. Nearly all are of the short answer or multiple-choice variety. Essay-type answers are virtually non-existent. The tests most open to abuse are the English-language examinations, where students are required to memorize every word of lengthy paragraphs from works of literature. These are then duplicated on the question sheets, with individual words or phrases left blank. The student must insert the exact word or phrase as used by the author. No matter that the word used by the student is perfect English; if it is not the same as in the original, it is wrong. With the most prodigious efforts imaginable, it is clearly impossible to accomplish this memory-work, so professors offer hints as to probable passages from likely books.

Some may give more detailed hints than others. Not corruption exactly, for it is very rare that money ever changes hands, but a pervading atmosphere in which anxiety, greed and simple human compassion interact leaves open the door to "corruption" of many degrees and kinds.

Preferential treatment, a sort of moral corruption, exists everywhere, encouraged by circumstances in Japan. With competition to enter certain universities and departments so stiff, it is not surprising that corruption is uncovered. In 1982, it came to light that Aoyama Gakuin University gave second-choice entrance candidates with special connections priority over those who passed the exams with higher marks. An administrator of the university admitted in 1982 that "this has been normal practice since the university was opened in 1949, and I don't think it is bad."[35] Yet the student candidates were led to believe that entrance was based exclusively on exam results.

It has long been known that some universities demand donations for entry to their dental and medical schools.[36] The criterion for entrance is the size of the donation, not the level of academic excellence. In 1977, the Aichi Medical College accepted large donations for back-door admissions. Two facts came to light, namely, that the large majority of entrants to medical schools were from medical families, and that the "donations" themselves were very large. In the case of Aichi, the list showed that 85 per cent of freshmen's parents were physicians, and the biggest donation, of more than 57 million yen, was made by a doctor in Osaka.[37] One tragic result of the affair was the suicide of a fourth year student, who was upset because *all* the students on the campus were viewed with suspicion.[38] He was one of those who was not admitted through bribery.

The number of institutions which demand to be informed of the applicant's family wealth has also been increasing. Saitama Medical College requires parents to give details about their families' savings accounts, securities, land holdings, as well as ownership in housing and forest areas. Other colleges telephone parents of applicants immediately after the entrance tests to discuss donations.

Wealth, however, cannot buy a medical degree. Indeed, because many students accepted have money but few other qualifications, fewer students have been able to pass the national examinations. Although the success rate in the national exams still remains high (it was 90 per cent up to 1973), it has declined since that date. In 1982, there were 85 examinees who had tried to pass as many as thirteen times. In some universities, fewer than a third are able to pass.[39]

Another factor encouraging ethical breaches is the treatment of professors, who are among the lowest-paid professionals in Japan. Moreover, their academic lives are filled with frustration. A scholar hesitates before openly disagreeing with his senior, even if his silence means publication of incorrect scientific results. Confined by the Japanese status system, ill paid, relying on lecturing at outside universities to make ends meet, and in most cases lacking the prestige of a pre-war degree, most professors are profoundly dissatisfied, and a few have been corrupted.

The 1983 scandal at the prestigious Tokyo Medical and Dental University was typical, although there was a twist. It involved an applicant for a professorship who bribed a member of the selection committee. The interesting aspect was that, when he failed to get the job, he went public and complained to a newspaper. He obviously was convinced that bribery was an accepted method of advancement and felt cheated when his efforts were in vain. Such an incident illustrates, too, the great temptations open to professors, particularly in medical schools. They have been compared with feudal lords, with absolute authority over their subordinates, and the ever-present opportunity to make considerable fortunes. Achieving such a position is a very great prize and the present selection system has led to unethical behaviour, including the accepting of bribes.

Although it is well known that corruption permeates even the inner circles of Japan's intellectual community, the 1970s case of Yoshio Unno came as a shock. Unno, one of Japan's finest international musicians, accepted "rewards" for pushing sales of instruments to his students and to the Tokyo University of Fine Arts and Music. The music industry, not without blame itself, claims teachers have been exploiting their students and universities for years. The student is the victim, for his future may depend on his professor. It is customary for teachers of music to act as judges in musical competitions, even when their own students are involved. The students, in turn, are the unwilling dupes, facing a none too subtle blackmail if they do not buy the recommended instrument at the price demanded.

Four Wasted Years

Once a student is admitted to a status university, for all intents and purposes his future is assured. Meanwhile, his counterparts in the mass of private universities know that, regardless of how hard they work or how high they graduate, the jobs in the traditional firms will be denied them. For both types of students, there is little motivation to work. One writer has called the university experience "four wasted years."

Japanese business helped create this sad state of affairs. In the early post-war years, the competition for graduates was so great that, instead of waiting until the students had passed their final exams, businesses gave them casual tests and promised jobs upon graduation. As universities became grossly overcrowded, it became common to graduate all, regardless of their standings. A direct result is that the undergraduate examinations are almost worthless and motivation to study has virtually ceased.

With such a lax system it is not surprising that the students, harassed throughout their lives, should start to take life easy. This attitude has resulted in severe criticism from many Japanese who view the typical undergraduate as little more than a frequenter of coffee shops, *mah jong* parlours, *pachinko* parlours and bowling alleys. The same detractor would say that students show up only for the exams and don't even know what their professors look like. Like most generalizations, it is partly true. Most students are serious, but for nearly half, their declared aim is not to get professional and technical qualifications but to lead a free life for four years.

All undergraduates are aware that professors are lenient in grading, even in the more demanding disciplines. For a university to expel a student, or for a teacher to fail a pupil is considered a public admission of a lack of ability and concern on the part of his professors. Undergraduates are permitted to stay virtually until they do graduate. A liberal arts student can remain on the roles for eleven years before having to drop out, while those at medical schools are allowed six years to earn enough credits. Such "professional" students are called *ryunen*.

Students would have to be paragons of virtue if they were not to loaf, but, all the same, much can be gained from Japanese university life.

Academic clubs offer discussion and debate, and the content of most liberal arts courses can be judged by the distaste in which they are held by the hierarchies. The pity is that Japanese universities cannot do credit to their students, and, for this, the system of tenure and advancement within the faculties must bear substantial blame.

As a general rule, the more prestigious the university the more inbred the faculties. Some hire virtually only their own graduates. The sciences tend to be much more open, but here, too, overall figures speak for themselves. At Tokyo and Kyoto, the faculties are made up of 95 and 89 per cent respectively of their own graduates, who are accorded lifetime tenure. Nationally, the figure is some 34 per cent.[40] These percentages are radically higher than those of universities in the West. British and French universities do not employ any of their own students on a lifetime basis upon graduation, and it is exceedingly rare in the United States or West Germany.

While Tokyo and Kyoto are almost entirely isolated from their fellow institutions in Japan, nearly all national universities are quarantined from centres of learning overseas. Out of a total of 110,000 university teachers, foreigners number fewer than 1,000, and they are mostly found in private institutions, teaching foreign languages. To compound the problem, Japanese law specifically bars any person not of Japanese nationality from ever being appointed as a tenured professor on the faculty of any national university. This racism, which has not been ameliorated by the modest easing of citizenship rules in 1984, is ultimately self-defeating.

Segregation is aggravated by the isolation of one department from another as well. Compartmentalization appears to be an accepted fact. In large universitites, this makes setting up common programs, common goals and interdisciplinary research a major problem.

Allowing for the fact that there is not a great deal of circulation among the personnel of different faculties, except for the "part-time" teaching in other universities, the situation is worsened by the "chair system." When the chaired professor retires, the assistant professor with seniority is advanced automatically. The only competition that exists, and that on a limited and partial scale, is among teaching assistants in the sciences. It is a system which results in poor teaching and disillusionment among the best students.

That students relish intellectual stimulation after becoming accustomed to force-feeding may come as a pleasant surprise, but such appears to be the case. Students' main complaints are that professors try only "to impart knowledge without stimulating the class to think,"[41] and that their classroom lectures are "far removed from actual problems."[42]

By the time Japanese youth have passed through university, they have few illusions about the value of their higher education. In a 1983 poll of undergraduates in Japan, the United States and Britain, one of the questions was, "Can only graduates from good schools and universities become great persons?" Only 9 per cent agreed in Japan, compared with 14 per cent in the United States and 31 per cent in Great Britain. Japanese students are realistically aware that success in the "examination hell," while it may assure them of good jobs, does not necessarily rate them among the "Best and the Brightest."

Graduate Schools

Graduate schools are one of the weakest elements in Japanese higher education. Most have to share their facilities with the undergraduate departments and, because they have no regular full-time teachers, are forced to borrow from the undergraduate schools. Administrative work, too, is performed by the same staffs for undergraduate and graduate levels. Neither students nor schools receive much in the way of government financial aid. This lack of incentive, combined with corporations' preference to hire those with Bachelor degrees, means that most potential graduate students go directly into the business world instead. In part, this is also due to a perception of undergraduate training as the culmination of study; for instance, medical, dental, engineering and specialized institutes are all undergraduate schools.

Business insists that young persons can gain advanced training on the job, although they realize that graduate schools have a role in the advancement of scientific knowledge. But business gives little incentive to those seeking graduate degrees. An M.A. is paid only slightly higher than a B.A., with the result that the commercial or social studies student looks upon the lesser degree as the quickest, least expensive route to business.

Young researchers who pursue their studies in Japan receive little further training. They usually end up as assistants to their professors, often in areas outside their specialty. Some of the best teachers, attracted by a better salary, and less restricted by the stultifying emphasis on rank, now work abroad. This exodus has resulted in a serious "brain drain," which may, in the view of some Japanese academics, threaten the standards of higher education in Japan in the long run.[43]

Students who study abroad often find it difficult to find employment upon returning. They may have fluency in a second language and picked up an M.A. and a Ph.D. along the way, but invariably, unless they are from a "status" university initially, they have to settle for being paid less than if they had remained at home. With so many unstable factors built into the system, it is hard to believe that it can survive the demands which lie ahead.

To compete with the world, Japan business needs a new generation who are willing to study and work at home, for Japan cannot afford a "brain drain." If this involves new ways of doing things, it is a risk the *zaikai* are increasingly being forced to take. Recognizing Japan's shortcomings in basic research, the Japanese government is investing heavily in scientific education and research facilities. The funding for scientific education will undoubtedly increase the number of researchers and engineers, markedly increasing as well the pool of such workers that high technology companies can choose from. But many doubt that the forced-march approach to creativity will be successful in the context of Japanese society.[44]

The Central Council for Education in Japan has suggested that graduate institutions should be set up separately from undergraduate departments but within institutions adequately equipped for research. The institutions designated as graduate schools would offer advanced specialized curricula leading to a master's degree, while "research centres" would train academic research workers and award doctorate degrees. These two categories of higher education are to be firmly separated from undergraduate programs so that professors teaching at the undergraduate level may concentrate on their teaching, and those engaged in research may devote their energy fully to that.[45]

Legislation proposed in 1975 would permit the establishment of independent universities to be exclusively devoted to graduate teaching and research. Foreign educationalists doubt, however, that the quality of teaching and research can be improved by separating graduate and undergraduate work into different institutions.

The System Won't Do

The present system won't do, traditionalists and reformers agree. Apart from all the other reasons, Japan can no longer afford the luxury of four wasted years at university. As in the West, there is a debate on how education can best serve the nation, debate which has divided the public into two warring camps. There are those who look upon education as a training school for industry, and others who believe it should develop knowledgeable citizens who can provide leadership in improving society and the quality of life.

In Japan there is a very strong historical sense of a close link between education and economic development. Many Japanese maintain that it was the educational reforms under the Meiji governments which permitted their country to become a modern industrial power. Further, they project that national education will enable Japan to achieve its third industrial revolution. There is no other capitalist nation that emphasizes the role of education as a basis for growth to such an extent.

The hierarchies generally believe that since the Meiji system proved its worth, it should have been left largely intact after the war, save for those changes required to teach new technologies.

A radical application of this conservative attitude is exposed by Konosuke Matsushita, head of one of the world's largest electrical firms, Matsushita Electric Industrial. He is a prophet of economic growth and, like his Meiji forebears, conceives of education as a way to train youth with technical skills and high standards. He advocates reducing the number of colleges and high schools by half. This would, he maintains, have two desirable effects: it would increase the value of college education and also save the government in the order of three billion yen per year.[46] Such views are supported by influential elements within the LDP and among the *zaikai*. An opposite view is taken by Japan's liberals and humanists, including Motofumi Makieda.

Makieda, once chairman of the Japan Teachers' Union, looks upon education as a force for social change. He maintains that the way to ensure a better society is to expand the role of public education, by reducing objective-type testing and abolishing the outside cram school system, both of which discriminate against children from poorer families. If the system is left as it is, Makieda argues, it will only perpetuate material and social differences.

The conservatives counter that Japan's present system is producing a generation of weak-willed, ill-disciplined and unpatriotic youth. Leftist American-inspired reforms, they maintain, are responsible for the lowering of morals, increased delinquency and other social ills.[47]

The reformers see the present system as one in which merit counts only if the student can afford it. In the view of one:

> Japan seems to have spawned a society in which upper-strata children tend to enter the best high schools and universities, preparing them for entry into the elite; middle-strata children attend second and third-rate high schools and universities and go on to take commensurate jobs; and

lower-strata children are apt to go to a low class high school or attend night school and then begin employment. In other words, the top remains at the top and the bottom at the bottom.[48]

The reformers advocate increasing the period of compulsory education from nine to twelve years and retaining vocational training in high schools. They oppose the Ministry of Education's plans for a two-track, university and non-university system. Those who wish to keep the "best" of the present system maintain that all should have access to higher education; the alternative, they contend, not only perpetuates an elite class, but discriminates against students in rural areas where a university education is seldom an option. Reformers do not deny differences in ability among students, nor do they reject streaming according to ability, as long as students can move from one group to another easily as motivation and performance change.

Education, then, has become a battleground for right and left. Conservatives emphasize service to society and condemn postwar education because it tends to be based upon the self-interest of the students. Greater consideration, they maintain, should be focused on the group, society and the nation. Without this grounding, they believe education serves no purpose. These traditionalists are in favour of a modified version of the 1890 Imperial Rescript on Education.

The reformers, including most teachers, claim the Rescript deals less with education than with submissiveness, obedience and loyalty, and its revival would have repercussions far beyond education. They have a very real fear that government and traditionalist forces are intent on reverting to the old "Imperial Way." Indeed, the government's educational reform has become a code phrase for a Meiji revival. What Yasuhiro Nakasone calls a "robust culture," is seen by critics as a call to authoritarianism.

5

FABRICATED TRADITIONS

Today, there exist no evils and we feel no necessity [for
a factory law]. We cannot agree to something that will
destroy the beautiful custom of master-servant relations
and wreak havoc on our industrial peace.
HEIGORO SHODA, Director, Mitsubishi Nagasaki Shipyard, 1910[1]

Although managers pay lip service to the notion of
the enterprise as a family, in actuality their treatment of
workers and staff is fundamentally different. The concept
governing labour-management is that, if the enterprise is
a family, the staff are family members and the workers
are family servants.
HOME MINISTRY *Review of Labour Relations*, 1941[2]

The Cloak of the Samurai

Japan's labour-management relations are built on traditions that
were fabricated at the turn of the century. These "beautiful
customs," as one employer labelled the emerging industrial
"peace," were invented and exploited by employers in order to
achieve a submissive work force.

Under feudalism, Japanese merchants were near the bottom of
the social ladder. With the Restoration, they saw their chance to
gain status by adopting the traditions of the *samurai*, who had
provided Japan's rebel leadership. Out of opportunism or conviction, they portrayed "competition" and "profits" as selfish
motivations, hence rejecting the glorification of the individual
and individualism, and substituted instead patriotism and devo-

tion to the emperor.[3] Such ideals were, of course, welcomed by Japan's new rulers.

Leaders and merchants, both seeking to industrialize Japan quickly, needed a willing work force. The ideology for the purpose was at hand. As the West had its work ethic, so did the Japanese – a mix of Buddhist and Confucian philosophies. The Zen Buddhist monks, like the Puritans, put a high value on simple living and productive labour. The Confucian ideology stressed these virtues too, as well as the ideal of each person having a particular role in society, a role shaped and nurtured by the education system.

In 1896, Takashi Masuda, president of the Mitsui Trading Company, argued that only education would prevent troubled labour relations.[4] He and his fellow industrialists had no faith in inborn human traits.

To ensure that relations remained peaceful, and workers submissive, the industrialists imposed a pattern of paternal control. And the myth of idyllic feudal labour relations was born.

Heigoro Shoda of Mitsubishi spoke, in 1910, in glowing terms of the historical relationship between employer and employed in Japan. Conveniently forgotten were the waves of bitter strikes in 1906 and 1907. Shoda proclaimed:

> Since ancient times, Japan has possessed the beautiful custom of master-servant relations based firmly on a spirit of sacrifice and compassion ...[5]

Shoda, Masuda and the other industrialists went to great lengths to oppose all moves to bring in factory legislation. When a factory act was finally legislated in 1911, they made sure that the "beautiful customs" were written in it. Paternalism was sanctified.

Labour's Early Years

The modern labour movement in Japan really began in the summer of 1897, after the war with China over Korea had ended in 1895. Industry had prospered through war contracts and the war indemnity taken from China. However, there was a period of post-war inflation, during which the workers demanded an increase in wages to cover the increased cost of living. One direct result was the founding of the Iron Workers' Union in Tokyo on 1 December 1897. With over 1,000 members, it was the first in Japan.[6]

As in Western industrial societies, the history of trade unionism in Japan is the story of many more defeats than victories. The spread between the two is far greater in Japan than in the West. Trade unions have proved to be so dangerous to the existing social order simply because they have, if only to a limited degree, curtailed the competition of employees among themselves. The Japanese companies recognized this united front as a threat. As a result, the first sporadic and unorganized protests, in the 1870s, were put down ruthlessly.

After the formation of the Iron Workers' Union, the nascent movement was moderate and reformist. However, in the decade between 1897 and 1907, a variety of Western radical ideas came to influence it. The most pervasive was anarcho-syndicalism, a philosophy which espouses the immediate destruction of private ownership and its replacement by worker control. While historians have argued that this extreme radicalism nurtured further oppression, there is no reason to believe that the government would have responded less brutally to the milder challenge that democratic socialism would have posed. In the midst of a police state atmosphere, the Socialist Party of Japan was formed on 26 February 1906. Several incidents of violence were shortly to result in a ban on the party.

The first great protest started 14 February 1907 at the Ashio copper mines. Workers rose up against the inhumane working conditions for three days before the action was put down by three regiments of troops. Meanwhile, disorder spread. The Bessi Copper Mine was struck on 4 June. Again the army was called in and the miners were forced back to work. This brutal repression culminated in a High Treason Trial staged in 1910-11, at which leading leftists were sentenced to death on charges of planning to kill the emperor. The government used this alleged treason bid as an excuse to stamp out all labour organizations.

Although World War I resulted in industrial expansion and in-

creased profits, the workers did not share in the prosperity. Their
discontent was fuelled by the success of the Russian Revolution
and by the ideals of Marxism. Employers were once again faced
with organized worker action. They responded with police oppression but, by 1921, labour unions briefly showed signs of
taking the lead in a series of bold and illegal strikes.

The employers continued to promote harmony and "beautiful
customs," but worker action forced them to re-evaluate their
policy. Employer paternalism had failed to silence the workers.
As one scholar observes:

> Management's professed view of the company as a pater-
> nal, benevolent institution concerned above all with its
> workers stands in stark contrast to the worker perception of
> the company as insincere and cold-blooded.[7]

Industrialists continued their close association with government throughout the post-war years but, as the Great Depression
descended, employers realized that a major reorganization was
needed. Management turned its attention to gaining effective
political control, a goal reached by forming the Hamaguchi Ministry in 1929.

Osachi Hamaguchi, the new prime minister, was a Japanese-
style liberal who believed in rigid protectionism and who strove
for effective authority of the Diet and for control by the civil
power. Those too were the aims of big business. For his troubles
he was shot in November 1930 by a right-wing youth who opposed his democratic ideas. Hamaguchi died the following year
as a result of his wound.

The real political and economic power of business was demonstrated during the years 1930-32. In 1930, cartels and trusts
were legalized and key industries were placed under the control
of four industrial combines. Meanwhile, the *zaibatsu* used their
new strength through the ministry to maintain maximum profits.

In 1932, labour legislation, slated to come before the Diet,
proposed some protection for the employees of small businesses.
The working conditions of these lowest of workers had become
well known through accounts in the press. Most lived with their
employers in a feudalistic relationship, working fifteen to nine-

teen hours a day. The bill proposed to enforce 10 p.m. closing, and four non-working days a month. But business opposition to the bill effectively killed it before it was even submitted to the Diet.

In the inter-war years, Japanese labour experienced insecurity and sharp divisions. Companies sought to maintain stability through authoritarian control. As part of this strategy, worker councils were introduced with the aim of creating a facade of worker participation. The myth of workers as members of one big family was a sham in all large firms, though it was to become a political cornerstone of labour-management relations in Japan, extending to the present day. And while the family likeness was closer to the truth in small and medium-sized businesses, often controlled by family members for generations, workers in these companies lost in material benefits, as smaller firms could pay their workers only subsistence wages.

Trade unions barely existed in the Japan of the 1930s. Membership never exceeded 7 per cent of the work force and, apart from those in a weak seamen's union, most unionists were in small and medium-sized enterprises. In 1939, all of these groups were dissolved and re-formed into a military front organization called *Sampo*, or "Industrial Patriotic Society," which aimed only to further Japan's war against China.

This labour organization, without unions, was formed by a broad coalition of bureaucrats, politicians and intellectuals, with some managers and a few groups of workers. Local police helped by urging or coercing thousands of companies to set up their own *Sampo* branches.

When the Allied Occupation began in September 1945, neither victor nor vanquished knew what kind of society would evolve. The working people lacked a strong tradition of labour organization so, without strong Occupation support, their immediate future looked bleak. The Trade Union Law of December 1945 established for the first time in Japanese history the legal right of workers to organize. At that time there were only five trade unions in the country, with a total membership of 5,300. But, for nine months, it seemed that an effective workers' movement might develop.

Post-War Hopes

Food, not ideology, was the spark that ignited the demands for reform. The period between August 1945 and January 1946 was one of skyrocketing inflation, black marketeering and mass misery. Members of the hierarchies, conservative politicians, industrialists and gangsters, all seemed to be able to live well, but the great mass of Japanese barely survived. It was under these circumstances that the workers staged a hunger march during which they demanded the resignation of the government and abdication of the emperor.

Radicalism reached its peak during 1946 and 1947. Worker control of factories became a commonly heard demand, as managers tried to cut down their work force and workers fought to subsist.[8]

There was a certain justification for labour taking control.[9] In the post-war confusion, managers lost full control of their factories. Some were dishonest and played the black market; some were controlled by rightists of the wartime school. A case in point was the first major labour takeover, that of a national newspaper, the *Yomiuri Shimbun*. The publisher, a notorious militarist and anti-unionist, was dismissed.

But most cases of factory control had a purely economic basis. When the Japan National Railways decided to dismiss a large number of workers, the employees refused to be laid off. Rather than strike, they took over management duties. They thereby maintained essential services, and were able, at the same time, to increase their own pay.

Another takeover occurred at the Keisei Railway Company. At the end of 1945, its workers demanded a five-fold increase in wages, a demand refused by management. Accordingly, on 10 December, workers offered free transportation for a short period, then charged fares from which they deducted the wages they had initially demanded. "From now on," they said, "we will undertake to repair the trains and transport the passengers. Let us see how our way of conducting the operation compares with that of the management."[10] Keisei's workers were able to increase the railway's efficiency, show a profit and at the same time realize their demand for a wage increase.

This action was followed by others, which the Japanese authorities, supported by SCAP, condemned as destructive of the economy. In this light, production control of a coal mine in Hokkaido, the northern island, was an embarrassment to the authorities. After taking over the pits, the miners increased production from 250 to over 650 tons per day, while cutting the work day from twelve to eight hours.

In most of these cases, as we have seen, the workers avoided strikes which would have crippled their livelihood and the economy of the country. Their real crime, in the eyes of the hierarchies and SCAP, was taking over private property, an act tantamount to treason.

On 20 May 1946, General MacArthur threatened to suppress all political demonstrations. The government was now on a collision course with organized labour. Matters came to a head on 31 January 1947, the day before a planned general strike, when General MacArthur issued a statement prohibiting it, on the grounds that he could not possibly permit so dangerous a weapon in the hands of the workers.

MacArthur's action was applauded by Prime Minister Yoshida and the authorities, just as it was condemned by leftists, one of whom wrote, "... if the strike had taken place, we would have discovered in no uncertain terms what a priceless thing is politics based on democracy."[11] The consensus is that it would have toppled the Yoshida administration, which was on the verge of collapse in any case. Although there is disagreement about the significance of MacArthur's act, one fact is indisputable. The aborted general strike of 1 February 1947 marked the farthest point of advance for the labour movement, and also the point of no return in the continuous push to the right of Japanese labour relations. When SCAP was forced to choose between potentially socialist unions and the Yoshida government, MacArthur came down on the side of the conservatives.

'Recovery of Management'

In the two years before the call for a general strike, workers had started to take over the management of their factories and businesses. This interest in "production control" spread through all sectors of Japanese industry. In April and May of 1946, 110 production-control struggles were recorded with nearly 75,000 workers involved.[12] In reaction, the employers co-ordinated a movement against worker seizure, called "recovery of management." One of their earliest strategies was to turn *Sampo*, the wartime labour front, into a grouping of co-operative and docile unions.

At the same time, the Japanese authorities, to whom any form of change is anathema, began to see communists under every bed. In the words of one Japanese scholar: "Yoshida believed organized labour in post-surrender Japan was little more than a pawn of the communists. Its activism irresponsible, at worst malicious. Its goals selfish, negative, destructive."[13]

A similar view is colourfully expressed by an admitted rightwing extremist, but one who became influential within the corridors of power. Yoshio Kodama wrote in his autobiography:

> The bestial roar of the Communist Party during the days from the general election of 1946 to the failure of their 1 February strike reached into my cell through the barred windows of Sugamo Prison. This year [1948] their shouts cannot be heard as clearly as in the past, yet I can feel the dull thud of the marching feet of thousands of Communists advancing towards the bolshevization of Japan reverberating ominously from the bowels of Japan.[14]

This fear of communism, bordering on paranoia, was not exclusive to Japan, of course. The pre-conditions of the McCarthy era were quickly coalescing in the United States.

With the growth of the Cold War, the United States' enthusiasm for democratic unionism in Japan noticeably cooled. In July 1948, the rights to bargain collectively and to strike were withdrawn from Japanese public servants. Beginning in the same month, MacArthur forced the Japanese cabinet to outlaw all demonstrations by government employees and to declare null and void all existing collective bargaining agreements. He stopped those in progress and set stiff jail sentences for unionists who did not comply.

Members of the National Railway Workers' Union reacted by walking off their jobs. This period of confrontation was climaxed by a number of tragic events including the apparent murder of the president of the National Railway Corporation, whose body was found on the railway tracks on 5 July 1949. Subsequently, a train was sabotaged, derailed and overturned. The engineer and his assistant were killed. Another train was later derailed at Matsukawa. This time, three engineers were trapped and burned to death, and three passengers seriously injured. This last incident resulted in a famous series of trials.

These events took place in the midst of persistent attempts by SCAP and the Occupation's military intelligence to discredit the Left. Instead of spending the slightest effort to discover who had caused the wreck, the authorities arrested twenty militant trade unionists and general troublemakers. The courts found all of them guilty and handed down sentences which included the death penalty and life imprisonment. Fourteen years and five trials later, on 12 September 1963, the accused were all found not guilty.[15]

On 14 August 1964, the statute of limitations on the Matsukawa case was up, precluding further prosecution, but the case was not closed. The defendants sued the government in order to prove that they had been framed and were therefore entitled to several million yen in damages. As part of this suit, the plaintiffs charged the government had known all along who were the "true criminals in the Matsukawa case." When the Supreme Court upheld the defendants by returning a "not guilty" verdict, the question remained: who was in fact responsible?[16]

Even today there is speculation about whether American agents sabotaged the train at Matsukawa as part of their anti-socialist campaign.

By 1949 union bashing became so blatant in Japan that the powerful and strongly anti-socialist American Federation of Labor was appalled by what it saw and called on the U.S. government to discontinue what it termed repressive action "... being carried on under the guise of anti-communism against legitimate trade union objectives and practices ..."[17] Shortly afterwards, what U.S. organized labour had labelled democratic unionism was largely dead.

Political strikes were banned in March 1949, but no concise definition of "political" was given, opening the door to government prohibition of almost all strikes. This move so incensed the workers that large-scale violence resulted. In response, Yoshida sought to mobilize two million volunteer firemen, to be added to 30,000 national and 95,000 local police, in event of "riots" or "emergencies." As before the war, a combination of police power and a divided labour movement was to assure his regime relative freedom from industrial unrest.

By March 1949, there were 6,910,000 workers organized into 36,500 unions, representing 30 per cent of all non-agricultural labour. But many of these unions were of the government-sanctioned co-operative variety. SCAP, in large measure, had achieved its object of an orderly, some might say submissive, trade union movement.

The Occupation's military intelligence, G.2, co-operating with the ultraright in Japan, infiltrated the newly born Japanese trade unions with *yakuza* and other anti-labour elements, in order to destroy self-governing unions and replace them with ones willing to co-operate with the employers.[18] Their success can be measured statistically. Three weeks before the outbreak of the Korean War, in June 1950, more than 5,500 unions "disappeared." Further, union membership declined by 880,000 in one year.

It is a common belief that co-operative enterprise unions evolved naturally. Nothing could be further from the truth. Co-operative unionism was imposed, often brutally, upon the workers. The destruction of the "old" Toshiba union was one of the early examples. The attack on the union came during a decisive phase of the prolonged labour-management dispute over dismissals. To resolve this dispute, management encouraged "moderate" workers to form a new union. It then immediately concluded a contract with the new group and recognized it as the sole bargaining representative of the workers.[19]

The employers set out to systematically divide the labour force, often by offering some workers security within co-operative company unions. This division of the workers into "permanent" and "temporary" employees had first been imposed at the turn of the century, to ensure a stable work force and to keep wages down. Under paternalism, the "permanent" workers were told they were part of the family. As a manager told his senior workers in 1904:

> You are chosen and are part of the . . . family. It wouldn't do
> to think of yourselves in the same category as these new
> temporary people.[20]

Since those days, enterprise unions have taken this division a step further. They cater to full-time employees, but most particularly to the white-collar workers – office and factory staff – as these employees tend to be more conservative and ally themselves with the employers. Hence, they are favoured by management and support its efforts to maintain a peaceful labour force.

Trade union leaders are usually "elected" from the white-collar employees with the approval of management. Jobs are then found for them within the company's executive ranks, where they do their part to assure peaceful labour-management relations.

Democratic trade unionism did not go down without a fight. A series of actions were called against major corporations. Toyota was struck in 1951, Nissan in 1953 and Nihon Steel in the following year. Each strike ended in defeat and many union leaders, as well as numerous rank and file members, were fired.

The Nissan strike was like a small-scale guerrilla war, reflecting Japan's history and the times. Nissan was a "new *zaibatsu*," a creature of the militarists in Manchuria. Therefore, in the postwar years its management was weaker than most. As well, the company founder, a militarist named Yoshisuka Ayukawa, and his executives had been purged, making the new management particularly vulnerable. At many companies – Toyota for example – the militant union was quite easily and quickly replaced by a management-approved union. This was not the case at Nissan.

The protagonists in the Nissan strike were bigger than life. The man who took over Nissan was a conservative banker,

Katsuji Kawamata; the union was led by the brilliant and charismatic Tatsuo Masuda. Both were of the upper-middle class, both university graduates, but Masuda's "alma mater" was the prestigious Imperial University of Tokyo, thus making him a traitor to his class. The third, the man who led the strike breakers, was Ichiro Shioji. A creature of Kawamata, he was to head the all-powerful All Nissan Union, imposed by management after the strike. When he joined Nissan he was already an experienced anti-labour activist and a born street fighter, although only 26 years of age.[21]

Tetsuo Masuda, a giant among Japan's labour leaders, could have succeeded in any of the nation's elites. Instead, he chose to back the underdog and fight for democratic unionism. He was worshipped by his fellows, and became the most forceful man in the entire auto industry. Even his enemies could never label him a communist and make it stick. A man of independent mind, a brilliant speaker, he dreamed of an industry trade union.

When the Nissan strike began 25 May 1953, Kawamata decided to wait it out and exhaust the union. Nikkeiren, the employers' association, was ready to aid the company financially. Nissan hired several hundred thugs, or *yakuza*, to protect a second union, to be formed mainly from men in the middle level.

Management refused to talk to Masuda. It planned to bait and provoke the union. Inevitably, the union moved closer to violence. On 5 August, Kawamata locked out the strikers and, on the 7th, the second union surfaced. When the management put up barricades, the unions responded with force. Masuda was arrested.

For the first time, Kawamata had the upper hand. He was well financed; the union was not. Once the second union was in place, its members, mostly white-collar workers, were allowed to come to work and were paid immediately.[22] In the aftermath of the failed strike, Masuda was jailed for two weeks. The strike had lasted 100 days. Strikebreaker Ichiro Shioji became head of the company union.

For a brief time the old order at Nissan became democratized by its collaboration with co-operative unions, but the basis of real power had never really changed. Over the next few years, thousands of workers were fired, and the union became one of the most subservient in Japan. Masuda died in 1964 of a heart attack. He was 50 years old. Some twenty years later, when Katsuji Kawamata was asked about Masuda, he replied, "Masuda? I don't really remember him. Besides, he is dead, so why even talk about him?"[23]

Nissan, grown into a giant, played host to Leonard Woodcock, then head of the U.S. United Automobile Workers, in 1973. On that occasion, Woodcock first learned of the union's past. He had never before heard of the 1953 strike, and asked Shioji, "Why did you not tell me of this before?"

"You never asked me," said Shioji.[24]

Democracy in enterprise unions is a sometime thing. Elections for union office commonly offer only one slate of candidates. In one union, workers were asked to vote for 182 union officials from a field of 182. Even after having taken such precautions, unions require employees to vote openly, in front of their supervisors, to ensure there are no "spoilt" ballots. Unity, however, still shows occasional cracks. In early 1986, some workers in an automobile plant appealed to their counterparts in Britain to seek support against what they claimed as "a denial of democratic procedure and a betrayal of workers' rights." They accused their union of being "an aggressive organ of management." The appeal fell on deaf ears.

Today, Japan's enterprise unions flourish, abetted by "equal responsibility," the basis of company indoctrination. The ideal, from the employer's viewpoint, is to play down the worker-management struggle within an enterprise and to divert attention to the competition of company A against company B.[25] One advantage of this philosophy is its power to weaken labour solidarity at the industrial or national level. Perhaps this competition can best be shown in a typical union song, where "our company" is emphasized:

Now to be born anew: the history of Japan.
Wave the union flag on high.
The sun thrusts up over the horizon.
The century of the working man arrives!
Our Hitachi! Hitachi where the muscles tense![26]

In the West, the weight of the big trade union provides a counterbalance to the weight of the big corporation. Nothing of the kind has been allowed to evolve in Japan, and the existence of enterprise trade unions has reduced the likelihood that it ever will.

Where large groups of workers exist, outside the confines of a single plant, the hierarchies prefer multiple unions, which enable them once more to use divide and rule tactics and whip up hatred against those who oppose their plans.[27] As a result, multiple unions tend to be found mainly in the public sector. The Japan National Railway had six organizations until it was privatized; there are four in the Ministry of Posts and Communications and eight among the teachers.

Drilling their workers in the values of company success and survival through the company union is management's first labour priority. It follows, from these early lessons, that strikes are to be avoided at all costs. The workers are taught by their leaders and by management that industrial action reflects badly on all concerned. Trade unions are designed primarily to control and contain disputes, not, as in the West, to become the instrument of these struggles.

Dissension and Violence

The use of gangsters in strikebreaking is accepted even by established and respectable concerns.[28] In one firm, a broadcasting company, use of strongarm tactics was condemned by the Labour Relations Commission. In that instance, an ultraright-wing group was enlisted to force active union leaders to retire.[29]

To understand the prevalence of violence in strikes, we must remember the long and bitter history of Japanese labour relations. The National Railway Workers' Union had been involved in militancy ever since the disastrous Matsukawa affair of 1949. Since those days the Japanese government had kept up its attempts to destroy the union. The conflict resumed in the early 1970s as the workers, united again after a lapse of many years, sought to share in the "economic miracle."

During the period from 4 April 1972 to 12 March 1973, national railway service was disrupted for a total of 81 days. In the crowded trains, commuters' passions flared, leading to shoving matches and physical attacks. Over 200 passengers were injured. Japan's worst anti-union violence was also experienced during that period. Frustrated by three weeks of delayed and cancelled trains, the travelling public went on the rampage. Railway property was damaged and destroyed and workers were assaulted.

In 1974, at the height of the first oil shock, the 5,211 strikes officially recorded in Japan actually exceeded the number reported for that year in either the United States, Great Britain, France or Italy. If work stoppages of less than half a day, not included in the official statistics, were counted, the number would more than double, to almost 12,000. In fact, in 1974 Japan recorded the highest number of strikes of any year in Japanese history. The number of strikes had risen gradually since the mid-1960s and continued to rise until 1979, after which it fell drastically. The figures reveal the volatility of Japanese labour-management relations.[30]

But numbers do not tell the whole story. For one, Japanese strikes are usually much shorter than in the West, and are not the principal labour tactic. They are far exceeded by other types of conflict, such as slowdowns, picketing, working to rule, and absenteeism. And sometimes even sabotage. In the view of one Japanese, who has been an active member of the Tokyo Metropolitan Labour Relations Commission, "Japan might be regarded as one of the most remarkable countries in the world in the sense that the greatest variety of acts of dispute occur there daily."[31]

'Dedicated' Workers

One of the favourite and more entrenched ideas about the Japanese is that they are by nature dedicated to their work, however menial or repetitive it might be. This "love" is claimed to be a national trait, a view accepted by many who have observed but never actually worked with the Japanese. One foreign scholar-diplomat who has lived extensively in Japan even praises its "protestant ethic" which, he says, is far stronger than in the West. He associates the work ethic with the Japanese climate, but also proposes that it has been strengthened by group orientation. He concludes that "the primary identification of the individual Japanese with his work group and his enthusiastic ever joyous participation in its activities are reasons why the Japanese work ethic even today appears strong."[32]

In the diary of one worker, who is not atypical, joyous participation is noticeably absent in his description of his working day.

> The conveyor starts at 6:00 a.m. and doesn't stop until
> 11:00 a.m. One lot of transmissions arrives on the conveyor
> belt every minute and twenty seconds ... After standing
> five hours, my legs are numb and stiff. My new safety shoes
> are so heavy I can barely move.[33]

By contrast, it is interesting to consider the views of a Japanese businessman at the turn of the century. Upon returning from a visit to the United States, he claimed that American workers were diligent and hard-working compared to the Japanese. "They came to work on time, never loafed, and would every day seek to double their output." What a difference, he lamented, from the ill-disciplined Japanese, who needed constant supervision.[34]

Constant supervision is still the rule: foremen in a typical plant are expected at the morning assembly to explain the slogan: "Use every minute, use every effort!"

> When the warning siren goes five minutes before the end
> of the lunch break, make sure that you are ready to start
> again immediately the next siren goes ... You should, for
> example, stop your ping-pong or other sports and wipe the
> sweat away, ... your mind and body should be already
> turned toward the next job of work to be done.[35]

When Japanese workers are asked to assess their own attitude to work, their views seem at variance with the Western image. According to the Japanese Economic Planning Agency, nearly six out of ten Japanese employees want to combine leisure with an average work pace, as compared to one-fifth who are willing to work harder, in return for more leisure time. Only 8.4 per cent wish to put hard work first.[36]

A well-known Japanese businessman tells of an experience he had in a barber shop in the Marunouchi area, one Saturday.

"Not many customers today?" he asked the barber.

"No, business has been off on Saturdays."

"When are you busiest?"

"Well, these days, around eleven, then around two or three in the afternoon on weekdays."

"Do you mean during working hours?"

"That's right. People these days don't want to spend their own time on things like haircuts."[37]

Many Japanese *do* work very hard, but if white-collar workers have a chance to get time off, they take it. A newspaper bluntly stated:

> If young people's sense of value and attitude toward life serve as an indication, the future Japan would be a country where a majority of people live leisurely.[38]

This view was based on a poll conducted by the Management and Co-ordination Agency in the summer of 1985, according to which most young university graduates look upon work merely as a means of making a living; they choose their jobs not for the challenges they offer, but for the security.[39]

Some say that such attitudes are limited to the young, but the Japanese are the first to admit this is not so. Most middle-aged married men are placing the emphasis on life outside the work place. This attitude is known as "My-homism." One writer put it in the context of the times.

> The home in Japan is not merely a place of rest and relaxation. It embodies a struggle between the value of self, of individual worth and family, against the social demands for productivity and mechanization.[40]

To the establishment, such views border on treason. They are condemned as threats to "public good, national defence and love of country." "My-homism" goes against the carefully nurtured and imposed work ethic, but it is the reality. All the evidence shows that interest in the quality of life, *ikigai*, is very much alive, and that the perception of Japanese workers as automatons is a myth which business leaders have tried, unsuccessfully, to make a reality.

The immediate post-war Japanese had to work very hard to subsist. Now, with a higher standard of living, leisure is becoming more important, even at the cost of increased income. Most place the opportunity to enjoy life and to extend relations and friendships with others as their top priority.[41] These issues are of such importance that public demonstrations have been held to demand an increase in leisure time.

This change in perception is making industry realize that the public demands far more out of life than work. In one sense, this is happening at a good time for business, as Japanese economists estimate unemployment will exceed 6 per cent by the early 1990s. A decreased working day is viewed as one way to make unemployment figures appear low.

One of the fabrications about Japan is that it has been a country with virtually no unemployment. It certainly *has* enjoyed far less unemployment than other free enterprise countries. But Japanese figures have always been artifically low by Western standards of measurement. Due to major differences in statistical criteria between Japan and the U.S. or other Western nations, the official Japanese unemployment percentages must be doubled to be more correctly evaluated in international terms.[42] One reason for the statistical difference is that employees who are laid off are not counted as jobless, as in other countries, but as on temporary leave. Those who have been dismissed but are helping their family business, for example, are not counted as jobless either.

In November 1986, Japan recorded 1,770,000 people officially unemployed, a rate of 2.9 per cent (5.8 per cent in real terms). In other advanced countries the rates were 6.7 per cent in the U.S. (December), 8.7 per cent in West Germany (October) and 11.5 per cent in the United Kingdom (October).[43]

Unemployment is hitting the cities in the prefectures particularly hard. Tokyo has not felt the economic pinch, thanks to a crazed land boom and the soaring stock market. Finance and service industries in Tokyo are continuing to grow, and have a big capacity for absorbing workers.

During nationwide local elections in 1987, Governor Moriteru

Hosokawa of Kumamoto Prefecture described the distress of regional cities, saying: "The bright hope that prevailed just a few years ago . . . has completely disappeared. Regional communities today feel like revolting against the central government."[44]

Shipbuilding, coal mining, steel making and the textile industry are in difficulty. Even the automobile industry is depressed.

Managing Director Shohachiro Takahashi of Mazda Corporation headquarters in Hiroshima City, who is in charge of subcontractors, commented on the harshness of the situation: "Co-operating companies [subcontractors] which cannot cut down on their cost any further will be weeded out naturally."[45] Regular workers in main plants are also feeling the pinch.

Katsuhiro Hamada, 42, worked at a dockyard on Innoshima Island in the Seto Inland Sea off the coast of west Japan. Hamada is the breadwinner in the family. Dependent on his pay cheque are his wife, a son in the first year of senior high school, and a daughter in the first year of junior high school. For twenty years, he worked for Hitachi Zosen Corporation, one of the five shipbuilding companies in Japan. On 31 December 1986, he was dismissed, one of 5,300 to lose their jobs in this one firm. His future is uncertain. His income is now barely enough to subsist on. He laments: "I don't know what I'll do when my unemployment insurance expires in six months. One of the boasts of Japanese companies was the lifelong employment system . . . Then all of a sudden we were dismissed."[46]

A shorter work week is beginning to make good sense in Japan. Regular working hours per month have begun to decline. In 1970, the number of hours averaged 186, falling to 161 in 1983. Despite a continuing reduction, it is still well above the 145 hours for most Western industrial countries. The reason for long hours of work in major companies is not hard to find. To maintain full employment for the permanent staff, their numbers must be kept low; to carry out their jobs effectively, they are required to put in much overtime, above and beyond the normal work day. Overtime of two to three hours and additional work on weekends are commonplace during peak-load periods. Employees seldom refuse to do the extra work, partly because it means added income and also because it ensures security and ups the chance of promotion. The "temporaries" work overtime under a different pressure: they can be fired at will. Love of work, in either case, has very little to do with it.

Yet those who still view the Japanese as "workaholics" have other examples to support their conclusion. Among these is the very low rate of worker absenteeism, which is a fact. One of the causes pertains to a very real sense of group responsibility among the workers. They know that their workload will be added onto the others since no substitutes are hired.

Publicity is also given to the numbers of workers who refuse to take paid holidays. In fact, most Japanese take whatever holidays they can get. During the Spring Break or Golden Week, four-day vacations are becoming more common, although a quarter of Japan's workers receive fewer than four vacation days a year above and beyond statutory holidays. The longest recorded company holiday is thirteen days. The shortness of most holidays is more a reflection of the impotency of the trade unions than the ideal of the average Japanese. This is not to deny that white-collar workers, especially those in middle management, forego their holidays voluntarily, as do their ambitious Western counterparts. But in Japan the number willing to make the sacrifice is diminishing.

When all is said and done there are actually many more similarities than differences between the attitudes of Japanese and Western workers. In one report on workers in both countries, "improvement of life style" was most often cited as the personal goal of working at a job – by 48.3 per cent in Japan, and somewhat less, 43.1 per cent, in the United States. Working for work's sake was mentioned so seldom it was not included among the responses. In answer to "What do you think of jobs in general?", most Japanese said they did not want their work to infringe on their private lives. To cap it off, the Japanese Institute of Labour itself admits that "Workaholic is not the appropriate way to describe the Japanese attitude to work."[47] It is an admission which only confirms that most Japanese have much the same attitude to labour as most of the rest of us.

Labour's Future

Labour's future may well be tied to one all-embracing labour federation under the control of Japan's ruling hierarchies, if the Liberal Democratic Party has its way. Such a federation would signal a return to the nation's labour practices during World War II. The reasons for this radical reversal are easy to find.

After SCAP dissolved the wartime labour front, *Sampo*, on 30 September 1945, two labour federations arose in its place, the left-wing and sometimes communist-dominated *Sanbetsu*, and the more moderate and later right-wing *Sodomei*. The former was backed by the Communist Party, the latter by the Socialists. A concerted effort, supported by SCAP, was made to weaken *Sanbetsu*. Unions affiliated with *Sanbetsu* were subject to widespread infiltration by right-wing activists, a practice which continued until most unions fit a co-operative mold.

The purge of militant workers signalled the beginning of the end for *Sanbetsu*. It declined after 1950, to be replaced by a new federation born with the support of SCAP. This was *Sohyo*, the General Council of Trade Unions, which became Japan's largest labour federation. It was founded in July 1950, immediately after the purge of the Japan Communist Party, and at the start of the Korean War. As the head of *Sohyo* wrote to the U.S. labour leader George Meany in 1965: "the history of the foundation of *Sohyo* is closely connected with the fight against the domination of the Japanese trade unions by the Communist Party."[48]

The new *Sohyo* federation did not, however, live up to the expectations of the U.S. and Japanese elites, which wanted it to become an apolitical and co-operative organization. Wages became the first bone of contention between *Sohyo* and *Nikkeiren*, the employers' organization. *Sohyo* rejected the Consumer Price Index as a guideline for wage increases, and fought for what was dubbed the "market-basket formula," based on its calculation of the minimum needs of the workers.[49]

The establishment, disillusioned with the federation that was intended as its front organization, quickly labelled it Communist-dominated. Meanwhile, *Sodomei* dissolved, splitting into two groups. One joined *Sohyo*, the other formed *Domei*.

Founded in 1954, *Domei* has antecedents dating to pre-war unions, with which it has much in common. It attracted the great bulk of the newly imposed co-operative enterprise unions. While *Sohyo* has always allied itself with the Japanese Socialist Party, *Domei* supports the Democratic Socialist Party, an essentially conservative group with policies similar to those of the Liberal Democratic Party.

Domei helps management keep a lid on wage demands. As a reward, many union leaders end up as executives within their own companies or corporations. If, as occasionally happens, a business is faced with a militant union, it uses gangsters to start a co-operative one of its own. *Domei* supports such action. In this, as in all things, the federation favoured by business does its best to deserve that trust.

Domei's individual unions, being enterprise-oriented, have difficulty organizing across company lines. It is therefore *Sohyo* which represents workers at many companies, in the style of Western trade unions. It is also *Sohyo* which started, in 1955, a national annual movement to set wages. A series of mass demonstrations, called *Shunto*, are held every spring. While it plays no active role, *Domei* allows its member unions to participate. In doing so, it takes some of the credit for improvements in wages and working conditions, without compromising its establishment connections.

Shunto, the most important event in union-management relations, publicizes demands for wage increases. Every year, March through May, more than 80 per cent of organized labour participates. The organizers choose a lead-off union which is in a particularly strong bargaining position. Apart from its militancy, it is usually connected with a large and wealthy firm. Upon achieving a good settlement, it becomes a "pace-setter" for the industry so that unions joining in the struggle may push for wage raises higher than they would have otherwise expected, a condition which, with variations, is common in the West.

Japan's employers have accepted the *Shunto* because it substantially decreases the chance of strikes. Indeed, it has become common practice for enterprise trade unions to agree not to strike over a period of several years, in return for management's acceptance of the increases given to other unions in the spring labour offensive.

But acceptance of the *Shunto* does not mean that Japan's establishment is satisfied; and it will not be until labour, as in wartime days, is completely under its control. A plan has been adopted by the establishment to unite the currently antagonistic federations into one big union. This federation, to be initially comprised of private sector unions, is intended to annex public sector unions, hence embracing all the major unions from the private and public sectors while it remains firmly under the control of business.

A major move was taken in this direction by the "socialist" *Sohyo* federation. *Sohyo* had been forced into a corner, its militancy rapidly dwindling. Representing workers in the public and the government sectors had been its strengths, but they were being co-opted by the establishment. The breakup and privatization of Japan's National Railway, during 1987, and the decline of the Japan Teachers' Union, are symptomatic of its weakness. At the same time, *Sohyo* has lost the support of most private sector unions, many of which formed a new group, *Zenminrokyo*, in 1982. All of these setbacks to *Sohyo* are the direct result of government pressure, part of a program aimed to undermine labour in general.

As a result, on 24 July 1987, *Sohyo* adopted an action policy calling for its dissolution in three years. The breakup of the 4.27-million-member *Sohyo* is designed as the first step in unifying all unions by 1990. According to *Tokyo Business Today*, the new single federation will be politically "neutral," and will carryout reforms within the framework of capitalism.[50]

In the view of its critics, this unification will result in *Sohyo*'s absorption by *Domei*, and by the big business associations.

This plan, promoted by the hierarchies, coincides with the collapse of some of Japan's export markets and increasing losses by a number of the nation's largest firms. The most active supporters of unification are those enterprise unions which represent the export sector of Japanese private industry. Their aim is to create a labour front, with right-wing unions at its core. The result would be an enlarged replica of the corporate world, where the "national interest" of competitiveness in the world market would be paramount. Ideologically, Japan's labour movement would find itself at the disposal of the employers. Some major unions, including the shipbuilding union, have begun to conform to this mold. It is a trend that fits in well with the aims of big business and of the Liberal Democratic Party.

The LDP has taken the plan of one large conservative labour federation a step further. In the party newspaper's 1982 editorial, it proposed "fully integrating the trade union movement with the ruling party which will directly absorb the voices of the urban communities, consumers, and the aged." This proposal envisages an ultimate union of all sectors of society, including a middle-of-the-road Socialist Party and an emasculated *Sohyo*. Only the Communist Party would be excluded.[51]

This ideal of a one-party capitalist society without dissent or antagonism is, in the view of its critics, disturbingly similar to an authoritarian state.

6

SOCIAL CONTROL

*You had to live – did live, from habit that became
instinct – in the assumption that every sound you made
was overheard, and, except in the darkness,
every movement scrutinized.*
GEORGE ORWELL, *1984*[1]

*Before lunch, we receive a uniform with the logo on it
and a cap with two green stripes. The two green stripes
stand for Seasonal Worker; one green stripe,
Probationer; one white stripe, Trainee; one red stripe,
Minor; a cap without stripe, Regular Worker; two yellow
stripes, Team Chief; a thick yellow stripe, Foreman; . . .
There are so many ranks I can't memorize them all at
once. It's as if we've joined the army!*
SEASONAL WORKER IN A LARGE JAPANESE FIRM, 1973[2]

Divide and Rule

A co-operative work force is the ideal sought by employers and, with vacillation, many employees. At times through force, but more often by indoctrination and manipulation, Japanese authorities have had greater success in approaching this ideal than any of their counterparts in other advanced free enterprise societies.

Inside the world of Japanese companies, control is exercised by putting workers into categories and erecting invisible walls around them. The major firms designate their employees "permanent" and "temporary." Permanent employees – the labour

145

aristocracy – enjoy reasonable wages, a degree of security and other benefits; the temporaries do not. But the hierarchical system does not stop there. There is a third class of workers, the so-called "outside workers," who are employed by subcontractors working inside the factory of the main company. In some cases, outside workers are assigned to the same jobs as regular workers but with less pay. Yet even these "less equal" workers have advantages over a fourth class – part-time employees who work in small firms and in home industries.

The division of workers into a myriad of categories, each with its own distinctive uniform, is but one approach to worker control in Japan. Practices vary from corporation to corporation, but there are some striking similarities – artificial competition among workers, intimidation, ostracism and, sometimes, physical violence.[3]

In Japan, a person's well-being is decided largely by whether he is able to become a "permanent" employee in a large enterprise. Such firms are usually connected with one of Japan's six large conglomerates: Dai-Ichi Kangyo, Fuji, Sumitomo, Mitsubishi, Sanwa and Mitsui. Each has direct controlling interest in over 40 to 50 large corporations. Combined, they make up only one-tenth of one per cent of all Japanese manufacturing business, and employ only 14 per cent of all employees, but working for one of them is the goal for most ambitious Japanese. Not least of all, these companies confer status on their employees. Even a worker in one of their main sub-contracting firms can proudly introduce himself as a Mitsubishi or Mitsui man.

To maintain this system, workers are subject to a degree of control and economic manipulation unequalled in any Western industrial nation.

Wage manipulation is one means of ruling the work force, as a large part of pay is subject to evaluation by management. An extreme case of arbitrary evaluation is seen at Nissan Motors, where only 13.5 per cent of the wage is the "basic wage"; the rest is largely determined by management evaluation. Loyalty is the number one criterion for a good evaluation and a high wage. Workers who would "complain" are blackmailed into silence

with near-certain wage cuts. The results of management evaluations are secret and not disclosed to the workers involved.
Under this system, flattery, dedication and submissiveness
become the routes to promotion. One worker gives an example
of how wage exploitation works in practice:

> A worker must complete his quota within his shift, re-
> gardless of how demanding that is. If he fails he has to work
> overtime until his target is met. Workers know if they apply
> for overtime pay this will count against them, they will be
> bypassed for promotion. So employees work overtime for
> nothing. The union of course does not interfere.[4]

All advanced free enterprise countries have relatively few very
big corporations which rely on numerous sub-contractors. Nowhere, save Japan, is this dualism as obvious, or as institutionalized. Of all plant employees, 58 per cent work in plants with
fewer than 100 workers, and wages at these plants are 30 to 40
per cent less than those at larger companies.[5]

In the West, wages are roughly the same in large and small
businesses, so corporations cannot rely on sweated labour to the
extent that they do in Japan. There, as well, poorly paid "home"
industries flourish. A memory of the past in the other advanced
nations, they are accepted and widespread in modern Japan, as
well as in Korea and the other newly industrialized countries of
East Asia.

The Japanese wage system has its roots in the country's history of industrial dualism – a parallel system of large parent firms
and small sub-contractors – the major purpose of which has been
to keep the base wage as low as possible. Sub-contracting firms
are often kept on the brink of bankruptcy, so that their workers
never make more than a bare subsistence wage. The Japan Institute of Labour admits that there are great discrepancies in wage
structures between small and larger firms and that these dif-
ferentials are vast compared with those in other countries.

It is perhaps fruitless to compare Japanese wages with those of
other industrial nations. The Japanese Ministry of Labour admits
as much: "It is technically difficult to make a fair international
comparison of wage standards due partly to the difference in the

quality of welfare facilities in different countries and partly due to the difficulty in evaluating the actual value of each nation's currency." Nonetheless, the ministry proceeds to do so. Taking into account only production workers in manufacturing, it uses a wage index of 100 for Japan. The ratings of other countries are: the U.S. (130.8), West Germany (131.8), Britain (83.4), and France (89.9).[6] This gives Japan a fairly respectable rank until one notes that the calculations for Japan, unlike those for the other countries, exclude all the lowest-paid workers in companies with 30 employees or less. The enormity of this omission becomes obvious when it is realized that well over half of the Japanese work force is in small firms, as compared with about one-fifth of the British work force. And such workers in Japan receive wages 40 per cent lower than those in large and medium firms, while employees in small firms in Western European countries get roughly the same wages as they would in larger firms. If this lower stratum had been included in the Ministry of Labour's statistics, Japan would have appeared at the bottom of the wage index.

Despite the mounting evidence, the myth of the privileged Japanese worker persists. Authorities in Japan and the West point out that the average Japanese salary and hourly wage is very close to those in the United States and West Germany. However, these relatively high figures reflect not a standard of living but the sharp upswing of the yen on international markets. The standard of living achieved by most unionized workers in the West is still largely a complete stranger to Japanese salaried workers, despite the fact that their income levels are about to rank first in the world thanks to the skyrocketing yen.[7]

Of course, the permanent workers in major industries can do well and it is they who are so often portrayed as "the average Japanese worker." In addition to good wages and very substantial bi-annual bonuses, they are provided with housing and a wide array of services. But to believe that these benefits are the result of benevolent paternalism is naive. As an example, consider the bonuses. They are not considered a part of the regular wages; therefore, they do not figure in calculations of the retirement lump-sum payments. This bonus system effectively reduces the pension burden on employers. Moreover, employers can reduce labour costs during recessions by adjusting bonuses, which is much easier than changing seniority-related wages. (As an added bonus to employers, the lump-sums paid bi-annually to workers contribute to a stable seasonal demand for consumer goods.)

Shame and Obligation

At one time a graduate from a good university could count on entering the major company of his choice and enjoying status and security. Like so many other elements of the Japanese myth, this is now often untrue. The corporate world can afford to be much more selective as the employment picture worsens. Its ability to discriminate is aided, not coincidentally, by the revival of the *oendan*, the right-wing college cheerleading groups, whose members discipline themselves in the virtues of duty and loyalty. Because of their disruptive role on campus, they were temporarily disbanded in the late 1960s and 1970s. The resurrection of the *oendan* in the 1980s has been welcomed by corporations and nationalists. Submissive youth are becoming harder to find, so members of these clubs have little trouble finding employment.

Another group which has seen job opportunities rise is women. The low-cost temporary positions they usually occupy are always available. Between 1978 and 1983, employment of women grew by 16 per cent, as compared with an 8 per cent increase for men. In 1986, 73.4 per cent of Japan's female college graduates entered the work force, more than had done so in any year since 1955. However, the vast majority became temporary office workers. A Ministry of Education survey shows that nearly the same percentage of female and male school graduates are now achieving employment. While this statistic is largely explained by the greater demand for clerical workers, it also reflects the relatively smaller number of higher-paid jobs open to male graduates.

Failure to enter the working aristocracy comes as a shock to hundreds of thousands of young men, and, literally, brings shame to their family. If students fail to be accepted by a recognized firm upon graduation they have little chance at acceptance later, and, as opportunities for permanent employment decline, the reservoir of discontented youth increases.

Recruitment of university graduates used to be a well-organized affair. The job-hunting season for large businesses traditionally opened on 1 October, a date arrived at by companies and universities so recruiting and job-hunting would not disrupt the students' studies, which end in May. This system gradually eroded during the years of economic expansion as firms desperate to snap up the best students began to accept them earlier, before they had graduated. As a result, final university examinations became a formality.

Until 1981, the Ministry of Labour served as a monitor to ensure that the agreement was honoured by companies and universities, but when violations became blatant, ministry officials gave up. At one point some businesses had their employees contact and recruit senior students from their own universities during the summer. However, when the recession gripped Japan in 1982, applicants far outnumbered jobs. The situation was reversed. In 1982-83, large numbers of students began to use contacts with former graduates in an effort to land jobs with their companies.

But, for most graduates from good universities, and for status firms seeking management material, the university placement office remains the sole link to the corporate world and the most important institution in a young graduate's life. (Major firms never accept personal applications for jobs.) The placement office deals only with those companies which recognize the university and which are on the approved list. On its part, the office recommends only qualified students whom it trusts to maintain the honour of the school. Each company recruits only from particular universities. Students not enrolled at one of them simply cannot apply. Most graduates inevitably end up with firms which aren't their first choices. It is a state of affairs which makes the teaching of company loyalty more difficult.

Universities have already done their part by teaching "traditional values" to their students prior to graduation. Waseda University's *Employment Guidebook* is typical. It states:

One cannot change his job in midstream simply because it does not suit him. Japan is a country with a system of lifetime employment. Not only is the graduate an employee of a firm but he is also considered a life-long representative of his university. A bad reputation can result in bad relations between his school and the corporation, with disastrous effects for all the students that follow. He is therefore always under an obligation to his college to be obedient and loyal.

Thus the "unique loyalty" the Japanese have for their firms often boils down to shame and obligation to one's university and fellow students, and the humiliation of "letting your side down."

The great majority of universities recommend a student to only two or three companies at a time. An exception is Tokyo University, where all applicants to a given firm receive recommendations, even if the number far exceeds those requested. The ties between a major firm and a university may be based on tradition, or connection with executives or shareholders who are graduates. The selection of universities by a business recalls the pattern of the feudal era when positions in the bureaucracy were filled from selected elites or *batsu*, a term applied to an informal and exclusive group which is concerned with the general welfare of its members. When ties are especially strong among the graduates of a particular university and a particular firm, the company is said to be dominated by a *gakubatsu*, or school clique. Under such circumstances the job interview is a mere formality, a chance for the company to assess the applicant's personality; for all intents and purposes the graduate passed the company entrance exam when he was accepted into the selected university. Those who enter a firm but become disenchanted for one reason or another and quit still find it extremely difficult to get another job with a company of the same status. Not only that, but when they cease to be members of the *batsu* they lose seniority, friends and influential support.

'Natural' Loyalty

Few would accuse Japanese business leaders of naiveté. They have never been under the illusion that loyalty is an inborn trait. That is why they have spent, and continue to spend, huge sums and vast efforts on indoctrination. Combined with a seniority wage system, loans and housing benefits, and a degree of security, indoctrination serves to tie the worker to the company.

Indoctrination of a new employee begins with his first day. The typical joining ceremony is "religious"; its aim is the propagation of faith, dedication and, above all, submissiveness. The nation, company and family are presented as a trinity. Disloyalty to one becomes disloyalty to all. A typical service starts with the company song, followed by a catechism embodying the company's ideals. The success of the firm is invariably linked to the welfare of the nation. Parent involvement is an important part of the procedure. While the president admonishes the new recruits to serve well, he also promises the parents to care well for their children. The ritual is designed so that, by invoking patriotism, family and school, the new worker is so caught in a web of moral obligations as to have no choice but to embrace the firm and its principles.

Each employee is introduced, not in alphabetical order, but by his school. A graduate of a national university precedes one from a private university. These, in turn, are called before two-year colleges, and so on. Furthermore, within each category, the graduate of the elite institution precedes the recruit from a lesser one. Tokyo University comes before Kyoto, for instance. In addition, the new employee is placed within a group, based on seniority. He remains a member of that *batsu* for all his working life; it becomes his "family." The concept of the group, and his responsibility to it, is instilled from the very outset.

Once inducted, workers enter training schools conducted along paramilitary lines. The trainees live in barracks, wear uniforms and adhere to regimented schedules and regulations. A typical day starts with the flag raising and company song, followed by a spoken pledge to the company, and physical training. Personal humiliation before one's peers is a technique used to uproot individuality. During these sessions, all workers must undergo self-criticism before their fellows, a practice which reduces some to tears. Everything in the trainees' lives must be uniform; even the precise angles of bowing to one's superiors have to be learned and practised. All of these programs are designed to instill the ethic that work, if it serves a purpose, is essentially good and should be respected. That such courses are popularly known as "hell weeks" shows what most Japanese think of them.

Japanese firms often do not stop their indoctrination with hell weeks; they also send their employees to special courses offered by the "Self-Defence Forces" for a good dose of hard military discipline and right-wing propaganda.

But the whole indoctrination program is proving of little avail. In a survey conducted jointly by the Japan Productivity Centre and the Junior Executive Council of Japan among the employees of 82 firms, only 19.2 per cent of employees answered "yes" to the question, "Do you want to stay with your present company until you reach mandatory retirement age?" In a study entitled "People and Jobs" and released by the Japan Youth Research Institute, United States and Japanese workers were asked, "Do you have a sense of loyalty to your company?" Forty-six per cent of the Americans answered "Yes, to a considerable degree," but only 24.5 per cent of Japanese.[8] The remarkable thing about these responses is they prove the diametric opposite of the view of Japanese loyalty circulated abroad.

Equally significant is a survey showing that, while 36 per cent of all Japanese workers are prepared to make personal sacrifices for the company, 57 per cent are not.

Of middle-echelon executives, from whom one would expect the greatest loyalty, the survey shows that 40 per cent want to quit their present jobs. According to the same survey, three out of four salaried men have at one time or other thought of casting off the corporate yoke and becoming independent. It is not surprising that the Japanese government should reach the conclusion that there is widespread discontentment with jobs.

No longer does the government claim that workers' resentment is just an aberration of youth. It too is aware of the evident, that Japanese workers' natural loyalty to their companies is no greater than any of their Western counterparts. Most stay where they are not because of loyalty, natural or otherwise, but because they are enmeshed in the corporate system from which there are few escapes.

The Best Provided Workers

The employers in big firms are not foolish enough to believe that indoctrination alone can ensure worker loyalty and submissiveness. The web of obligations they create for their workers also plays a part. Japan, it must be emphasized, spends less on social welfare than any other developed nation. Hence, accommodation at a reasonable price, and access to medical, health and education facilities, as well as to recreation and athletic programs, is more important to Japanese employees than to their counterparts in Western countries.

Company dormitories play a role in Japanese society that would be inconceivable in the West. In the first instance, they provide an inexpensive and convenient way of housing single workers, while keeping them under company discipline. They also serve to board children of those forced to move from city to city. Continuity of education is exceedingly important for the Japanese youngster's future, so accommodation for children is another bond tying the father to the company.

The dormitories are grim and cheerless, without private toilets or central heating. Baths are taken in public bath houses some distance away. The sleeping rooms are often the size of a large Western bathroom. It is common for two workers to share these cramped spaces.

The buildings are all but undecorated. The few wall ornaments are signs which list the rules and restrictions. The buildings are given names which would be comic under other circumstances. One is called "Sei-shin Wafu Ryo" (Sacred Heart and Pleasant Breeze Dormitory). It is likened, by one of its inhabitants, to a prison camp.[9]

Housing is one of the greatest problems facing the Japanese. Urban accommodation is priced beyond the reach of most, so that subsidized housing and low-interest loans are of immense importance to the family. No one exploits this situation more than major Japanese companies. The home-loan system sounds attractive and benevolent; in fact, it is another brick in the company wall.

A left-wing trade union leader of the General Workers' Trade Union has said that the company home-loan system alone would be enough to keep enterprise workers submissive and loyal. As he puts it:

> An employee of a big private company can borrow from the company to buy a tiny house on the condition that he repay it with his severance pay at the age of 55 when he has to retire. This agreement ties his fate to that of the company. If he should resign prematurely, his severance pay would be much less than his debt to the company. For a worker, being hired by a big company is like mortgaging his whole life; also the company housing loan is usually not enough to enable a worker to buy a house, and so he borrows from other sources as well. If the company should go bankrupt, he also goes bankrupt as he cannot repay his debt to the private company, and his house will be confiscated.[10]

The seniority wage system also works to mortgage the worker's life. The longer an employee remains with a firm, the higher his salary, the greater his expectations, and the better his standard of living. Adding to this system is the forceable constraint that the skills he learns in one company cannot always be used in another. When these economic ties increase over the years, many find they have no choice but to remain with the firm.[11] This is another example of "loyalty" which allows of almost no alternative. While the hierarchies have been successful in enforcing a system of conformity in Japan, the evidence increasingly shows how little of the brainwashing has penetrated the minds of the Japanese people.

One of the few areas of social services well provided by most large firms is health care. Company hospitals and medical clinics are often exemplary. Full-time employees also have the benefits of group insurance and other financial aids, costs of which are shared with the company.

But other large Japanese companies show little interest in their paternal obligations. Workers know that, if they are badly injured on the job, it is they and their fellow workers who will have to pay in lost wages. Although companies are legally obliged to pay an indemnity to injured workers, they are unwilling to take financial responsibilities and some Japanese companies have devised an array of stratagems to avoid paying compensation.

The *Municipal Administration Study Monthly* details how one Japanese firm penalizes everyone connected with the victim.

> If an accident occurs, the ones responsible for the group have their bonus reduced: 40 per cent for the team chief, 30 per cent for the foreman, 20 per cent for the general foreman and 10 per cent for the section manager.[12]

Japan's workers have no one to turn to, if, as in the vast majority of cases, their enterprise union is essentially a company one. The workers are fully aware of what may befall them.

> We often hear about accidents – one guy was killed and another was injured. But we never hear the line's been stopped because of it.
> A lot of the team chiefs and foremen have no hands, you know.
> I know a foreman who lost the fingers from both hands. He can't even wash his face.[13]

These cases might not be typical, but comments about serious injuries to workers are common among employees, even more so in smaller industrial plants.

Whatever benefits the permanent workers – the industrial aristocracy – enjoy in the large firms, the vast majority of Japan's workers see no such benefits. The average business employing fewer than 100 persons has little capital, inferior equipment and low productivity. Where welfare provisions exist, it is by grace of a single man – the employer. Characteristically, there are no retirement plans for long-time workers, and neither the government nor trade unions are doing anything to improve the situation.

Most workers are conditioned to accept temporary employment under these terms. It is a system which enables business to establish a labour aristocracy with its "lifetime employment."

The very term "lifetime employment" was not used in Japan until the end of World War II when it was invented by American experts on Japanese management. Real lifetime employment is rarer in Japan than in any Western country. It may be applied to a select group of white-collar staff, but others are "fired if they are sick, or unwanted." Even Japan's state broadcasting channel is calling the lifetime employment system a myth.[14] Paternalism is used as a way to ensure stability within the working aristocracy when economic conditions are good, and it is disposed of, grudgingly perhaps, when things are bad.

The system, at any rate, is only a gentlemen's agreement, a general understanding between the company and "permanent" employees that their relations are to be continuous. Management is publicly ambivalent toward the system. Close to half of Japanese employers claim to be in favour of it because it promotes a sense of stability among employees. However, somewhat more than half of employees believe the system also has the adverse effect of "preserving old and unnecessary employees."[15]

Company responsibility for its employees is an issue that never arises. In management's view, the system is nothing more nor less than a means of control. The advantages of the system to management depend on the state of the economy. In a growth situation, the system works well. But in times of recession, despite all their precautions, companies find themselves overstaffed. In such conditions the temptation is to retain as many temporary low-paid workers as possible and to retire or transfer the permanent ones. This is exactly what happens. Where once workers would be sent out to affiliates and subsidiaries on temporary loan, nowadays they tend not to come back to the mother company. The new practice is named, with appropriate cynicism, *"Katamichi no shukko"* – a one-way ticket.[16]

Economic and social controls over employees are disintegrating as workers are swept away in a storm of cost-cutting measures. Steel manufacturers, the coal industry, ship and automakers are all trimming staff. Nissan sent 2,500 factory workers to car dealerships in 1986, and planned to transfer another 2,500 in 1987.[17] Companies are assisting, even paying, their permanent employees to search for jobs with other companies. High-tech workers are being courted by other firms, and others are leaving their status companies to start up on their own.

Nevertheless, the traditional system would not be retained if big business did not consider it, on balance, to be in its long-term interest. One of the advantages of the present system, in the view of some executives, is that the well-defined schedule of promotion based on seniority, age, and education denies subordinates the chance to leap-frog over their colleagues to the executive suite. On the other hand, any sign of individualism is quickly quashed and promotion is denied to offending workers. A lot of first-rate people become disillusioned in the process. And it also results in a bloated middle management which slows down an already cumbersome decision-making process. Some of the least competent managers are called *madogiwa-zoku*, or "those who sit along the windows." They get paid, but they do not do any work. Finally, the arrangement has a demoralizing effect on the younger workers who see little opportunity for significant promotion up the corporate ladder.

Despite the system's advantages, management is seriously concerned about some of its effects. The Japan Institute of Personnel Administration (JIPA) discovered that nearly half of major firms have qualified persons whom they cannot promote because of lack of posts. The ambitious are being driven, and sometimes explicitly encouraged, to seek jobs outside their company. Thus both "lifetime employment" and the seniority system are being undermined.

After 55

The Japanese retirement system is based on an earlier era when life expectancy was short. Today, workers are forced to retire at a much earlier age than their counterparts in other advanced industrial countries. The age for women is commonly 50 and for men normally 55; however, the Labour Ministry is encouraging private firms to raise the retirement age to 60. Even if this age becomes universal, it still leaves the male worker with five very difficult years until his savings are augmented by a state pension at age 65.

Under the retirement system, a permanent employee, leaving a company with 1,000 or more workers is given the equivalent of three and a half years' salary to last him the rest of his life. That is the most that can be hoped for. Those of medium-sized enterprises get only half of that, and employees of small firms are fortunate to get one-third. A quarter of the companies employing fewer than 100 workers have no mandatory retirement, thus no pension. In reality "lifetime employment" is more a system of mass dismissals than anything else.

For the moment, the situation is good for business. After "early" retirement the corporations rehire those they need at a fraction of their previous salaries, sometimes to do the same work. Workers are only too happy to get any kind of employment, and it is not unusual to find a stationmaster with the National Railways ending up as the manager of the coffee stand, while a senior foreman with a construction company considers himself lucky to get a job as a night watchman.[18]

Most men and women in the West look forward to an active retirement after 65, but not in the Japanese sense. More than half of retired Japanese work not for enjoyment, but just to subsist. This compares with 12 to 18 per cent of older people in France, West Germany and Britain. This situation exists in one of the world's wealthiest industrial nations. No wonder the Japanese have gained a reputation as "savers." What to foreigners appears as miserliness and a reluctance to spend more on imported consumer goods is often nothing more than a need to save for old age.

The Japanese male worker knows that after retirement he will have to fend for himself – an undignified prospect for a man who has been taught respect for the aged. With the realization that forced retirement means a decreased standard of living, even poverty, alienation sets in. The image of a paternalistic society thus becomes counterproductive, a two-edged sword in the hands of the ruling class. Both the young and the old become alienated.

"Late" retirement has been making a slow intrusion into the labour market, but even the largest corporations allow only 27.6 per cent of their permanent workers to continue to age 60, and none beyond 60. After that, if they are lucky, they may be rehired as temporaries. And lucky they must be, as 80 per cent of the unemployed are in the 44-64 age bracket. This is not a reassuring statistic, especially since fewer than half of the whole labour force is covered by unemployment insurance, and benefits range up to only 60 per cent of wages. Very few workers over 55 years are entitled to unemployment insurance at all.

Japanese-style retirement, however, has obvious advantages for the government. It keeps welfare costs to a minimum, while holding down labour costs. Yet the Liberal Democratic Party is not satisfied and is seeking ways to cut costs even further.

In the summer of 1984, the government proposed revisions to the Health Insurance Law that would have cut benefits by 10 per cent in 1984-85, and by a further 10 per cent in 1986. This reduction would have particularly hurt the retired. Public outcry was immediate, led by the Japan Medical Association, which declared the legislation to be disastrous for the poor. Elements of the JMA, a very conservative organization, took the radical step of organizing a series of rotating strikes to protest the measures.

The Company Family

Japan's largest and most modern colliery is Mitsui's Miike mine, situated in the city of Omuta in Kyushu. A bitter labour struggle developed there in 1960 during a severe industry depression. To remain profitable, the company resorted to laying off workers, increasing overtime and, according to Mitsui's biographer, economizing on safety.[19] Some 1,200 miners were forced to "resign" and many others were phased out. At the same time, the company tried to boost production by carrying on operations in three shifts, 24 hours a day, with no breaks for maintenance. Safety regulations became a formality; drills and safety checks were cancelled. As a direct result, accidental deaths tripled and serious injuries increased five-fold over the pre-strike average. During one year, fifteen men died and 1,800 suffered severe physical injuries. Such tragedies were the result not only of a ruthless employer but also of a weak and compliant union.

The inevitable tragedy occurred on 9 November 1963, when 458 workers were killed in an explosion. No company doctor was on duty at the time and the water spray system was damaged. The company president reflected his concern by publicly lamenting the accident, and adding sadly that it occurred just as the mine was beginning to show a profit once more.[20]

Despite this profit, and the fact that the mine was part of a huge and wealthy conglomerate, the company claimed it had no money to compensate the victims' families. Fortunately, the Japanese cabinet gave the company one billion of taxpayers' yen. As if the tragedy was not bad enough, the fate of the survivors was determined by archaic labour legislation.

The *Asahi Evening News*, in 1965, commemorated the second anniversary of the disastrous dust explosion. A columnist wrote:

> As of 1 November, 1965, 286 disaster victims are still hospitalized, unable to go home two years after the accident. Among these are about 20 who have remained unconscious for two years. They are like "living corpses."
>
> According to the Workers' Accident Compensation Law, compensatory aid lessens if the victim is not cured within three years.[21]

Moved by the inhumane circumstances, he went on to say: "It is most heartless to penalize victims of a disaster caused by oversights on the part of the company before they are completely cured."[22] Yet the government did nothing.

The Yamano Coal Mine in Kyushu was the site of another disaster which resulted from the company's decision to put profits above worker safety. On 2 June 1965, 485 miners died in another explosion. Management was fully aware of the situation. Workers had previously complained of lack of ventilation. And it was known that the temperature in the pit had risen to almost 40°C, yet the union took no action and the workers were still sent down. A security inspector had to cut off power when he found the gas content of the air in the mines was 9.5 per cent, well above the danger level. The company refused to do anything. It told the inspector to check again. The explosion occurred before he could do so.

The Japanese press prefers not to attack big business as such, and, although in this case it lamented that production and profits had been placed above safety, it balanced these remarks by deploring those who attacked the authorities. Typically, one paper expressed concern for the victims while attacking "leftists" for turning the mine disasters into a pretext for political propaganda.[23] No remedial legislation was passed and the tragedies have continued into the 1980s.

At the Hokkaido Hokutan mine, the sensitivity of the gas sensors was deliberately reduced so that miners continued to work even after the alarms sounded. The resulting blowout, on 16 October 1981, caused 93 deaths. Management's reaction was similar to the reaction at the Yamano mine. Shortly after 2 a.m. on the day following the accident, the company president proposed flooding the shaft to put out the fire, knowing full well that the fifteen men alive below would be drowned. He retracted his proposal only after protests from miners and members of the victims' families.

The affair led the Minister of International Trade and Industry, a wholehearted business supporter, to put on his public mask. He told the president publicly on 17 October, "You don't have any compassion."[24] On 2 November, seventeen days after the accident, the mine president came to the belated conclusion: "From now on, our company will give priority to safety." It was then that the first openly critical newspaper article appeared in the *Japan Times Weekly*. It was entitled, "When 'Money First' is Motto, Mine Disasters No Surprise." It noted that 93 lives was the price of the president's enlightenment.[25]

A leading MITI official pointed out that the Hokutan group owns and runs seven hotels, a TV station and 38 affiliated businesses, and raised a question regarding the management's sincerity and seriousness about the business of coal mining.

I wonder if the government subsidies given to the Hokutan

group (Y 600 for every ton of coal produced) are really used for their intended purposes. It is very difficult to trace how the money has been used.[26]

Oppression is not restricted to any one section of Japan's work force, nor is it based on the whims of individual executives. Rather, it grows out of a philosophical belief widely held in the business community. Nikkeiren, the Japan Federation of Employers' Associations, specifically encourages its members to dominate their work forces. From the start, in August 1948, Nikkeiren consistently sought to restrict the power and scope of unions. In September 1949, it called for the re-establishment of management authority and workplace hierarchy.[27]

Toyota is one firm that takes Nikkeiren's admonishments seriously. There is a saying that the difference between workers in the West and those in most Japanese factories is that Western employees "work for" their firm, while Japanese workers "belong to" their firm. This perception is borne out by Toyota, which owes its status as the world's largest car exporter to its highly disciplined work force. Joining such a firm is like joining the army: for example, each rank in the hierarchy has its own uniform. There are different ones for seasonal workers, probationers, trainees, regular workers, team chief, foreman, general foreman, workers from subcontractors and so on.

The military aura is reinforced by the ex-members of the Self-Defence Forces, who are commonly employed as foremen and team chiefs. None has any experience in automobile plants, and none is needed. Already indoctrinated with anti-labour attitudes, their job is to ensure instant obedience.[28] One company measure for reinforcing compliance and submissiveness among the recruits requires them to keep diaries which are open to inspection and criticism by their superiors. This depersonalization process, of course, harmonizes with the military-style discipline techniques which pervade the workplace.

Despite suppression of individual will, worker dissension in many such companies continues. At Nissan, in 1982, several employees were severely beaten by company and union officials for protesting working conditions. This immediate crushing of protest may account for the survival of the myth of harmony and co-operation. In reality, Nissan's aim, shared by Japan's largest corporations, is the absolute submissiveness of its workers.[29]

Another remarkable firm, in a different line of business, is Matsushita Electric Industrial, which manufactures under such trade names as National, Panasonic, Quasar and Technics. It is, in some respects, a very progressive company. It was the first to introduce a five-day work week in 1965. It then divorced pay scales from seniority and, in 1966, gave equal pay to women. Management claims that the ultimate aim is to give every male employee his own home by age 35. But, unfortunately, all is not well. Worker health is a great cause of concern, as it is in many Japanese firms: according to a Ministry of Labour survey of 10,000 businesses, a half of the workers said they felt "strong anxiety, worries and stress in connection with work or place of work."

Matsushita's response to health problems has not been to slow down production but to provide a compulsory fitness program which, owner Konosuke Matsushita claims, enables his employees to live and work longer. Blending *samurai* philosophy with psychological therapy, he set up a "self-control" room containing a stuffed dummy of himself. Workers are provided with staves so they can unleash their aggressive feelings on the dummy.[30] He is one employer who admits such anger exists. In some ways, the firm still fits the standard mold. Every morning and evening, the employees gather and are required to sing the company song, "Grow industry, grow, grow, grow! Harmony and Sincerity! Matsushita Electric."

Matsushita, the founder, is a philosopher of sorts, who imposes his views upon his workers. These views are incorporated in the "Seven Spirited Values," which employees are forced to recite:

1. National Service Through Industry
2. Fairness
3. Harmony and Co-operation
4. Struggle for Betterment
5. Courtesy and Humiliation

6. Adjustment and Assimilation
7. Gratitude

While many of these virtues are certainly laudable, it is worthwhile to remember that "National Service Through Industry," the
first of Matsushita's "Seven Spirited Values," was the motto of
the militarist government-sponsored Patriotic Industrial Association during the war, an organization modelled on the Nazi
Arbeitsfront (Workers' Front).[31]

After the recitation, group leaders inform the workers of the
competitive situation in the marketplace. Before going home for
the day, employees are advised of the next day's tasks. The aim
is to turn workers into "company people."

Like Matsushita, the Honda Motor Company is often
portrayed as "different." To some extent that is true; while
Soichiro Honda does not like unions, he was wise enough to hire
outside consultants to handle management-labour relations. The
result is an enterprise union which has ensured a co-operative
work force. Another Honda difference is that workers are encouraged to express and use their personal initiative. Competence is the yardstick for promotion, while education and seniority are secondary considerations. One visible result of this encouragement is that section chiefs tend to be much younger than
in other plants. Most remarkable, for Japan, is that incompetent
workers are demoted. The company's wage and salary policy is
also pragmatic; the same wage is paid fror the same work regardless of seniority or education. Such attitudes, alien to Japanese
practice, have proved successful in attracting capable young
workers to the permanent force. But in other ways, Honda is like
all Japanese firms. Like George Orwell's Big Brother, Honda
uses high technology to aid in the constant surveillance of its
workers. This omnipresent industrial surveillance reaches its
apotheosis in the new Honda headquarters in Tokyo.

Completed in August 1985, the building is equipped with systems that tell the employer when a worker arrives, how much he
pays for lunch, and what he is doing and where he is at any particular time.[32] It is reminiscent of Orwell's words, ". . . every
sound you made was overheard." But it is not only Honda which

scrutinizes its employees. The *Asahi Journal* notes of Japanese corporations:

> Company regulations range from permission to leave premises for lunch, affidavits from train company if trains are late ... In applying for vacation leave, employees are asked the reason and destinations.[33]

In such an atmosphere, many workers learn that it is best to keep quiet, as this conversation at a Toyota plant demonstrates:

> "If we speak out now," one of the regulars said, "we'll suffer for at least 10 years."
> "How about the union? Won't they take care of you?"
> "The union works for management," one of them replied, and shrugged his shoulders.[34]

Sony, a name synonymous with quality and industrial efficiency, has been described as "... unlivable for workers."[35] Symbolically, Sony's fifteenth anniversary in 1961 was marred by a violent strike which forced the cancellation of a visit by the prime minister and other government dignitaries.

Part of the problem lay in the attitudes of "over zealous managers," who worked on the assumption, in the words of the company report, "that people were machines or domestic animals."[36] The management concluded "that the essential trust was missing in the personal relationship of management to the workers."[37]

The 1960s saw Sony at the vanguard of the world's electronic firms. In one year the production line was speeded up on three occasions, with serious consequences for worker health. Other hardships for workers arose in 1972 when Sony first introduced two shifts. Workers, mainly women from the poor Tohoku region, were on the 5 a.m. to 12:30 p.m. shift. Those from the Tokyo area worked from 12:30 p.m. until 8:20 p.m., making home life difficult for the women and, because they prepared the meals, for their families as well. The real effects of these industrial troubles are concealed within the company walls where worker protests are met with job transfers and, occasionally, violence.[38]

One example of this violence involved three women hired by

Sony's Shibaura plant in 1969. They registered a complaint about working conditions. A violent confrontation developed when the plant's security guards were called in. After physically assaulting the women, they threw them bodily out of the plant.[39]

As the company grew into one of the world's leading electronics firms, basic organizational changes were implemented. A system of worker cells was set up. Each discusses production techniques based on information from other groups and studies how best to improve work and production. Such cells, or Quality Control Circles, are not peculiar to Sony but have been common within all large Japanese concerns since the first ones were organized in 1952.

It had long been a myth in the West that Quality Control Circles were of Japanese origin. This view, like so much else about Japan, is false. They had their roots in the quality control technology developed immediately after World War II by Professor W.E. Deming of the United States. American business was prosperous and showed a marked lack of interest in his theories, so Deming went to Japan where, by the late '50s, he had become something of a god. One Japanese wrote in his diary: "Here was this . . . American telling us that we would be an important force in five years if we did what he said."[40]

As adapted in Japan, Quality Control Circles are not simply opportunities for employees to have input into the production process, they are also tools of management control. Workers are expected to make suggestions; promotions and bonuses often depend on their participation. The circles also provide a platform for passing on management ideals. All circles are held after the full working day, and after overtime, so even if a genuine trade union exists, there is no time for its meetings. Sony QC Circles have been an instrument not only of quality control, but of assembly line speed-up

Japanese employers, who rarely do things by halves, stretched the original Quality Control Circles to their ultimate conclusion and labelled them TQC – Total Quality Control. The Japanese corporate world has proposed widespread introduction of Total Quality Control, declaring that this is just what is needed to save Japan. The objective of Total Quality Control is the same as its predecessor: the reduction of production costs and the improvement of quality. The difference is its degree of exploitation.

TQC created a boom among Japanese corporations at the beginning of the '80s after it was first proposed by the Japanese Union of Scientists and Engineers. A Deming award for employee quality control work, instituted in 1951, is still awarded. A minimum requirement for receiving the award is at least one year of compiling data and writing self-criticism. This means endless hours of overtime.[41]

Not all workers co-operate. In some workplaces, union members refuse to attend group meetings. One says:

> The atmosphere on the working floor becomes worse. We feel suffocated by the autonomous goals imposed on us: write suggestions, write about our group, help each other, accomplish norms etc. It is said that group discussion is an excellent method to solve problems. But if the results of group thinking are predetermined, group discussion would be a waste of time. I always refuse to speak at meetings to express my disgust for pro-management group activities.[42]

The quasi-religious fervour of TQC groups resulted in three employee suicides due to harassment and criticism in the first year it was introduced industry-wide. A section manager at an automobile manufacturer took his life in the company pond. Yet the list of Japanese corporations which have adopted TQC is impressive – Toyota, Bridgestone, Komatsu and Fuji Xerox, to name a few.[43]

Successful Japanese firms such as these teach employees that labour is *not* alienated from its own production because workers are a part of management. The small group is the key to propagating this philosophy. Workers who are appointed group leaders tend to feel superior to their fellow workers. They are sent to training courses and encouraged to think of themselves as chosen and aloof. They cease to go to union meetings and begin to organize group activities to increase production.

These workers come to see themselves as autonomous or independent, although in fact management guides them carefully, thinking only of the interests of the company. The successful realization of this theory has contributed to the well-known rigidities of the Japanese workplace and to the ultracontrolled patterns of thought and conduct in the broader society.[44]

Self-criticism and the worship of production is far from coming to an end. Less scientific methods continue. Some corporations go so far as to gather their middle management at the foot of Mt. Fuji and subject them to seven days of mutual torture – marathons lasting from 5 a.m. until 10 p.m., during which managers abuse each other until each participant admits he has been neglecting the quality of the company's products and its well-being. He is then given various menial tasks designed to debase him.

The Japanese, by their own admission, go through a number of "hells." This one they term the "Seven Day Hell."

'The Improvement of Women's Well-Being'

"One's upper body should lean forward at an angle of 30 to 40 degrees. At the same time the female employee must let both hands meet slightly in front." Office ladies, O.L.s, spend a lot of time doing this and, like their British sisters, making tea. In April 1986, an Equal Opportunity Employment Law was passed prohibiting distinctions on the basis of sex in employment, salary and advancement. It includes no penalties for employers who do not obey, and is therefore virtually useless. So, while women in the work force of the industrialized West remain second class citizens, the reality for Japanese women is worse.

For instance, Kinokuniya, one of Tokyo's largest bookstore chains, advertised in its 1983 guidelines for hiring female part-time employees:

> Don't hire divorced women, women who live alone in apartments, wives of writers or teachers, or women who wear glasses. At all costs, avoid hiring ugly women.[45]

Most women work in offices or factories and an increasing number are employed at making electrical equipment, precision instruments and armaments. The electronics industries now employ the largest numbers, with whole factories staffed mainly by women. At Matsushita Electric and Sanyo Electric, a half or more of all employees are female and, at the Toshiba Transistor and Hitachi plants, the proportion is about 80 and 74 per cent, respectively. The average age of working women is twenty and almost 80 per cent of them are under 25. The pace of the production lines is so fast that few older persons could withstand the pressure. In any event, management knows it will replace its young women within three or four years when they leave to get married. The work is repetitious and requires minimal skill. Training usually takes a week. Women, it is conveniently maintained, are especially adaptable because of their skill in delicate assembly. They also, conveniently, happen to be cheap. While the working environment is often excellent in the main plants, the constant pressure, double shifts, and company dormitories remain the same in large firms and small.

Part-time women workers are the natural choice for many employers. Apart from the lower wages, employers are relieved of maintaining a lifetime employment system with its costly benefits. Temporaries are given no break when it comes to working conditions or productivity expectations. According to a Special Labour Force Survey, over a fifth work for the same hours and days as the regular employees, and about a half work for more than 35 hours per week, which is almost full-time. And they work these hours at lower salaries and with fewer fringe benefits than full-time male employees.

A female worker at the Radio Division of Matsushita Electric Company is typical. She is 22 years old and has worked there for seven years. Here is one day in her working life:[46]

8:00 - 8:15	morning meeting (*chokai*)
8:15 - 10:00	routine work
10:00 - 10:10	10 minute break
10:10 - 12:00	work
12:00 - 12:45	lunch
12:45 - 2:20	work
2:20 - 2:30	10 minute break
2:30 - 4:40	work
4:40 - 4:45	evening meeting (*yukai*)
4:45 - 5:00	supper break
5:00 - 6:00	overtime (depending on
- 7:00	business conditions)

As a part-time worker she is in no position to refuse if overtime work is required.

The number of part-time workers is increasing conspicuously. While women by no means make up all the temporary workers in major firms, the ratio is increasing. The proportion of part-time workers to the total number of female employees is also rising, from 9.6 per cent in 1965 to 22.1 per cent in 1984.[47] As unemployment rises, the lot of the temporaries becomes worse.

In May 1984, the LDP brought up the Working Women's Welfare Law for revision and immediately removed the few safeguards it gave women. For example, it abolished the two-hour limit on overtime for women in industry. This was, of course, a convenient arrangement for business but, many thought, an unusual way to promote equality.

There are few areas in which it is possible to compare male and female workers. Banks are an exception, as both men and women work as tellers and clerks. However, it took 28 years after the passing of the Labour Standards Law before a case of equal pay for women was brought before the courts. In 1975, complaints were heard against the Akita Sogo Bank, which had introduced separate promotion rates for men and women upon reaching the age of 26. By the age of 50, women were being paid 60 per cent of what men received. The court decided in favour of the women, leading to numerous other cases of litigation against the banks and other employers.[48]

Such a ruling has had no more effect in Japan than similar settlements in other countries. Equal pay for work of equal value remains a dream for most. Wage statistics are hardly reassuring. In 1975 full-time women workers received 61.4 per cent of the salaries of their male counterparts; in 1984 it had fallen to 58.6 per cent. But these figures are hardly surprising. Japanese companies are showing deficits for the first time in decades, and women employees are the first to suffer. Most work in small firms lacking even co-operative unions to support their cause.

Meanwhile, Japanese women who work in offices have even less chance to advance than their sisters in the West. A typical example is the regulation of one of Japan's biggest trading companies, under which women workers cannot become supervisors, regardless of their ability. This corporation also refuses to hire female university graduates because, for a long time, they had all left the company within two years, giving job dissatisfaction, not marriage, as their reason for leaving. Job dissatisfaction can arise for many reasons, but the requirement that women make and serve tea, a practice well known elsewhere, is one.

While women account for about one-quarter of Japan's total business and industrial work force, less than 1 per cent of these working women are senior personnel. Over 80 per cent of the major corporations have no women in this category. The highest percentages of female decision-makers are in the service industries with 0.5 per cent, in wholesale and retail with 0.3 per cent and in finance and insurance with 0.2 per cent. The remaining industries list nil.[49]

A few women have indeed achieved great responsibilities. In 1986, Takako Doi was elected leader of the Japan Socialist Party; another woman is the president of Takashimaya, Japan's most upper-crust department store chain. But in Japan, as in most advanced Western countries, such successes are rare.

Of course, many Japanese women have neither the time nor education for administrative positions. Given the pressure on women to stay at home, it is somewhat surprising that a fifth of female university graduates say they want to hold a supervisory post at some time.

There is a common belief that Japanese women remain at home once married rather than seek jobs. The truth is that, very much as in the West, married women are making up an ever increasing percentage of the work force. In 40 per cent of Japanese families, both husband and wife work. But the large majority of Japanese men want their wives to stay home after child bearing, although their wives are much more willing to get jobs.[50]

Having a working wife remains a social stigma among elements of the upper-middle class. Most Japanese men are reluctant to admit their wives work, for to many it involves a loss of face, an admission that they are not good providers. (This attitude, of course, is not confined to Japan.) But the promise of a larger family income is winning out, for, low as women's wages are, everything helps to pay the skyrocketing mortgages and the often ruinous costs of educating the children. Japanese women are under few illusions about the types of jobs open to them or about discrimination in the job market. Those with professional training, for example, find it virtually impossible to return to their original jobs after child bearing without losing seniority and wages.

Returning to work at a larger enterprise means working at lower wages, and being "let go" before their male fellow workers. Such early retirement is now illegal, but women workers are invariably temporary and can be dismissed at will, so the question becomes academic. In addition, because women are mostly temporary and draw lower wages, they receive few of the retirement benefits of their male counterparts.

Another of the obvious inequities is the mandatory retirement age for women. This form of discrimination received the official seal of approval in 1971 when the Tokyo High Court ruled that female workers are physiologically inferior to male workers and that they can be legally compelled to retire at the age of 50. The presiding judge said, "the physiological capability of a 55-year-old woman is equivalent to that of a 70-year-old man, so that a five year difference between the retirement ages is no injustice."[51] This judgment remained law until 1981, when the Supreme Court ruled that Nissan's discriminatory retirement law was unconstitutional. The early retirement law was overturned. Nevertheless, most of the basic inequalities are still practised and condoned.

The Working Women's Welfare Law of 1985 does little to change things. Equality in the work place, as advocated by the United Nations, is watered down by the addition of a qualifying phrase, "While maintaining harmony with family life." The law makes no pretense at aiming for equal pay for equal work. Rather, the objective is stated as "the improvement of women's well-being." This act is a poor substitute for the Equal Opportunity Act that women's groups had been fighting for. We must keep in mind that the liberation of women in Europe and other Western countries is far from complete, a fact which should temper criticism of sexism in Japan. Feminist groups in Japan are concerned about increasing religious and ideological rhetoric which is elevating the family to the status of a cult, but which, many women fear, will ultimately serve business and the state rather than the wife and mother.

The Bottom Rungs

As in all societies, people on the bottom rungs of Japan's economic ladder come in for more than their share of suffering. The temporary workers, in large or medium-sized Japanese firms, struggle to make ends meet, but they are almost universally better off than those in sub-contracting firms within or outside the major plants or than those myriads who work in home industries. These lowly employees are, in turn, better off than the seasonal or casual workers and day labourers. Working conditions for these very lowest workers are often appalling, and any labour laws that cover them are frequently unenforced.

The Japanese people are aware of these inequities but, like people in other countries, they become used to looking the other way. An editorial in an English-language Japanese newspaper is entitled "Looking Behind the Facade":

> ... And when you pass by labourers working on a railway, or on a highway construction project, give a thought to the loneliness of these people – persons who are forced to leave their wives and children to run their impoverished farms while they try to bolster the family income by taking jobs no one wants in the city.[52]

The writer sadly concludes,

> ... and right now, we're a lot further away from being first in the 21st century than a lot of other countries in this world.[53]

A glaring case in point is the wide-scale use of home industry, which is virtually non-existent in the industrial West. In Japan, it is big business. The total number of household workers exceeds 1.25 million, representing some 10 per cent of Japanese homes. Of these workers, 93 per cent are women.[54] They are paid on a piecework scale and are fortunate to receive two-thirds of the pay of even a temporary factory worker. In fact, Japan's minimum wage laws are so blatantly ignored that fully two-thirds of the country's businesses pay below the required minimum. As the large majority of companies are small sub-contractors, they depend on low wages to sell at competitive prices to the major corporations.

A study of plastic goods in Aichi Prefecture discovered that, among 158 firms, over a third of the work is farmed out to 3,500 housewives in their homes and is paid piece-rate. These women represent nearly half of all workers involved in plastic production. Domestic industry has grown faster in Japan than in any other highly industrialized country. It is widely used by car and engine manufacturers, and in the clothing and electronics industries. The sub-contracting firms in these industries themselves sub-contract out, using housewives as their labour force. This combination of sweatshop labour and twentieth-century technology has served big business well by keeping costs down, and is at the heart of Japan's "economic miracle."

These "less equal" workers suffer not only economically, but their health and well-being suffer too. There are few official statistics broken down by sex, but it is generally known that small businesses with a large proportion of women have the highest rate of industrial injuries and health problems. In fact, more than 90 per cent of all industrial injuries occur in the smallest enterprises.

Many such businesses are situated on the premises of the major firms. This is particularly true in industries such as shipbuilding and iron and steel production. In the automobile and electrical machinery firms, sub-contractors operate outside the parent firm.

In both cases, however, there remains a substantial disparity in the number of industrial injuries between the sub-contractors and the prime contractor. In shipbuilding, severe injuries are four times as great among the suppliers as among employees of the main companies. The lower on the employment ladder in Japan, the greater the risks.

At the bottom of the heap are the day and casual labourers who work under the so-called *hamba* system. The *hamba* is a prefabricated building near a main factory. Typically, it is made of the thinnest plywood. There is no heating, and the "bath" is a converted oil drum, outside the building.[55]

Workers, many of whom come from nearby Japanese "skid rows," or *doya-gai*, are paid token wages and provided with food and shelter in the *hamba*. It is quite common, too, for the largest Japanese corporations to start their own *hambas* in order to attract workers who are cheap, can be forced to work long hours and are easy to lay off. Discipline is often exercised by underworld organizations or mobs.

Labourers refer to the *hamba* as an "octopus room," because, like the octopus traps used by Japanese fishermen, there is no getting out once one has gotten in.[56]

7

RICH COUNTRY, POOR PEOPLE

Japan may be the world's richest nation, but something is terribly wrong when white collar workers in top firms cannot afford to buy a house, or even pay for their children's education.

HIDEZO INABA, Chairman,
Industrial Policy Research Institute, 1987[1]

Japan has grown into an economic power. But we do not feel that our country is an economic power . . . you must understand that we live in small homes called "rabbit hutches," work hard all year long and still worry about our life in old age.

HIROSHI KISHIDA, company employee, Urawa City, 1987[2]

Public Priorities

Art lovers around the world were shocked when Yasuda Fire and Marine Insurance paid $39 million for Van Gogh's painting *Sunflowers* in March 1987. Japan's Ministry of Finance took the company to task for "distorting" the international art market. Many Japanese in the street thought corporate wealth could be better spent.

Corporations in Japan have been prospering since the 1950s, their wealth accumulating rapidly. The assets of one Japanese finance company, Nomura Securities, easily exceed what the government spends in a year on its social security programs.[3]

Recognition of the imbalance of wealth is beginning to cause concern among some of the privileged. The managing editor of a business magazine observes:

> The first step Japan should take immediately is to "bring the gold coins out of the warehouses and spend them on improvement of the nation's living conditions."[4]

Post-war Japan is seen to be a relatively equalitarian society. As far as salaries and wages are concerned, it is, but an economic division is forming between those who have assets, and those who do not.

On one hand, a group of "new rich" is gradually making an appearance on the Japanese scene. By and large unknown to the public, they have astronomical sums at their disposal, often gained through land speculation during the recent upsurge in land prices. Typical is Kichinosuke Sasaki, who owns assets worth over 250 billion yen, acquired after he gave up medicine for real estate in 1977. Many of the new rich conceal their wealth by forming limited liability companies; with 6.7 million such companies, Japan is the world leader.[5]

By contrast, the average Japanese employee takes home an annual income, in 1987 terms, of US$29,000. If the figure seems high, it should be remembered that Japanese income earners do not live in a dollar, but a yen, economy. And the costs of housing, utility payments, education and above all food are so high that many cannot make ends meet, while others have little left over to save.

Early in 1987, the Organization for Economic Co-operation and Development in Paris noted that, for 1986 as a whole, the average yen-dollar exchange rate was 169 to 1. Early in 1987, when the dollar plunged into the 140s, Japan was clearly the "richest" major country in the world. But the OECD went on to expose the single most illuminating statistic to come out of Japan. When it adjusted incomes in each country for purchasing power, it found that the "real" exchange rate was 223 to 1. In blunt terms, this means that consumers are paying through the nose to make Japan "a rich country."[6]

This reality is revealed as well in a second key statistic. The authorities have accumulated vast sums through land speculation. Japan's land is altogether "worth" more than America's, although the United States is 25 times as large. This is an important fact because of what it says about the repression of consumer interests in Japan. The gap between the official and "real" exchange rates – between something in the 140s to the 160s and 223 – is the wealth the corporations have accumulated in order to preserve their market share, the wealth denied to their own consumers. In other words, for 140 yen, a Japanese consumer could buy a dollar and use it to buy essential goods abroad that would cost him more than 200 yen at home.[7]

As a high-ranking member of Japan's National Institute of Public Health declares:

> Japan is not really a developed country; industry has developed but the country as a whole has not. Our economic growth rate and GNP may well make the government proud, but the living conditions of the people should cause it shame.[8]

Most Japanese cities are ugly and uncomfortable. Ninety per cent of Tokyo's roads have no sidewalks and some city rivers are little better than open sewers, although Tokyo's Sumida River is less filthy than it was in 1964 when a newspaper was provoked to print:

> Sumida River with the Tokyo Olympics so near
> Water falling from the oars of boatman
> Going up and down the river
> Scatter methane gas;
> To what can this foul odor be compared?[9]

As far back as the seventeenth century, Japan's cities, such as Edo, Kyoto and Osaka, were among the largest in the world. Yet Japan remained an agricultural country. As late as 1920, when the first national census was taken, less than 20 per cent of the population lived in urban areas, and the towns retained their feudal character. A deeply communal quality remained. The newly arrived urbanites retained their ties with the rural areas and carried their customs with them. In the process, the new towns became a conglomeration of independent villages, each largely insulated from the other. Such fragmentation made urban planning and the development of civic pride very difficult. Under feudalism, the fief, village or family was all-important. Anything larger was difficult to comprehend; indeed, the term society, *shakai*, only came into existence in the early years of the Meiji era. Thus the sense of widespread social responsibility remains weak.

Historically, life in the countryside was harsh. Famines and peasant revolts recurred frequently. A few gentry owned most of the land. This pre-modern character of rural life stayed largely intact until after World War II, when the Occupation divided the larger land holdings. As a result, over 70 per cent of farmers outside of Hokkaido cultivate very small plots of less than one hectare. The plots are so small, in fact, that only by huge subsidies can most farmers make a living from the land. To ensure a good life, many work part-time at factories in the cities, as seasonal employees (a pattern growing more common in the West as the economy makes small-scale farming more precarious). It is a way of life that has taken its toll on the family. In the off-season, some villages appear to be inhabited only by women and the elderly.

Farmers with large lots in good locations, however, can do very well indeed. Due to lavish subsidies, many concentrate on rice. One author describes the life of a farmer friend. His work keeps him busy for a few weeks a year.

> ... The rest of the time he does casual work in the nearby town, drinks (a cynic describes most of the local generation as sun-burned alcoholics), chats up the Filipino girls supplied to the local *Sunnakku*, snack bar, by the local gangster, and plays pachinko. In short, he is preserving traditional culture.[10]

Meanwhile, the foodstuffs he used to grow on the hillside now have to be imported.

If some farmers have never had it so good, urbanites are increasingly dissatisfied. As a Japanese author writes:

> The Japanese people are fed up with paying 7 to 10 times the international price for the rice they eat. The last straw

was the folly by the LDP, which recently overruled a rec-
ommendation for a cut in the price the government pays to
producers.[11]

The Ministry of Agriculture, Forestry and Fisheries admits
that Japan's domestically produced rice is 8.3 times as expensive
as that of the United States, 3.7 times that of Great Britain.[12]

In some senses the Japanese are rich. They have the highest
living standard in Asia, boundless consumer goods and are liter-
ate and long-lived. Yet they suffer a quality of housing on a par
with the Third World and a government which spends less on social welfare than any other advanced country. Japan, too, as a
nation has 330,000 people in mental institutions, 80 per cent of
them behind bars.[13] "A rich country but a poor people" is the
phrase Japanese citizens most often cite to describe their plight.[14]

Tokyo

Tokyo is huge and dynamic. Its hotels and department stores are
among the best in the world. It is also ugly. Its few sizeable en-
claves of natural beauty include a handful of medium-sized
parks and a large green area reserved for the virtually exclusive
use of the emperor. Figures tell the sad story. The average
Tokyoite has a mere two square metres of park as compared with
30 and 46 square metres for his London and Washington
counterparts. This is an unfair comparison, for land is sadly
lacking, but it does reflect an important difference in the quality
of life. For some tourists in the most luxurious hotels there are
exotic mini-parks, and for all there are several hundred small but
beautiful areas, usually surrounding temples and shrines. Yet
even when these are added together, they are poor compensation
for the Japanese city-dweller. It is not surprising that there has
been a small but growing reverse migration from the huge urban
sprawls.

Westerners sometimes say of their own largest cities, "a mar-
velous place to visit, but I wouldn't want to live there," and the
Japanese feel the same way about Tokyo. The *Tokyo Business
Today* bluntly states there has never been a city as unpopular. It

quotes a survey conducted by one of the nation's largest newspapers, the *Asahi Shimbun*, in which 70 to 80 per cent of non-Tokyoites claimed to be disenchanted with Tokyo.[15]

For a few who live in the city, however, Tokyo really is a home of which they are proud. According to them, the criticisms of those from the "prefectures" are likely born of jealousy. Tokyo is becoming a centre of fashion, and of new cultural trends. Many find exhilaration in this dynamic metropolis.

To those who have lived in and loved Tokyo, there is the charm of the unexpected and the conviction that the élan of the East, perhaps of the world, is concentrated here.

One of Japan's leading intellectuals, Kazuki Kasuya, points out how the city has matured.

> Tokyo has become more settled in the past 10 years. There is even a new type of people, called Tokyo-jin, who are born and bred in Tokyo ... they are becoming the driving force of a new culture.[16]

But even for the most affluent Tokyo-jin, finding a place to live at an affordable price is most difficult. Downtown accommodation is virtually unobtainable.

Conglomerates own much of the real estate in the major cities, as indeed they do in Western countries. In the Tokyo business areas of Marunouchi and Ohtemachi, the Mitsubishi group possesses some 85 per cent of available commercial buildings. In another prime area, Toronamon, where the Imperial Hotel is located, the Mitsui Group owns 60 per cent of the land. The 1973 recession gave the *zaikai* further opportunities to increase their holdings by buying up vacant lots.

Central Tokyo was the scene of an unprecedented construction boom in the 1980s. In one district, more than 260 new construction projects were launched between 1982 and 1985. The National Land Agency predicts that by the year 2000 there will be a need for approximately 5,000 hectares of new floor space in central Tokyo alone. But land costs in this core area are skyrocketing. A National Land Agency Report released in May 1987 showed a 163.4 per cent rise in land prices in the central area of Tokyo during 1986.[17]

In the same area, real estate is selling for up to Y37,500,000 or some $250,000 a square metre. In terms of space, an average one bedroom apartment in a European or North American city would be worth $25 million on this scale. It is not surprising, then, that the number of apartments being constructed in Tokyo is falling. Within all Tokyo wards in 1985, the number of new apartments fell 30 per cent from the previous year, but within the city centre it declined at the astonishing rate of more than 66 per cent. Aside from luxury suites designed for foreign executives, it no longer pays to build housing downtown. Small businesses are being hit worst. More and more are being driven from the city centres. With fewer apartments and local stores, downtown is becoming a place where no one actually lives, a place deserted after the working day winds down.

During the early 1980s, the rise in land prices had been concentrated in the commercial districts, but by 1986 it began to be felt in the surrounding residential areas. In one such area, land prices rose by an average of 18.8 per cent in 1986, as compared with an increase of 3.8 per cent in the previous year. This jump in value is, of course, tied to inflation. The same year saw the exchange rate of the yen jump by 30 per cent. The total market value of the land in Japan, a country roughly the size of California, is now greater than the value of land in the entire U.S.[18]

Aside from the rise of the yen, there is another reason for these skyrocketing prices. The government has adopted a laissez faire attitude to the whole problem. Its land use programs and overall national development plan lack enforcing power. The government has set a poor example by paying huge sums for expropriated lands. The result is virtually unbridled land speculation.

The consumers are the greatest victims, but they remain unorganized and divided. Instead of demanding an effective land policy, many people attempt to reap profits for themselves. Some resistance to this spiral of land costs became evident in the early 1980s, but it was not enough to worry the owners or developers, who, if they fail to find a market, can always obtain tax incentives to hold or build empty commerical buildings. Under such circumstances, there is no end in sight to spiralling land costs.

Home Sweet Home

A classical Japanese home can be among the most beautiful of buildings. In simplicity and elegance, Japan's traditional architecture is a source of inspiration world-wide.

For a foreigner staying with friends in one of these homes, or as a guest at a first class inn, Japanese living is a joyous experience. And yet most of Japan's housing is inferior to that of any country in the industrialized world.

The Organization for Economic Co-operation and Development (OECD) compares the standard of the housing in Japan with that in the Third World, and coined the name "rabbit hutch" to describe a typical Japanese dwelling.

Home for millions of Japanese is a single room with a shared kitchen and toilet. In the Tokyo-Yokohama-Kawasaki triangle, there are 9.2 million households; 2.9 million households are situated in private rental housing, but only 650,000 of these live in modern non-wood buildings, and of that number a scant 8 per cent live in housing which is described by the Ministry of Construction as "adequate." In other words, only 52,000 families out of 2.9 million in the area live in "adequate," modern housing, by the government's own admission.[19] By "adequate," the Ministry means one room of at least 40 square metres, the bathroom and kitchen being invariably shared with one or more families. Tokyo's 40 square metres compares with 115.3 square metres, the average size of a dwelling in Sweden, and 102.5 square metres for a dwelling in West Germany. On average, accommodation in the Republic of Germany is two and a half times larger than an officially adequate housing unit in Japan.

The quality of public housing is little better. In the same urban triangle, barely more than one-fifth of public housing meets the tragically low minimum standards.

Since World War II, the Japan Housing Corporation and local bodies have tried to improve the quality of housing by building public apartments for rent, called *danchi*. Most consist of two small rooms and a dining-kitchen room, the whole known as a 2DK. This setup at least creates the possibility of two bedrooms, with the living room doubling as a bedroom, but still does not allow for the separation of the sleeping quarters of children of different sexes. Nor does it allow old people to live with their married children.

Most 2DK apartment buildings are situated in the suburbs and are of unattractive ferro-concrete construction. The rents are reasonable but the income requirements are very high. This virtually restricts the applicants to white-collar workers in the relatively high income brackets or to those with working wives. Very few manual workers live in a *danchi* for, by the time they have saved enough, they are usually quite old and have been long settled in other accommodations.

In December 1985, the Housing and Urban Development Corporation conducted a survey of the living conditions of housing complexes in six central wards of Tokyo. The survey covered both public rental housing built by the corporation and private units. Of the units surveyed, 43 per cent were at least of the 2DK type, designed for a couple with two children. But such apartments accounted for only 30 per cent of the private rental accommodations. Seventy per cent were even smaller.

The *danchi* used to be a middle step on the ladder for the Japanese middle class but, since 1975 and the recession, it has become the end of the road for many. The only alternative is to live in privately built and owned apartments euphemistically called *mansions*. The rents are often high, especially in the downtown areas. However, lengthy commuting under crowded conditions makes even a few *danchi*-dwellers think of moving in-town.

Mansions vary widely. Some are rows of grey doors reminding one of a cell block, yet others are colourful and airy. Most are very small.

There are even *mansions* standing on plots of 200-300 square metres.[20] These buildings are nicknamed "pencil mansions," or "chimney mansions." Such structures are expected to degenerate into slums, yet in Japan there is no effective legislation restricting their construction. Their developers are primarily medium and small-scale real estate firms that exist on the fringes of the business world. Luxury condominiums do exist, but they are so expensive that few can afford them.

Most Japanese like to think of themselves as middle class, owning a separate house with its own garden. They are willing to put up with the inconvenience of commuting to obtain that dream. But for the vast majority, it will remain nothing but that.[21] The market price of a house in suburban Tokyo – a miniature dwelling by Western standards – is about $500,000. To afford a house, an increasing number of Japanese are involving their families in multi-generation mortgages. The would-be homeowner arranges a down payment with the help of his parents and relatives, then settles down to paying for it, knowing that his children and their children may also have to carry the financial burden.

In light of this situation, why is housing so low on the government's list of priorities? Certainly a nation capable of building the huge ports and the massive infrastructures needed for its economy could, if it wished, solve its housing problems. But efforts have been pitiful. There *have* been a few projects, such as the Tsukuba Academic City for scholars and scientists, often heralded as a model, but even in Tsukuba, facilities are poor. Central heating in living quarters is inadequate or non-existent. Apartments and dormitories are squalid and dreary, far different from the attractive and spacious research institutes nearby. This has led some Japanese observers to call housing Japan's "not-so-secret weapon." They say that the Japanese are willing to toil long hours six days a week because, in part, the white-collar worker's office is usually more pleasant and roomier than his home.

According to the "study data book of 13 nations' view of value," researched by the International Value Conference, the percentage of people satisfied with residential living in Japan is 44 per cent, the second lowest among the thirteen countries studied. Only Korea had a lower satisfaction rate. Satisfaction in some of the other countries polled were: U.S.A. 71 per cent, Canada 78 per cent, Britain 71 per cent, Singapore 80 per cent and Korea 33 per cent.[22] However, as the Japanese Economic Planning Agency observes, these subjective evaluations are affected by the culture and tradition of each country, so they cannot be simply compared. As a rough guide, however, they are instructive.

The housing scandal nevertheless belies the commonly accepted view of Japan as an efficiently planned society. The gravity of the crisis is evinced by the extremes to which some downplay it. One prominent Japanese citizen claims that Japan's urban housing is fully adequate, since the home is only a place to sleep in any case. He points to the vast array of services provided by the cities that, in his view, more than compensates for the size and other drawbacks of Japan's dwellings. But it is a sad comment on Japan that he must also boast that restaurants and coffee shops can double as drawing rooms, *mah jong* parlours as card rooms, *juku* schools as children's rooms, and public bath houses as bathrooms. This gentleman, a banker, has little knowledge of how his fellows live. Nowhere is that clearer than in his observation that in Tokyo, "good sanitation . . . makes the high price of residential land quite reasonable."[23] This statement is as inaccurate as it is insensitive: the city's sanitation system is worse than any other in a major capital in the advanced world. Sewage disposal is still accomplished mainly by the ladling or pumping out of cess pits. The proportion of the Japanese population with drainage facilities is 28 per cent, compared with 97 per cent in Britain and 82 per cent in Sweden. In Tokyo, it is about 50 per cent.

Yet this viewpoint is not the aberration of just one member of the ruling elite. These groups in Japan are as isolated from reality as are some of their counterparts in the West. Yatsuhiro Nakagawa, deputy director of the Nuclear Fuel Division in the Office of the Japanese Prime Minister, declares:

> And while Japanese housing conditions are, to be sure, surprising in many aspects, on the whole they are incomparably better than those that obtain in England and the rest of Western Europe.[24]

To do the establishment justice, it is fair to add that his views are not universal. A corporation president, in reply to a question, admitted, "The Japanese are quite well off in what they wear and eat, but when it comes to homes . . . well I'm not convinced."[25]

The common people are convinced. Only 16.1 per cent of Japanese express overall satisfaction with their housing.[26] If further proof is needed, a glance through the letters to the editor page of Japanese newspapers for any week should be sufficient. In one column, a housewife writes:

> My heart aches as I see our sons squeeze their bodies into the beds we bought when we moved into the apartment. In the next couple of years, they will be as big as my husband and outgrow the small beds. They will find the limited space in our apartment unbearable.[27]

Despite their silence on the issue of housing, government leaders are the first to stress the importance of family life. After recent annual Family Day celebrations held by the LDP, one newspaper commented pointedly that a better way to improve family life is to provide adequate housing.

Marriage and Family

It is ironic that many foreigners criticize Japanese marriages, while defending those in their own countries. If commitment is a marital virtue, certainly few Westerners have a moral right to criticize: some 52 per cent of U.S. marriages in recent years have ended in divorce. The Japanese divorce rate, although rising, is far lower.

Before the war, the family system was feudal. After marriage, the eldest son continued to live in the same house as his parents, a custom destroyed by urbanization and one-room homes. In the 1947 Constitution, the term "head of the family" was abolished as a legal category. In its place, the one married couple and nuclear family system was established. The direct-lineage system survives as a convention, and the son's wife still lives with his parents where circumstances allow, although the custom is gradually disappearing.

Thanks to the Occupation, women have gained rights over their property and are able to transact business without their husband's consent. Thus the post-war Japanese family is no longer *legally* a male-dominated autocracy. And in practice, the idea of the traditional family is largely restricted to Japan's ruling circles, where status, discipline and male superiority remain strong.

There are three systems of marital match-making in Japan.

Miai, the traditional method, involves a formal introduction, usually by a go-between. *Shokai* is less formal, based on a meeting arranged by mutual friends, and *Renai* is like the usual Western practice, a meeting in almost any social situation. No system carries any compulsion to marry, and it is usual in Japan for the couple to date for some months and to seek the consent of their parents.

Miai is still customary in the countryside and among some establishment families.

Surprisingly, *Miai* helps break down the hierarchical structure of Japanese society. A less well-off family with an attractive daughter will seek a husband from a higher social stratum. In the same manner, a son who graduates from a "good" university but is of modest means is more likely to find himself a rich wife. His lower social position is offset by his educational status and the bride's family will be compensated by having their daughter marry a man in a prestigious government department or corporation. Such marriages of convenience can be to the advantage of both and often end up as true love matches.

Marriages in Japan have traditionally occurred among those sharing the same "place." In olden times, courting was limited to the village, and, in recent days, it usually occurs in the same place of work. This is of particular interest to the corporate world, as marriage is one further link that binds the employee to the company. Leading businesses such as Mitsubishi and Mitsui encourage in-company marriage and operate marriage bureaus. The intention is to strengthen the couple's "obligation" to the company. The Mitsubishi service is typical of a large concern, offering "support" to employees of the corporation's 28 companies and 31 affiliated companies.

Maintaining a division of labour in the home as well as the workplace is of importance to the Japanese hierarchy, and the state encourages traditional gender roles. For most young couples in urban Japan, the husband and wife's activities are clearly distinct. The man tends to be involved in household chores even less than his Western counterpart, partly because there is less housework and partly because the man's work keeps him away from home for longer hours.

For a woman, marriage involves management. She is in

charge of the accounts, and responsible for calling plumbers, carpenters and electricians. As well, her chores include most of the physical work around the house. Japanese wives take out the garbage and, above and beyond all this, the disciplining of the children and encouraging and cajoling them to pass their exams – all this falls on her shoulders as well. Japanese men are sensitive to foreign criticism of their treatment of women, not least in marriage. They go so far as to say that the real power is held by the wife. Typical "proof," which is heard commonly in the West as well, is the assertion that the women control the purse strings. It is true that most Japanese husbands hand over all or most of their pay cheque to their wives, who are responsible for the family accounts. It is also true that wives help determine the husband's monthly spending allowance. What many men fail to admit is that up to a third of their yearly salary, in the form of semi-annual bonuses, is often retained by the husband for his own use. In addition, the expenditure of any major sum must invariably be approved by the man.

Still, the vision of an average modern Japanese housewife as helplessly dependent on her husband's every whim is overstated. While a wife must still show deference toward her husband in public, in private her views often prevail in budgeting matters, and in the children's education. But her lot is not an entirely happy one; in fact, most Western women would find it intolerable. For instance, few wives of Japanese businessmen go out in the evenings. Their husbands expect them to stay home and welcome them back with a prepared meal, whatever the hour. In a sense, both are the victims of a business society which places far greater demands on the white-collar employee than would be tolerated in the West. On the man's part, many of the "demands" take the form of compulsory socializing, including such activities as drinking in the evenings or perhaps a round of golf on Sundays. Many Japanese men enjoy this, but many do not. Either way, the rigours of working life hardly strengthen the Japanese family.

While they stress harmonious family life, the authorities do much to destroy it. Unhappy Japanese marriages are often caused by the business-managed society. The father-son relationship suffers in particular, for when the father reaches middle management he is expected by his firm to devote most of his "free" hours to socializing with business associates. At this time, the son is normally approaching his teens, and the father is increasingly absent from the home. The company father rarely takes his son to the city and never to his business. When he is home, the father often finds that he and his son have little in common. As a result, the mother takes on the father's role. This too is in the interest of business, for it ensures that the division of labour is to the employer's advantage.

Things are changing, however. As the economy slows, husbands can take more time off. In 1987, the government undertook the first survey of its kind dealing with family relations. Some of the results are startling and no doubt upset the image held by many Westerners. Sixty per cent of respondents say a three-generation family is better than a nuclear one, and 90 per cent support the traditional division of roles between husband and wife, in which the man brings home the pay cheque and the woman looks after the house. Another response is remarkable, not for what it says, but for the reaction of Japanese sources. In the words of one Japanese report: "A surprisingly high 9 out of 10 couples said they have dialogue as husband and wife."[28]

Despite the belief in traditional roles, an increasing number of wives are returning to the workplace, not out of any need for fulfilment, but because of the overriding need for money. In Japan, youngsters of working parents are known as "key children," because they go home from school to empty houses. As Japan lacks virtually any day care facilities, this lack of supervision has been one of the contributors to the country's increasing juvenile delinquency rates.

The authorities lay the blame for delinquency on the Occupation's educational reforms and on the family. Parents see it otherwise. Only 3 per cent blame the schools, and a minority blame themselves.

Exporting the Aged

The youth and the elderly of a nation are often the first to suffer in times of economic hardship. In Japan, the young are promised a good future if they sacrifice their adolescence. Meanwhile, the aging are assured of respect. When neither promise comes true, both are disillusioned.

Japan's youth want to enjoy the fruits of the economic miracle: their "ism" is consumerism. An increasing number are looking to a good life of leisure. They deny, as we have seen, the loyalty and "workaholic" tendencies attributed to them by others. By every measurement, young Japan is placing quality of life above production and profits.

An interesting example of this involves the young wives who led the fight against Matsushita's practice of escalating prices of domestic goods in order to undersell abroad. Some observers have gone as far as painting Japanese women as a new revolutionary class. Far-fetched as this may be, it offers a new perspective on the increasingly active role of the rising generation of Japanese women. As young people of both sexes rebel against what they consider injustice, it is becoming obvious that the youth can no longer be taken for granted.

Every culture has what may be called a style of aging, as it has a style of growing up, and a style of maturity. The style of aging in Japan is not a graceful one. In theory, according to Japanese tradition, age demands respect; but in fact, it gets blessed little. Foreigners look upon the Japanese somewhat angrily as a race of "savers" who will not buy Western goods. But the average Japanese needs to lay away all he or she can just to subsist through old age.

As older people are forced into early retirement, their incomes are drastically cut. Society leaves them almost useless, with little status. A Japanese man, in particular, may become very depressed at being cut off from his "lifetime" career and close associates. He is less likely to have hobbies or household skills than his Western counterparts. So, with little to do, his feeling of isolation increases. His wife may also find it difficult because she must not only continue to do all the housework, but serve as

mother and nurse as well. It is seldom the best of times for either
husband or wife.

New medical techniques and the declining death rate have increased the proportion of those in the older age groups. In the
year 2000, Japan's population is expected to reach 128.1 million, of whom one out of five will be 60 years of age or older.
Yet Japan's provision for the old is far behind Britain or
Germany or even the United States.

The Asahi Life Insurance Company reported in December
1986 that elderly people living alone must have a monthly income of at least Y170,000 to survive. But public pensions were
at that time Y126,000 for men and Y109,000 for women over 65
and living alone.[29] That is why Japanese save.

Housing for the old is a major source of worry. As the extended family gives way to the nuclear one, homes become smaller
and public building for the aged remains grossly inadequate. As
a result, the number of older people living by themselves has increased, by 300 per cent between 1981 and 1986, according to
the Tokyo Metropolitan Government's Bureau of Social Welfare. There is every reason to believe the situation will worsen,
because an increasing number of the elderly will not or, more
probably, cannot do anything about it.

In the 1980s, well over one-third of the young generation
polled denied any responsibility for housing their parents, a
proportion nearly double that of a mere two decades earlier. Yet
the old more and more expect to spend their retired years with
one of their children. Both young and old face a terrible dilemma, worsened by the refusal of government to invest in low-cost
old-age housing. It is true that old-age pensioners are forced to
subsist "on the other side of the tracks" in other advanced countries, but in those societies there is little proclaimed reverence for
the old.

Japan's traditional rulers believe that old people should live
with their children, a view not altogether motivated by love of
family. It is no coincidence that this method of caring saves the
state large sums. Because there are very few modestly priced
senior citizens' homes, some 600,000 elderly Japanese who do
not live with their offspring live by themselves – many under the

very worst conditions. They subsist in single rooms, lacking heating or baths and sharing kitchens and toilets with others. It is only in recent years that authorities have begun to install phones in the tiny rooms occupied by the elderly. Yet, fewer than half have phones or even bells to summon aid in emergencies. The degree of the government's concern can be gauged by comparison. In Japan, there is one professional home-helper for each one thousand eligible senior citizens, as compared with Sweden's one for sixteen and Britain's one for ten.[30]

Private wealth, of course, can bring peace of mind. But in Japan one has to be very wealthy indeed. A retirement residence offers a "lifetime lease" on a one bedroom apartment at US$730,000, plus a monthly management fee of US$1,300 for a single person, or US$2,100 for a couple. For those less well off, the government has come up with an imaginative scheme.

Faced with an aging population, MITI proposes to export senior citizens and establish inexpensive retirement "villages" abroad in such countries as Spain and Portugal. The idea is to take advantage of the strong yen and enable older Japanese with modest savings to live better.

The scheme is euphemistically called Silver Columbus. MITI stresses that the future expatriates will be volunteers and that they will be setting off "to discover new horizons."[31] It is difficult to imagine any proposal that more completely destroys the officially hallowed concept of the extended family.

The people who will be retiring in 1990, the year that the first retirement village abroad is scheduled to open (and approaching the 500th anniversary of Columbus' discovery of the New World), are the very generation who rebuilt Japan from the ashes of World War II. A man who will be 65 in 1992 was 18 in 1945. His entire adult life will have been devoted to turning Japan from a devastated country into a prosperous one. And now his government is saying, in effect:

> You won't be able to enjoy the fruits of your labours in Japan, because it's too expensive to live in Japan. Now that your work is finished, it's time for you to go elsewhere.[32]

The proposal would tear old people away from their families

and friends and settle them in a different culture, half-way around the world. Japanese critics have compared it to ancient traditions when the aged, no longer of use to the village, would walk into the mountains to die.

Under these circumstances, middle-aged Japanese view retirement as a dark and insecure future, and the overwhelming majority want improvement of old-age pensions and other welfare. With the increasing "greying" of Japan, the problem becomes ever more acute.

Splendid Welfare State

The idea of a cradle-to-grave system of government care is as distasteful to Japanese authorities as it is to many Western governments. Like Western conservatives, Japanese elites have set themselves sternly against the "creeping socialism" of the "welfare state." However, aware of the inadequacy of their own system, several high-profile Japanese citizens extol the virtues of Japan's own welfare measures. Under the title "Japan – the Welfare Super-Power," one maintains that Japan is, in actual point of fact, "a splendid example of a modern welfare state and to deny this, or to attempt to persist in labelling Japan as 'backward' or 'deprived' of welfare, is to perpetuate an erroneous image of the country and to allow oneself to be completely governed by uninformed preconceptions."[33]

This banker has the wholehearted support of another leading establishment figure, whose views on housing were previously quoted, Yatsuhiro Nakagawa, the scientist and technology officer in the Office of the Prime Minister. He indeed believes Japan is a splendid welfare state, and authored a lengthy article to that effect.

> A comparison of Japan with other countries shows that the Japanese worker is assured a high standard of living ... His working conditions protect his health and his safety. In his old age, he finds himself most satisfactorily provided for. Japan is not only a "Welfare Super-Power", at one and the same time, it also manages to be a "Paradise for the Worker."[34]

Not all of Japan's privileged agree. A survey by the Nikkei Industry Research Institute (NIRI) focused on the attitude of Japanese business people, who voiced a consensus that Japan still lags far behind North American and European countries in providing a high quality of life for its citizens. Most rate improvement of medical and other services for the elderly, and the nation's medical system as the highest priorities.[35]

While the welfare system is based on the assumption that the elderly will live with their children, those who do so are penalized. The government requires a long waiting period before these elderly become eligible for the full benefits others receive much earlier. Despite this inequity, the worst off are still the elderly who live alone. Upon reaching the age of 70, citizens are eligible for a non-contributory pension which barely allows for subsistence in slum dwellings. It is a practice which allows Japan to spend only one-third of its gross national income on welfare, compared with between one-half to nearly two-thirds in countries such as Sweden, France, West Germany and Britain. Even the United States allocates a larger percentage.

The fact is that Japan's welfare system is one of the least developed among the industrial states. Critics are particularly concerned that, while other advanced countries at least seek equality in their welfare programs, in Japan many of the most disadvantaged receive the least.

This inequality is the welfare system's major weakness. The belief that the old should be looked after by the young accounts for a few of the deficiencies, but it is clear that the majority are a direct result of Japan's policy of "cheap government," a policy which maximizes funds for industrial and business investment and growth. It is only recently that this balance has begun to change. The oil shock and the recession of the mid-1970s has had its salutary effects. Hardships proliferated to such an extent that the government could no longer simply point to the Gross National Product as justification for its inadequate social programs. The Japanese people had long been dismayed by many aspects of their life, but as long as wages rose and industry churned out consumer goods they could be persuaded that their sacrifices were worthwhile. Since the end of 1973, however,

even the LDP and the bureaucracy have had to admit that the
people have undergone extreme hardship.[36]

Published unemployment figures in Japan, as we have seen,
must be doubled to be calculated in the British or American fashion.[37] Hence, unemployment is expected to double by 1990 to
some 6 per cent, or 12 per cent by foreign statistical standards.
To add to the problem, unemployment insurance compensation
remains low and of short duration. The law stipulates that all
workers under 30, and those with less than one year of employment, cannot receive more than 90 days of unemployment insurance payments. In fact, under the formula for calculating
benefits, they receive considerably less. It is no wonder that
government spokesmen can boast of modest direct costs to the
taxpayers for public services. "Cheap" government has been
achieved, lamentably, at a high cost to the disadvantaged.

The medical insurance plan is also inequitable. Under it, each
citizen chooses his private doctor and pays a subsidized set fee,
determined by the national plan, for the particular service. The
balance is paid by the state. Medical insurance is divided into
eight types, according to broad categories of occupation, and
there are discrepancies between them, in both the amount the patient is required to pay and the level of benefits he or she
receives.

One plan, the government-managed Employees' Health Insurance Program, covers most workers in large firms. Up to
1983 it paid all medical costs for workers, but only 70 per cent
for dependants. This plan was renegotiated in 1984, but the administrative difficulties and inequities of coverage remain. The
government medical health schemes cover only care of the sick;
preventive medicine is available only as a supplementary benefit
to be negotiated with the employer, and covered through private
health insurance companies. From the point of view of big business, such arrangements are beneficial. They strengthen paternalism by increasing the dependency of the employees and ensuring a healthy and stable workforce. Thus, the social insurance
policy in Japan has favoured the employer's convenience in personnel management. This is certainly the case when a health insurance society is established *within* a given enterprise and is op-

erated as if it were one of the benefits provided by the management.

The least generous system is National Health Insurance, which covers mainly farmers, the self-employed, and the retired or others without jobs. Participants make a monthly payment to their local government office in order to cover 70 per cent of necessary medical, dental and hospital expenses. All citizens under 70 years, including the needy, must pay the balance.

Once again, as in the pension scheme, the government maintains that it runs a uniform system. However, at present, wage earners are divided into categories depending on whether they work for large corporations, small businesses or national or local governments; different rates and fees are charged to each. The best benefits and lowest costs are enjoyed by employees of governments and the largest companies, while employees of smaller firms get benefits at a somewhat higher cost. The self-employed and jobless receive less and pay relatively more. This pattern serves to reinforce the attachment of workers to their employers, and like so many programs, government and private, it is designed to strengthen the supposedly unique group loyalty of Japanese workers. The Japanese health care system is used by the business world as another instrument to maintain the economic dualism which has made "Japan Inc." such a success, if one requiring so many qualifications.

Those who defend this system often use tortuous arguments. Japan's bureaucrats boast that the average stay for those confined to hospital is over 50 days, a figure radically higher than in Europe or the United States. One would not imagine that this figure is cause for pride, yet the government offers it as proof that its hospitals, both in their total number of beds and in their comprehensive medical and therapeutic facilities, are the best in the world. It is a specious argument which ignores the virtual absence of rehabilitation facilities, an almost total lack of convalescent centres, and little allowance for care at home.

The same people who praise the Japanese standard of health care are intent on cutting it back. The Liberal Democratic Party tabled a revision of the Health Insurance Law on 5 July 1984, which proposed a 1 per cent cut in benefits for health insurance in fiscal 1984-85, plus an additional 10 per cent cut in 1986. Such proposals aroused great opposition from the Japan Medical Association (JMA). The Osaka branch bluntly called it "an attack upon the poor." As a token of the concern felt by many doctors, they took strike action, which briefly closed hospitals and clinics in the Osaka area. Certainly, the fight against "socialized medicine" that hobbles public health measures in the U.S., for example, is not so evident among the medical establishment in Japan. Fierce opposition, led by the JMA both inside and outside the Diet, has forced the government to shelve its planned revisions. But their introduction in the first place, during a recession and just after military spending allotments had been raised to an all-time high, is a measure of where social programs fit into the government's priorities.

The reason for its opposition to equitable welfare is crystal clear: many Japanese leaders are philosophically opposed to a welfare state and see in it a fundamental threat to the traditional Japanese reliance on family, community and company. What is sad is that those who suffer are, as always, those least able to care for themselves.

Prosperity Without the Amenities

For those who measure a civilization's quality of life by car ownership, Japan is hard on the heels of the United States. Over 60 per cent of households own cars; in addition, nearly half have air conditioners or microwave ovens. Space is also found for at least one colour television set in 99 per cent of the homes and a refrigerator in 98 per cent.[38] Also in an increasing number of homes, stereo sets and VCRs are piled on top of whatever is handy.

The mass of consumer goods which pours forth from Japanese work and technology is one of profusion and variety. The glut can be sensed in the air of Japan's shopping districts. Department stores are jammed seven days a week. Television is filled with advertisements for gimmicks and labour-saving gadgets – the kind of things that a nation that has everything, yet nothing, spends its money on.

As we have seen, the average breadwinner in Japan grosses about as much as his North American counterpart and more than his European, but there the similarity ends. If you were to follow an average housewife on her shopping rounds, in October 1987, you would note these prices in U.S. dollars: a melon, beautifully packaged, cost $46.00, six oranges were $10.00, one grapefruit sold for $3.60, and a watermelon for $55.00. Rice, the staple of the Japanese diet, cost three to five times as much as it did in the United States. Meat, always a luxury in Japan, sold at $45.00 a pound for the best cuts, but more typically at $17.00 a pound.

The reason for these exorbitant prices is the notorious Japanese distributing system, which involves fully 20 per cent of Japanese workers. To streamline the system would bring prices down, but it would put several million Japanese out of work. In the meantime, the consumer pays for an inefficient hierarchy of middlemen.

The average Japanese, of course, is fully aware that the prosperity of his country has been achieved at the expense of his standard of living. Yet the myth of a contented Japanese consumer society is perpetuated by some foreigners who visit Japan. The publisher of one of America's most prestigious daily newspapers was quoted in a Japanese paper as saying: "Even though Japan is one of the world's super powers, it holds the illusion that it is small and poor." This caused a housewife and clerical worker of Aichi Prefecture to reply:

> I would like [such foreigners] . . . to see the gap between the
> wealth of our nation and the poverty of our everyday lives. I
> would like . . . her to see the homes of powerful financial
> and political leaders, university professors and elite busi-
> nessmen, but *also* experience, even if only for a short time,
> the lives of average workers.[39]

Japan is rich, but is having considerable problems managing its new-found affluence. As one Japanese columnist observes in an article entitled, "Is Good Life Beyond Reach of Japanese?":

> Incomes have grown steadily over the years, but the cost of
> essentials – food, housing, education – has risen even fast-
> er. Although we boast the world's highest per capita in-

come, our standard of living is not world class. People who
work hard just get deeper in debt.[40]

Indeed, few Japanese feel they are the richest in the world.
According to an estimate by the Economic Planning Agency, the
food cost is twice, utility cost twice and service charge 1.5 times
as high in Japan as in the U.S. Concerning housing, Japanese
pay 1.5 times as much for their "rabbit hutches" as Americans
pay for their vastly larger homes. Most importantly, the real annual income – what a salary can buy – is about half that of the
U.S., 10 per cent less than West Germany, and only slightly
above that of Singapore.

The Japanese had increasingly come to consider themselves
middle class, until 1986. Since that point, the decline in the middle class has, in fact, been marked. According to the Prime
Minister's Office, 89 per cent of Japanese had a "middle-class
consciousness" in 1982, but this had fallen to 68 per cent by the
end of 1986.[41] The reasons for this change are easy to find. The
year 1986 brought a major blow to Japan's economic scene, as
the yen's exchange value jumped some 30 per cent in a matter of
six months. In the meantime, taxes increased considerably and
insurance payments ballooned, while costs of education and
public services grew by 3 to 10 per cent.

At the top of the list of complaints are not only poor housing
and long working hours, but generally high prices of increasingly important consumer items, such as leisure goods and services,
and education.[42] All of this leads to a sort of demoralization.
Many Japanese, like other people, seek escapism in shopping, in
playing or watching sports or engaging in cultural pursuits.

Most Japanese make any excuse to leave their cramped
dwellings. A favourite haunt is the local department store, which
is an important part of the social fabric. It serves the same purpose as the American and European movie palaces of the 1930s,
where average people could escape their own squalid surround-
ings to gape at the great chandeliers and stairways and be transported for a few hours to another world. In one famous store, the
shopper can view a giant statue of *Tennyo*, the Goddess of
Sincerity, soaring three stories high. Even the store names,
Mitsukoshi, Takashimaya, Daimeru, Matsuya and Matsuzakaya

have as romantic a ring to the foreign ear as the great ocean liners of ages past.

Excellent service, which is characteristic of much of Japan, is nowhere more evident than in its department stores. Every morning, at opening time, the staff, from managers down, welcome customers entering their doors.

The exhilarating kaleidoscope of Japanese consumerism makes for some of the most exciting shopping anywhere in the world and – given the styles, the variations, the sheer choice – the most bewildering.

The largest of the stores provide the services for virtually an entire life cycle. It is possible for a couple to rent clothes for their wedding, have their hair styled or cut, be married in the wedding hall, and buy tickets for their honeymoon trip all in one large store. After they have a child they may come to the store's clinic for advice on raising a baby, or they may leave the infant at the nursery while they shop. The store, then, is an integral part of the Japanese lifestyle and does much to make it agreeable.

Kuniko Inoguchi, a political scientist in Tokyo, brings the life of the average Japanese into perspective. She observes:

> We live as we do in order that the economy may prosper even more. Long working hours, family members being forced to live apart, discrimination against women: all such practices that distort or devalue our lives have been foisted upon the people in the name of the propagation of wealth.[43]

She claims that wealth has been accumulated only to strengthen the economy, not to make a better life for the Japanese people.

Perhaps this realization, and the hopes of the average worker in Japan, are best summed up by a company employee in Tokyo, Hiroshi Maekawa.

> There is no country in the world where the imbalance between working and living is as bad as it is in Japan: But no country can survive indefinitely with such an imbalance. I believe this imbalance will surely be redressed somehow.[44]

8
SOCIETY'S SHADOWS

*After long hours of questioning and sleeplessness
day after day, I began to wonder why did I have to
endure such hardships.*
FALSELY ACCUSED SUSPECT IN POST-WAR JAPAN[1]

*Not a few workers are still lying in their beds,
completely deprived of their normal human
functions and unable to see the last days of the mines
themselves. Downstream on the Watarase River, local
residents continue to suffer from copper poisoning
brought to them by the continuous flow of the river.*
MAINICHI SHIMBUN, 25 February 1973[2]

Justice, Japanese Style

All countries have aspects of their societies which they would
prefer hidden – practices, attitudes and anti-social elements. One
thing, however, makes Japan singular among Western-style democracies: its elites and many of its citizens deny the very existence of most of these social shadows. Two such practices involve Japanese justice – forced confessions and treatment of the
mentally ill.

Japan is ranked among the leading countries in guaranteeing
political freedom and civil rights. Its police are often held up as a
model for Western forces, and the brutal practices of Japan's
feudal past are believed to be long gone. But there is ample evidence that police still regularly use violence to secure confessions.[3]

Confessions dominate Japanese criminal courtrooms for several reasons. The traditionalists stress that Japanese values predispose prisoners to confess to anything the authorities want them to. Representative of this school is Professor Tadashi Uematsu (Hitotsubashi University), who remarks that the Japanese are "not completely free of their feudal consciousness. They cannot maintain their point of view in the presence of superiors."[4] A Tokyo metropolitan police inspector puts it this way.

> Often they [suspects] feel very guilty and confess and then give the police tips on how to prevent the type of crimes they were involved in.[5]

The other school of thought on confession, which includes social critics, points out that many confessions are obtained by force as in pre-war days. Both are partly right. Values do differ in Japan, but not enough to explain the huge number of confessions.

In Japan, confession is the king of evidence. Suspects are expected to confess; it is considered the final proof of guilt. In pre-war Japan, 99 per cent of all criminal convictions were based on "confessions." Since 1945 the percentage had dropped only slightly, to 86 per cent.[6] This staggering figure is the result of a combination of psychological and physical abuse of the suspect by police. Many of these forced confessions have proven false.

A Prison Act introduced in 1908 encourages coercion. The Act was a temporary measure to deal with a lack of prisons. It stated that "places of detention adjacent to police stations may be used as substitutes for prison." As a result, police cells are defined as "substitute prisons" and suspects may be kept in custody there for an indefinite period of time without legal aid. In practice, the prisoner is confined until the examining official has got a "confession." The law was never revoked.

Such practices are, of course, forbidden under the Japanese Constitution. Article 38 specifically guarantees that no person shall be compelled to testify against himself, that confessions made under compulsion shall not be admitted in evidence, and that no person shall be convicted on his own confession alone. But this article appears to be a dead letter.

Not only do Japanese practices go against the letter of the law, they violate its very spirit. Typically, a suspect is apprehended early in the morning and taken to the police station without charge to answer questions about "friends." He then finds himself placed in a "bird cage," a cell designed for total surveillance, without solid walls or any privacy. Thus, as one Japanese lawyer observes, "the suspect is already in an abnormal psychological state."[7] After a lengthy period without any chance to receive legal help, the prisoner is taken to an interrogating room.

There are far more rooms specially designed for interrogation in Japan than there are in the West. Each is about two metres square, and soundproof. In sworn testimony, victims have spoken of treatment including deprivation of food and water, kicking, head bashing and other abuse carried on hour after hour, sometimes weeks on end.

The interrogating officer can prolong custody and withhold visits from a lawyer. Most important, the lawyer can do nothing to put a stop to actions against his client or to release him. Neither can a judge or prosecutor intervene. The investigating officer has licence to do what he will. One falsely accused suspect, a middle-aged former public servant, was taken by three detectives to a windowless small room and subjected to violence from 9 a.m. to 10 p.m. According to his testimony, his interrogation included:

1. Forcing his head down and bashing it against the floor while he was sitting down.
2. Bashing his head against the wall.
3. Twisting his fingers, using various tricks on the joints.
4. Pressing a large fountain-pen type ball-pen between his fingers and twisting. (Severe pain in the bones.)[8]

It is tragic to compare this recent treatment of suspects with pre-war practices described by the *Japanese Advertiser* of 9 April 1930.

Policemen use bamboo-swords frequently, make suspected men hold pencils between two or three fingers and then press their hands forcibly causing after a little time intolerable pain ...[9]

Left-wing activists, then as now, are often singled out for special treatment. The Matsukawa case in 1949 was a remarkable example and, because of its political overtones, became the most publicized of the post-war cases. It was tried during a period of violent anti-socialist operations by the Japanese and Occupation authorities. Twenty-eight railway workers were indicted for alleged sabotage of a railway line at Matsukawa. Eight workers had initially confessed, and five had been sentenced to death. Not until September 1963 were all found innocent and released. It is popularly supposed that police agents, and members of the Occupation's military intelligence, planned the whole affair to portray activists as terrorists.

Police oppression and forced confessions have continued throughout the post-war era. During the course of student uprisings in 1969, at least 8,000 people were arrested. In one case, a student leader at Nihon University spent ten months in solitary confinement before appearing in court. During demonstrations against the Japan-U.S. Security Treaty in 1970, many students were arrested. Many spent up to ten years in prison before being found innocent and released.

Up to 1972, the five most important criminal cases in post-war Japan involved "a false, coerced, or contested confession, and each one required eight to 15 years to reach a settlement."[10]

Nineteen eighty-three has been described as "the year of the falsely accused," having seen the largest number of confessions that proved false since 1945.

The practice continues. An editorial in the *Japan Times Weekly Overseas Edition*, dated 28 November 1987, notes:

> In the past couple of years there has been one case after another of convicted criminals being retried and found innocent on evidence that their confessions had been forced. Recently, the Yokahama District Court, in acquitting a man of the charge of murdering his ill wife, criticized the police investigation methods, which included a threat to involve the accused's son in the case if he refused to confess.[11]

One of the most notable cases in the post-war era concerned Sakai Menda, who was under sentence of death for 33 years before being ultimately declared not guilty. Menda was 23 years old when arrested, 57 when released. His story is an epic of human survival. He was detained on death row longer than any other prisoner known to Amnesty International. His conviction was based on a forced confession.

Originally charged with robbery and the murder of three people, the charge had been concocted by the interrogating official using methods similar to those perfected by the *Kempeitai*, or wartime military police.

As in most countries, the state targets minority groups for discrimination. One case of great notoriety involved a *Burakumin*, or outcast, named Kazuo Ishikawa, who was arrested for rape and murder. On 1 May 1963, a high school girl did not return home from school. She was found dead four days later. On the day she disappeared, her parents received a ransom note and offered the ransom demanded. But the police failed to catch the criminal who came to collect the money. Having lost face, the police rounded up 120 *Burakumin* youths off the streets. On 23 May 1963, Ishikawa was arrested. For more than a month, he was held and interrogated. Although he initially denied the charge, he finally "confessed." On the basis of this confession alone, he was sentenced to death. More than ten years later, his sentence was reduced to life imprisonment. There is still strong evidence of his innocence. His case remains the object of mass demonstrations by *Burakumin* groups throughout Japan.[12]

The Liberal Democratic Party has promised for years to revise the Prison Act and abolish the substitute imprisonment system, but it then brought forward new laws in April 1982 designed, in the view of many, to make the system permanent. One lawyer felt deeply enough to exclaim, "Japan is now preparing to move rapidly in the direction of a dark age."[13]

If criminal suspects often suffer at the hands of the justice system, there is yet another minority whose legal rights have also been infringed. They are the some 1,340,000 persons, or about 1 per cent of Japan's population, who are officially mentally ill.

The law gives mental patients less protection from arbitrary detention and less opportunity for legal redress than criminal suspects. And further abuse of patients' rights is encouraged by a health insurance scheme which rewards remotely located hospitals that accept as many patients as possible, and keep them as long as possible.

Japan has been locking up more mentally ill people, some 340,000 in 1987, and keeping them locked away longer than any industrialized country, at a time when most industrialized countries have been de-institutionalizing patients.

In September 1984, the Hotokukai Utsonomiya Hospital scandal broke, uncovering some of the worst abuses of Japan's mental care system.

"At Hotokukai scandal revolved around reports of violence. At least two patients had died from disciplining beatings by male nurses using steel pipes." The report continues, "Staff nurses had illegally dissected patients' bodies to remove brains for study by University of Tokyo medical school doctors, who reciprocated by referring patients to the hospital."[14]

The Hotokukai scandal exposed one of Japan's biggest government-sponsored rackets. Japanese laws allow families and society to hospitalize anyone alleged to be mentally ill. Vague definitions of "mental disorder" allow those who are deemed "embarrassing" or "troublesome" to be labelled and committed.

In May 1985, three specialists representing the International Commission of Jurists (ICJ) and the International Commission of Health Professionals investigated Japan's mental hospitals, in response to a request from Japanese lawyer Etsuro Tutsuka on behalf of the Japanese Fund for Mental Health and Human Rights.

> In May 1984, the International Commission of Jurists had written to Prime Minister Yasuhiro Nakasone to suggest that he appoint an independent group to study the treatment of mental patients and related laws. Nakasone did not reply, implying that how Japan treated its mentally ill was its own business.[15]

However, the publicity surrounding Tutsuka's request forced the government to take action. The Ministry of Health and Welfare, in response to the ICJ report and domestic opinion, drafted revisions to the Mental Health Law. Approved by the cabinet in March 1987, the bill encourages voluntary admissions and introduces stiffer medical criteria for involuntary detention.

Reverence Toward Nature

In North America's vast areas, Europe's compact countrysides, and Japan's islands, the hunger for land and profit has left little room for respect toward nature. Yet the West's earliest images of Japan were of beautiful mountains and cultivated fields. These postcard pictures, combined with the Shinto identification with nature, gave the impression of a people at one with its environment. If this impression was ever true, it ceased to be the reality when Japan embraced the consumer values of the West.

The Japanese face greater difficulties in overcoming geographical obstacles than the residents of most countries. Only 28 per cent of their land is flat enough for agriculture, industry or settlement. With a population of 120 million, Japan is the seventh most populous country in the world, and by far the most densely populated among the most advanced industrialized nations. The struggle for space has led to great social conflict.

The farmers are among the first to suffer, as scarce land is torn up to make way for roads, dams and factories. Rivers and streams are polluted. The takeover of farms – often by force – has led to repeated and sometimes bloody confrontations. A classic case took place in Sanrizuka, a farming village about 40 kilometres east of Tokyo. In July 1966 the government, without consultation, announced that the area would be the site of a much-needed new Tokyo International Airport, Narita. Angered at the confiscation of fine farm land, the Sanrizuka farmers replied with force. The resulting confrontation divided the nation, and offered one of those rare opportunities when individualism is expressed in Japanese life.

Sanrizuka is in the midst of some of the finest agricultural land in Japan. Some families have tilled the same soil for generations. They are not radicals. In the early days, public sympathy sided with the farmers, and the press published angry, if naive, letters. One person wrote, "What the rotten government is doing is more than criminal. Making us give up our land by using overwhelming force is terrible." But, as the violence continues, the public has become disenchanted, and the hierarchies continue their acts undeterred.

From 22 February until 25 March 1971, the period which the government called "phase one" of forceful expropriation, more than 25,000 police and officials were pitted against more than 20,000 farmers and their left-wing student allies. During those months, over 500 civilians were injured and almost the same number arrested. Waves of farmers and students attacked the police barricades. At one stage, in March 1978, youths seized the newly constructed control tower. This was two years after the airport was scheduled to have become operational. Yet not a single scheduled airliner had been able to land.

The authorities had taken the peasantry for granted, and had little guessed where their arbitrary action would lead. They had apparently forgotten that farmers, with their history of conflict, and the Left, with its history of violent resistance, had joined forces many times in Japan's past.

The airport remains surrounded by high fences and guarded by a thousand police. Narita still has only one 4,000 metre runway, although two more are supposed to be completed by 1990. Of the 515 hectares needed for the second phase of construction, only 21.6 have been secured. Twenty years after the decision was made to confiscate land, the tourist's first view of Japan is one of barricades and checkpoints.

Under popular pressure at the height of the Sanrizuka confrontation, the Environmental Agency (E.A.) was founded. But it was given only minimal powers. In the Sanrizuka case, it has no choice but to agree to the government action or be totally ignored.[16] Largely impotent though it is, the agency's existence remains anathema to big business and its allies; so much so that, in 1981, the head of the LDP's Environment Division caused a sensation by questioning whether it was needed at all.

The E.A. has no direct control, as regulation of major areas of pollution are shared by other ministries, including MITI, Health and Welfare, Agriculture and Fisheries, and Construction. Most of these ministries have close relations with the business hierarchy and are opposed to any meaningful (and expensive) anti-pollution measures. In addition, the E.A. has only advisory powers over the regulation of water disposal, sewage and chemical farming products (fertilizers, pesticides, and herbicides).

Furthermore, while it is legally responsible for soil pollution, it has no power over agricultural chemicals, which are the main cause of pollution. It also lacks control over many other areas, such as storage or disposal of nuclear wastes. The agency lacks the power even to enforce existing laws as the prefectures are independently responsible for their own areas.

Business opposition to all environmental protection has been consistent. When the Environmental Agency tried to introduce a bill in 1976, the Federation of Economic Organizations and the LDP opposed it. The cabinet even refused to submit it to the Diet. The bill was returned to the agency five times for revision. On each occasion, the agency made the bill's provisions weaker.

The interference with the legislative process caused a furor and the matter was heatedly discussed in the Diet. In 1981, having failed to pass any legislation and realizing that this was its last chance, the E.A. proposed a draft that was a parody of its earlier versions. The Federation of Electric Power Companies then appealed directly to the prime minister and other leaders of the LDP, claiming that, if enacted, the Environmental Impact Assessment Bill would enable lobbyists to hold up the construction of nuclear power stations. As a result, the government passed an emasculated act with atomic energy excluded from its limitations.

'This Isn't Pollution – It Is Murder'

"There was an ophthalmologist by the name of Tanigawa in Minamata who one spring day in 1956 was playing *go* with Dr. Hosokawa, head of Chisso Hospital, when news of the outbreak of a strange disease reached him. As more and more reports of cases came in, Tanigawa's son, Gan, urged Dr. Hosokawa to read Henrik Ibsen's play *An Enemy of the People*. This is a drama about a young man who is driven out of his village as an enemy of the people for pointing out that the local spring was poisoned. It was a most appropriate play to recommend."[17]

Minamata is a city on the southwestern coast of Kyushu. Toward the end of the 1950s, nearby villagers began to die from unknown causes. All that was certain was that the victims had eaten fish and shellfish from the coastal waters. It became clear that the LDP and big business were suppressing the facts behind these deaths. Only one ministry, the Ministry of Health and Welfare (MHW), was tackling the issue. It identified the cause of the deaths as methyl mercury poisoning and the polluter as the Chisso Fertilizer Plant. However, the Ministry of International Trade and Industry (MITI), the friend of the corporations, stepped in and supported Chisso's argument that mercury was not the cause. It was not the first or last time that the bureaucracy was split. Business brought pressure on the LDP to disband the study team within MHW, and MITI obligingly arranged for the Economic Planning Agency, over which it had influence, to complete the investigation. As a result, all research was simply suspended![18] In this, and other subsequent pollution cases, the enterprise unions did nothing. It was left to independent scientists to obtain evidence for the victims' lawyers, but not before the death toll had reached 46. One victim, Michiko Ishimura, cried

> I can hold nothing in my hands or arms, not even my husband's hand, not even my own dear son. I can't even hold a bowl of rice. I feel as if I'm on my own, a long way from earth. I feel so alone . . . [19]

Of the survivors, the most pitiful were the 25 congenital cases. All were born from mothers affected by the pollution and all were "human vegetables," lacking speech and motor functions. Thirty-eight per cent of all children born in Minamata between 1953 and 1960 were mentally handicapped.[20]

Chisso Corporation enlisted the help of the *yakuza*, gangsters, to disperse demonstrations by victims and supporters. At one point Minamata protesters assembled in an auditorium and were physically attacked. One badly injured youth had to be sent to hospital. At company shareholders' meetings, thugs stopped those present from questioning Chisso executives. One meeting lasted five minutes, another nine. Bo Gunnarsson of the Swedish daily *Expressen* asked of Chisso's president, Kenichi Shimada:

> I saw the stockholders' meeting for the first time, and it

was terrible. Do you mean to say that you have money to
pay gangsters but not patients?[21]

Shimada blinked.

The District Court finally found Chisso Corporation fully responsible for this horror. On 20 March 1973, the corporation was
consequently ordered to pay compensation of 937 million yen.
Chisso admitted its guilt:

> Chisso deeply apologizes to all of society . . . for its re-
> grettable attitude of evading its responsibility and for delay-
> ing a solution, as this has caused much inconvenience to
> society.[22]

Justice, of a sort, had been done. It had taken fourteen years.
One effect of the horror was the political disillusionment of many
local workers. As one seriously diseased patient, Hamamoto
Tsuginori, a former fisherman whose mother and other family
members died from the disease, remarked:

> I used to be a conservative, but I'm against the LDP be-
> cause it sided with Chisso. I don't really like the JSP very
> much either. But I have to be realistic. There's no place for
> me to go.[23]

Minamata was not an isolated case. The illness reappeared late
in 1964 in Niigata Prefecture. Once more the corporations hired
scientists to claim that mercury poisoning was not involved, and
once more there followed years of political, bureaucratic and
corporate stalling. In March 1966 the MHW concluded that the
Minamata disease in Niigata was caused by mercury originating
from the Showa Denko plant, which used the same process as
Chisso. Once again MITI intervened on behalf of industry and
insisted that MHW investigate in more detail before drawing
conclusions. By this time the scientific debate had been revived.
In May 1966 the Niigata University Medical School found that
Showa Denko was discharging organic mercury. The report
radicalized public thinking.

When the survivors and the families of the deceased eventually demanded compensation at the company's general meeting,

they were physically attacked by company gangsters. The police arrived too late to prevent injury. In February 1967, Showa Denko's president proclaimed over national television that, no matter what the findings, his company would not accept or comply with them. Rarely had corporate morality been expressed so clearly or publicly. Meanwhile, the Minamata victims were being exhibited to delegates at the International Conference Against Pollution in Tokyo. Appalled, one delegate exclaimed, "This isn't pollution. This is murder."[24]

Showa Denko finally reversed its position after a lawsuit had been launched and public anger had reached its peak. Two days before the verdict, it announced it would not appeal the case. The Niigata District Court declared for the victims, in a victory not only for the Ministry of Health and Welfare and the local judicial system but for a number of grass-roots citizens' movements. Its ruling was equally a defeat for MITI and its business associates.

A third case of note was Yokkaichi, a project typical of Japan's period of rapid growth. Yokkaichi, near Nagoya, was designed as a port for the new supertankers which would transport oil from a vast new petro-chemical complex. Increasing sickness among the nearby residents had already surfaced by 1963 when the second stage of expansion was under way. The fishermen, in anger, marched on the electric power plant and demanded an end to chemical pollution; but they left frustrated. Meanwhile, there was a remarkable increase in asthma cases due to air pollution. The local hospital had to set up a special "pollution-free" room for asthma sufferers, where they came when the pollution was especially bad.

Many people were desperate. On 10 July 1966, one elderly man, an asthma victim, hanged himself in his home opposite a refinery. He left a note explaining that things would be better in the next world, because at least medical care would no longer be necessary.

The pollution was described in a diary of the period:

> After five in the afternoon the smog became terrible. Because of the sulfur dioxide, I couldn't stop coughing ... Damn! Why doesn't Mayor Kuki try asthma and see what

it's like? Then would he understand? ... Ah, but I don't
want to die from pollution ...[25]

The resulting court case lasted nearly five years and eventually
brought a major triumph for Yokkaichi asthma victims. They
were awarded a total of 48 million yen, or $286,000, in dam-
ages, to be paid jointly by the six major petro-chemical firms.
The ruling was a landmark: in Japan's first multiple-source air
pollution suit, the industries were held "collectively responsible," and all the plaintiffs' allegations were supported except the
charge of "intentional negligence." In spite of the ruling, the five
companies that were defendants in the Yokkaichi asthma case
continued to discharge poisonous fumes.

By the early 1970s, Japanese industrial expansion had reached
its peak. Most major companies chose to ignore the environmental laws in their hurry to expand. Despite the tens of thousands of
victims of pollution throughout Japan, no arrests have ever been
made under the 1971 Law for the Punishment of Environmental
Pollution Crimes Relating to Human Health,[26] nor has the press
ever demanded arrests.

It was during the height of expansion that the Mitsui Mining
and Smelting Company's plants at Kamioka, Gifu Prefecture,
were accused of contaminating rice fields and water with cadmium deposits. More than 500 people were stricken. Cadmium
poisoning affects the liver and kidneys and softens the bones.
The body is twisted out of shape, causing the victims to cry *itai-
itai*, meaning "it hurts." This cry of pain gave the illness its
name, the *itai-itai* disease.

Mitsui's permanent employees rank among the elite of Japan's
industrial class. All are steeped in the doctrine of loyalty. However, faced with personal tragedy, hundreds of workers and
members of bereaved families surrounded the Mitsui administration offices demanding a hearing. When they were refused, they
invaded the building, only to be expelled by hired company
"police." A private medical doctor, overcome by the plight of his
patients, helped them to organize, but he found it difficult to
persuade anyone to file a suit against the firm which they had
been taught to revere.

But the myth of Mitsui as one great family was already wearing thin. Eventually, some victims, including employees, took the corporation to court. Despite the evidence, Mitsui denied that there was any connection between cadmium and *itai-itai* disease. But the Ministry of Agriculture and Forestry claimed otherwise and said they were "inclined" to have Mitsui pay compensation. This was as far as the bureaucracy was prepared to go.

Although the case was the third pollution suit filed, it was the first to arrive at a verdict without stalling, and thus set an important precedent for future pollution litigation. The verdict, delivered on 30 June 1971, was virtually a complete victory for the plaintiffs. Mitsui appealed, but the complainants, encouraged by the first verdict, doubled their demands for damages and added a further 20 per cent to cover legal fees. The high court not only sustained the new demands but also awarded the victims all of their newly enlarged claims for restitution. Despite the verdicts, Mitsui still refuses to acknowledge any guilt or to show any remorse toward the bereaved families or toward employees living in agony.

None of these major pollution cases could have been brought to justice without the perseverance of grass-roots citizens' movements. Their emergence is perhaps the most outstanding development in post-war Japan and an example for the people of the world. The effectiveness of a "citizen's movement" in Japan can best be illustrated by the case of Mishima.

Mishima is worth mentioning not only because it shows democracy in action but also because it shows that enterprise unions are not always subservient. The city is a well-known beauty spot not far from Mt. Fuji. It was there, in the 1950s, that a large petro-chemical complex was to be built. Local residents organized to defeat the project with the support of groups not normally in the forefront of anti-pollution activities – the middle class and the enterprise trade unions. When the plan's defeat seemed assured, movement leaders decided that some type of permanent organization should be formed for continuing to study local policy problems. Thus, the Mishima Improvement Association was established. Even independent conservatives supported the demands of the more radical elements in the area. As a result, the LDP has failed to win a mayoralty in Mishima for sixteen years.

In the midst of these struggles, the *zaikai* could have had little doubt of the people's contempt for them. Millions in Japan had come to recognize that corporate love for employees was a tragic farce. Perhaps inevitably, the hierarchy sought to polish its image. Most notable is the belated reaction of Keidanren, the Federation of Economic Organizations, a group comprising many of the architects of Japan's "economic miracle," executives renowned for their foresight and intelligence. At its general meeting in May 1970, delegates adopted a resolution stating "that pollution of the environment and increase in public hazards has been unforeseen until now."[27] It is worth keeping in mind that Japan's business leaders reached this conclusion fourteen years after the Minamata pollution was exposed. Perhaps the site of their meeting – Tokyo – helped them to gain this insight. The metropolis had become the most polluted of the world's capital cities. When the resolution was adopted, one-fifth of the city's public school students were suffering from pollution-related illnesses.

Pollution Politics

The mass of the Japanese people have been slow to react to the environmental destruction. Having survived the poverty of the early post-war years and built an advanced consumer economy, no doubt most were satisfied with their material gains and had little inclination to protest. It was not until the late 1960s that the ordinary people began to add up the cost of their achievement. The result was "pollution politics," so called because the issue which united the people was protection of the environment.

By 1970, some 100,000 persons in Tokyo were known to be suffering from chronic respiratory diseases caused by pollution. In one newspaper column, headed "Slow Death by Poisoning," the journalist stated:

> Tokyo residents are slowly being put to death. This is not an

exaggeration. We are horrified when we scan "Facts About
Automobile Exhaust Gases" made public recently by the
Health and Welfare Ministry.[28]

The situation was made immeasurably worse as most homes
are sited directly on narrow streets without sidewalks. One can
reach out and touch passing trucks. Elevated highways wind
around thousands of homes, without benefit of any zoning by-
laws.

At the same time, business leaders were saying: "Pollution is
the price we pay for high G.N.P. You can't have one without the
other."[29] It was not surprising, then, that increasing numbers of
citizens began to question this view.

The years 1970 and 1971 were momentous ones for citizen action. The Japanese people had forced the government to hold the
"Pollution Diet," which passed a number of environmental
protection measures. They had also awakened Keidanren to the
problem of environmental destruction, and had elected reformist
governors in the nation's largest cities. In April 1971, Tokyo
voters chose Ryokichi Minobe as Tokyo's new governor. A record 1.8 million cast their ballots, two out of three voting for
Minobe. The winning coalition was led by Socialists and
Communists but was supported by a large cross section of the
population.

"I can see Mt. Fuji" was the election slogan, expressing the
hope of seeing the distinctive landmark after the veil of air pollution had been dissolved away. It was a hope symbolized by the
campaign button, a white circle on a field of blue, representing
clear air and blue sky.

The slogan was more than a gimmick. Few Tokyoites would
have been around in 1877 when Mt. Fuji, 100 kilometres from
Tokyo, could be seen clearly from the city centre on roughly 100
days of the year. But most remembered 1965 when Mt. Fuji was
visible on only 22 days of the entire year, and 1966-68, when it
was not visible on a single day during June to September.
Things, it was thought, could only get better.

Optimism was high following Minobe's victory, but was
short-lived. The new governor had little real power, for the

Tokyo government had been, and remains, an agency of the national administration. The governor has to share control of his revenues as well as control over the police, housing and the various pollution agencies with the central government. His only effective weapon is public opinion. But reform *did* start, and with an important urban issue – garbage disposal.

Garbage is rarely a burning national issue, but, for a time, it became front page news. Up to that time, garbage had been used as land fill in Tokyo Bay. It was transported by 5,000 trucks rolling through the narrow streets of Kohto, a working class area which had supported Minobe largely because he had promised to cut the garbage traffic by building incinerators.

When an upper-middle class district fought this proposal, reaction in Kohto was swift and violent. Kohto's ward leader warned that his people "were willing to shed blood and lose lives," and, to lend substance to his threat, the garbage convoys were attacked. This wrath, unleashed after years of smoldering, was the closest thing to a class war ever seen in a Japanese city and illustrated the deep divisions within urban society.

The issue was resolved in November 1973, when plans to build local incinerators were hastened and the amount of bulk garbage being transported by truck was limited. The plan gave neighbourhood residents the power to inspect incinerators and order stoppages if pollution standards were being violated. A Kohto incinerator was among those constructed. Nevertheless, the ward continued to serve as Tokyo's dumping ground. Furthermore, the land reclamation sites on the bay still remain the final destination for garbage and the ash from Tokyo's incinerators.

Most conflicts tackled by the municipal government did not end as successfully. In 1975, a major chemical firm in Tokyo was found to be causing lung cancer by polluting nearby school and residential areas. In a typical "incident," the enterprise, the labour union and the national government collaborated in a massive cover-up. Among those who tried to hide the facts from the people was the Tokyo metropolitan government.[30]

While the municipal government was struggling with governing, the LDP was using its vast repertoire of dirty tricks, including false accusations and bribery, to overthrow it. Businessmen and their political associates in the governing party detested the progressive leaders of Tokyo and Osaka. They labelled the capital "The Tokyo Commune," after the Commune of Paris. Each election was vigorously contested with no holds barred. In April 1971, the LDP put up the former police chief as its candidate. It promised the voters of Tokyo that the government would allot four thousand million yen for the rehabilitation of Tokyo if the LDP candidate was elected.[31] The government lost in this instance. The bitter antagonism ended only when the conservative forces regained office in Japan's two major cities, in April 1979.

This political reversal was due largely to the economic recession, which brought a shift in the public's priorities: jobs, wages and housing became of prime concern, while ecological improvement was put on the back burner. The corporate sector was quick to take advantage of this change of heart. It proclaimed to Japanese and foreigners alike: "Yes, pollution was a problem, but now things are under control." Unfortunately for business, the Construction Ministry admitted in August 1985 that, of Japan's 109 major rivers, only 44 met environmental standards. Yet the people hardly needed to be informed of this fact.

Smog warnings, alerting people to stay indoors on certain days in the major cities, doubled from 1981 to 1983. Osaka and Tokyo are still considered danger areas for those suffering from bronchial asthma. More than 88,000 residents are recognized as victims of air pollution under the very strict definitions of the Pollution-Related Health Damage Compensation Law.[32]

Kawasaki City, sprawling along Tokyo Bay, is typical of areas where pollution has reached crisis proportions. The local government, a centre-left coalition, was elected in March 1971 on a platform of promises to clean up the environment. In 1983 it was caring for 3,374 patients suffering from pollution-related illness, among them a 47-year-old housewife. She died of lung disease on 20 March 1983, becoming the 639th fatality from pollution since records were first kept in Tokyo in 1973. Her death, and others, have not changed the attitude of the corporations.

Nissan's political candidates in Kawasaki are pledged to vote against all anti-pollution measures. Its union leadership makes every effort to persuade its members to finance and vote for company nominees.[33]

Of all forms of pollution, none arouses greater fear than nuclear contamination. While the world was aware of the nuclear accidents at Three Mile Island and Chernobyl, a comparable Japanese incident never gained the same attention. This accident resulted in a serious leak at the Tsuruga Nuclear Plant in central Honshu in March 1981. It was far more dangerous than the release at Three Mile Island because it was not controlled as early. But the whole Japanese incident was not reported by the daily press for over a month. Moreover, it was only later learned that more than 30 other accidents, which had occurred at the plant over ten years, had been also covered up. Only under public pressure did MITI finally criticize the operation of the Tsuruga plant, but it staved off any meaningful enquiry. And it continued to press for further nuclear expansion, backed by the uncritical support of the LDP and the press.

The United States government, for its part, was silent on the Tsuruga accident, although five years later, it led a world-wide campaign of criticism of the delay in announcing the Chernobyl nuclear accident in the USSR.

'Hammer Down the Nail Which Sticks Out'

It would not be difficult to make a rational defence for a social philosophy which keeps a society from becoming "cosmopolitan." Tightly knit, relatively cohesive communities have values, for which one can make a good case – values of common manners and morals, assumptions, and style of living. But this exclusiveness can, and often does, lead to a belief in cultural, religious and racial superiority. This is one of the tragedies of Japan.

It is true that the Japanese can be, and are, among the most hospitable of people. This is particularly true if you are a white Westerner. Once accepted by a Japanese as a friend, there is little he would not do for you. Indeed, the generosity can be embarrassing because it places you under obligation which is often hard to know how to meet.

Nonetheless, Japan is one of the most racist and discriminatory nations on earth. To the Japanese, all foreigners are *gaijin* – outsiders – or, as portrayed on Japanese television, figures of fun – *hen na gaijin* – "queer outside person."

The attitude of the Japanese toward foreigners is also applied to the tens of thousands of Japanese returning to Japan after living abroad. One teacher, referring to a new student who was to join the school after studying abroad, observed to the class before his arrival: "Here comes this boy, who isn't Japanese anymore, he will be *'hen na Nihonjin'* [the queer Japanese]." His life at school was made miserable; he was beaten up and robbed constantly. Now an adult with his school experiences behind him and with children of his own, he reminisces:

> We Japanese are fond of the proverb: "hammer down the nail which sticks out." Not to stick out is to be Japanese.[34]

This proverb is illustrated by a conversation with a student who had recently returned after spending eight years at boarding school in England and was attending a Japanese university.

> I am really trying to learn to be Japanese. I want to be accepted in Japan too. But everything I say and do seems wrong.
> I say what I think, and I have my own opinions – well, that's not done. And because I don't always remember when to use *Keigo* (polite Japanese) when I should, people think I'm rude or stupid or both.[35]

For Japanese women who have lived and worked abroad, the transition is equally difficult. Ordinarily a Japanese O.L. (Office Lady) wears a uniform, makes tea and smiles a lot. It is a somewhat limited existence. One woman who lived abroad talks freely of the difficulties of adapting:

> When I am with Japanese people, I am very Japanese. Deferential and reserved. It makes me uneasy, but it's the only way to survive.[36]

The treatment of this woman, like other Japanese tainted by foreign influence, is just a taste of the underlying xenophobia.

All foreigners in Japan, including non-Japanese whose ancestors have lived in the country for generations, are, by law, fingerprinted. Under pressure, the Japanese government in 1985 offered a concession. For foreign residents who dislike fingerprinting, the Ministry of Justice offered to change from black to colourless ink, apparently to obviate the embarrassment of bearing an emblem which announced that they were *gaijin*.

The present law requires that all aliens over the age of sixteen who have lived in Japan for more than 90 days register at municipal offices, submit a recent photograph and let a clerk take a print of their left index finger. The office then issues an Alien Registration Certificate, a sixteen-page booklet with a photo, fingerprint and other information, which must be shown to "competent authorities" when requested. Failure to carry it at all times could result in arrest, prosecution and fine or imprisonment.

One exception to this picture of intolerance was the revision of the Family Register Law in 1984. It removed one irritant of "homogeneity" by allowing all children of mixed marriages to acquire Japanese citizenship. Previously, only children of a Japanese father were eligible.

Japanese racism, like racism anywhere, has colour overtones. The older generation still considers lighter skins preferable. So it is that white races are preferred over other foreigners. An off the cuff remark made publicly in 1986 by then Prime Minister Yasuhiro Nakasone brought this racism out into the open: "The average intelligence level in the U.S. is lower than in Japan because of the presence of blacks, Mexicans and Puerto Ricans."[37]

It is hardly surprising, given this pervasive racism, that during the war the Japanese routinely referred to themselves as the leading race of the world – *shido minzoku*. Such make-believe is reinforced by myths such as the legend of *Kotodama*, "the spirit of the language," which maintains that Japanese has a soul that distinguishes it from any other language. Government-supported literature has described the Japanese language as a unique gift that sets it apart from other varieties of the human linguistic ex-

JAPAN: The Blighted Blossom

perience. This view now has little popular support, but it illustrates the attitude of a segment of Japan's current leadership.

Such a myth plays on the sense of being different and superior, which is very close to the surface in Japanese society. This pride in their difference helps explain why most Japanese distrust and dislike foreigners, of any group or race, who achieve fluency in their language. They interpret it as an attempt to acquire racial identity and to enter the Japanese community. Language is considered both as a barrier against "foreignism" and as a sign of uniqueness and racial superiority.

The Japanese prefer to picture themselves as a homogeneous people, without ethnic differences. The pretense is that the nation has no minority races or groups. To maintain this myth, Japan is the sole advanced capitalist country which has closed its doors to the mass of world refugees, accepting fewer than 5,000 since 1951.

Japan's image as a nation of uniform structure and composition is used to hide the treatment of minority groups within it. By denying their very existence, the authorities feel free to treat them as they will. Under such circumstances, figures are hard to verify; but the consensus is that Japan includes some 600,000 Koreans, around 50,000 Chinese and Taiwanese, 50,000 of the indigenous *Ainu* people who were the first settlers of Hokkaido, and 1.15 million Japanese "outcasts." The latter are descendants of a feudal "class" of the Tokugawa era, known as *Burakumin*, and sometimes referred to as the "invisible Japanese." If one also admits over one million Japanese from the island of Okinawa, who still face discrimination from the "main islanders," there is a total of almost three million people, among a population of 120 million, who experience outright racism or varying degrees of social and economic injustice based on their "difference" from the majority of Japanese.

One of the worst examples of discrimination is the treatment of Koreans, Japan's largest cultural minority.

After their country was colonized by the Japanese in 1910, many Koreans were brought over as virtual slave labourers. Racially they are of the same strain as the Japanese and physically they are indistinguishable, yet they were victims of persecution from the outset. Japan's rulers followed a pattern common in other countries. By systematically inciting their own poor against the Koreans, they diverted anger from themselves. The seeds of this policy bore fruit after the Great Kanto Earthquake of 1923. In its aftermath, "patriotic" organizations spread rumours that Koreans were poisoning the water supplies. They then encouraged atrocities in which thousands of Koreans were slaughtered.

During the war years, some 670,000 Koreans were brought to Japan, mainly to work in mines and heavy industry. It is estimated that 60,000 or more died in these conditions.[38] By the end of World War II, there were approximately two million Koreans in Japan. All benefited from the United States Occupation and its sympathetic attitude in the first six months or so after the Japanese surrender. The Japanese establishment, however, carried on as before. Massive unemployment and lack of foodstuffs led to government black marketeering. Scapegoats were needed, and the Koreans filled the bill. Through the press, politicians once more seized every opportunity to pit the Japanese poor against the Koreans, who were worse off still. Thus, they killed two birds with one stone. Excluded from unemployment, some Koreans turned to crime, which further fuelled Japanese hatred of them.

After 1945, the great majority of labour and military conscripts were repatriated. But the 600,000 Koreans and 40,000 Taiwanese who chose to remain in Japan were deprived of their Japanese nationality. Up to that time they were nationals, but not full citizens. Now, however, they are subject to alien control laws, passed to ensure that they and their offspring will be denied citizenship.

One group of Koreans, however, has obtained equality – those who died while serving Japan's Imperial Army. At the Yasukuni shrine, the remains of some 20,000 of these Koreans are buried. Yet their relatives are not even admitted to the sanctuary. Those who protest are told that all fallen soldiers (including the Koreans) are Japanese, but that their surviving family members remain Korean. Consequently, these "non-Japanese" dependants have no "Japanese" veterans' pension entitlement.[39]

Among the legal requirements after the war was a rule that Koreans adopt Japanese names – a humiliation to most. Fortunately, the revision of the Family Register Law in January 1984 has done away with that injustice. This, and the easing of a few citizenship rules, has gone some way to ending legal discrimination, but intolerance is strong and government discrimination remains.

Koreans must, like foreign residents, be fingerprinted if they remain in Japan and must also apply for permission to have their children enter public school. They must carry alien registration cards and cannot, as "non-nationals," work as civil servants or teachers without special approval. Nor are they allowed to run for office. Finding jobs in major corporations remains very difficult. Social discrimination, too, is unchanged. Among Japan's white-collar workers, having a Korean wife is still considered a disadvantage.

On 18 March 1987, Chong Gyan Yong, a man of Korean ancestry who was born in Japan, refused to apply for a visa extension when his three-year visa was cut to one year after he refused to be fingerprinted. He explained:

> Many foreign residents, myself included, live here not because we originally wanted to, but because we were forced to by Japanese colonial policies. Our lives are inseparably tied to this country's history. Our roots in this society run deeper than law.[40]

Foreign communities in Japan are full of stories of lengthy police interrogations of aliens caught outside their homes without their registration certificates. Kawasaki Korean Christian Church Minister Lee In Ha has compared these certificates with passbooks in South Africa, claiming they have become symbols of Japanese "apartheid."[41]

The great mass of Japanese oppose blatant expression of prejudice. All Japan Prefectural and Municipal Workers' Union (Jichiro), for example, is opposing a proposed bill, drafted by the government on 13 March 1987, that would extend the powers of the controversial Alien Registration Law (ARL). In 1983, the National Council of Mayors adopted a resolution calling for an end to the fingerprint system and the requirement to carry the registration booklet at all times.

In June 1985, Kawasaki City was the first municipality to formally defy a May 1985 Justice Ministry memorandum to report fingerprint refusers to the police.[42] Kawasaki's stance inspired many other municipalities to declare their support for those refusing to be fingerprinted. The assemblies of about one-third of Japan's 3,300 cities, wards, towns and villages – including many of the large municipalities where most aliens reside – have expressed their opposition to the fingerprint requirement. These developments indicate a very significant shift in popular attitudes toward overt discrimination.

The *Ainu*, the 'Invisible Japanese,' and Others

Ill treatment of native peoples is common to all colonial powers, and, at its worst, leads to genocide. Japan's native people, the *Ainu*, have, however, been the object of a particularly cruel hoax, as the Japanese have refused to accept them officially as a separate minority people. Of a different physical appearance from the Japanese, and of Caucasian extraction, the *Ainu* might have come originally from Siberia. They settled the archipelago long before the races that became known as "Japanese."

In 1980, the Japanese government submitted a report on human rights to the United Nations which stated that "Minorities of the kind mentioned in the 'International Covenant on Civil and Political Rights' do not exist in Japan." Japan, therefore, has the unenviable distinction of being the only advanced democracy to deny the original inhabitants their birthright.

The official policy of denying the existence of the *Ainu* as a minority people reflects the thinking of most Japanese. When the *Ainu* issue comes up for discussion, these stereotypes are sure to be aired.

> The *Ainu* have intermarried with the Japanese to the point where there are almost no pure *Ainu* left.
> The only people who speak the *Ainu* language today are a few old people.

> Most *Ainu* don't like the word *Ainu*. They just want to be
> left alone.[43]

The *Ainu* Liberation Federation puts out a newspaper, *Ainu Shimbun*, in which it appeals to the Japanese to abandon the pretense that the *Ainu* are not a minority race. Prime Minister Nakasone tried to turn the *Ainu* appeal into a joke. Speaking before the Diet, he drew attention to his heavy beard, smiled, and claimed that he, too, is part *Ainu*.

Racists have little sense of the absurd. While the national government claims the *Ainu* do not exist, the Hokkaido government and agencies help them unofficially. Under a government program set up in 1974, the *Ainu* are, in effect, treated as a minority people.[44]

According to one census conducted in 1986 by the Department of Social Welfare of the Hokkaido Prefecture Government, 24,381 members of this non-existent minority live in the northern island.[45]

If minorities have the right to use their own language, as the UN covenant declares, *Ainu* must be guaranteed the right to learn their mother tongue. But even at prestigious Hokkaido University, not a single *Ainu*-language course is offered. As one *Ainu* expressed it: "What they're really telling us is, 'Be exterminated in silence.'"[46]

Japan is also unique among the advanced industrial democracies in having a caste system with a hereditary social class whose members are restricted in occupation and are socially deprived. The authorities go to great lengths to hide this fact from its people and from the world. These unfortunates, the "invisible Japanese," are known as *Burakumin*, literally "village people." They are believed to number some 1.15 million and live in 4,374 ghettoes or segregated slums, accoring to 1975 statistics.[47]

A typical *Buraku* is the Sawia-Oji District of Izumi City, Kyushu, which comprises 3,000 densely packed houses, many of which are tenements. The proportion of families living in one room is twice that of the rest of the city. Roads in the ghetto are narrow and often dangerous, so that fire engines and garbage trucks are unable to reach many of the dwellings. The sewage system has never been completed; as a result, sanitation is poor and living quarters flooded even after the lightest rainfall.

During the Tokugawa era (1603-1867), there were four great classes of the nation: the lords, the *samurai*, the farmers and the merchants. Outside of these, and hopelessly lower in social standing, were the *Burakumin* (then known as *Eta*), or "non-persons," regarded scarcely above the status of animals. They were not recognized as Japanese. Their status has been popularly attributed to their trades as butchers and tanners, both considered unclean in Buddhist teachings. These occupational histories are pure myth; few *Eta* worked in these trades. In reality, the formation of the caste arose out of complex political developments during the feudal era in which the nobles saw it to their advantage to deflect the people's hatred.

From a strictly legal point of view, there is no such people as *Burakumin*. Article 14 of the Japanese Constitution states: "All Japanese are equal under the law, and they shall not be discriminated against in political, economic and social aspects by the difference of race, religion, sex or social status."

Although the outcast system is now legally abolished, it is unofficially condoned despite the spread of democratic ideas after World War II. The Japanese government set up the Integration Policy Deliberation Committee in 1960 to help end discrimination against the *Burakumin*. During the twenty years between 1953 and 1973, government expenditures on the *Burakumin* issue totalled 930 billion yen, though the annual expenditure has declined since 1976, probably due to the economic recession.[48]

It was not until 11 April 1974 that the Prime Minister's Secretariat for *Dowa* Measures was organized to promote and coordinate projects regarding the *Burakumin*. Living conditions have improved, as the budget allocated to help the *Burakumin* find work increased nearly 90 times between 1969 and 1980. However, unemployment is still a severe problem for many. In the ghettoes in Nagasaki Prefecture in Kyushu, unemployment is 50 per cent, in Osaka, 29 per cent, and in Kochi Prefecture in Shikoku, 26 per cent.[49]

Wide-scale efforts have been made by the government to improve housing. The budget allocated to assist the *Burakumin* by the Construction Ministry was 3.6 billion yen in 1969 and increased to 111.2 billion yen in 1980.[50] However, most of the *Buraku*, or ghettoes, remain virtually untouched.

Discrimination against these ethnic Japanese is easy because they live in known ghettoes. Traditionally, great care is taken in Japan to document details of all citizens' lives, down to place of birth, home and occupation of parents, so it is a relatively simple matter to identify the *Burakumin*.

Despite spending to help the *Burakumin*, the government has failed to undertake a public education campaign against intolerance. The history or present situation of the *Burakumin* is not on any school curriculum, and all mention of them is censored from textbooks as part of a nationwide cover-up. Even imported books by foreign authors have had references to the "village people" deleted. The Japanese people are aware of the issue and perceive it as an embarrassment. When confronted by foreigners, they tend to deny any knowledge of it or else portray it as a historical problem, rather than one of racism or social injustice as yet unsolved.

Graffiti about the *Burakumin* have appeared on the campuses of two of the nation's most prestigious schools, Tokyo and Osaka Universities. Walls at both campuses were defaced with such phrases as "out with the *Eta*," and "*Burakumin* aren't human." (When applied to the village people, "*Eta*" means "filth.") Perhaps such views simply reflect those of the students' parents, and theirs those of their parents before them. Be that as it may, these undergraduates will one day be filling the most powerful posts in Japanese government and industry, and as one poll shows, they have little doubt about the existence of discrimination in Japan; only 1.4 per cent of students claim it has been eliminated.

Certainly the business community is well aware of the issue and its potentially explosive effects. Corporations are careful to avoid employing *Burakumin*. Illegal lists of their settlements and addresses are continually drawn up and sold to large firms. One company, the Kubota and Yasuda Trust Bank, admitted, "we re-

ject for employment *Burakumin*, who are looked down upon."[51]
It could hardly be put more clearly.

Acts of discrimination are ignored by the authorities. The
Ministry of Justice has repeatedly refused to take action against
the companies or the compilers of the lists. The government has
made no effort to get at the root of the problem, and, in fact, has
treated the symptoms of discrimination but not the disease. The
Burakumin problem remains.

Another group which is also "racially" Japanese, the Okinawans, faces discrimination of a much lesser degree. As most live
on Okinawa, outside the four main islands, they are not faced
with the daily bigotry experienced by the *Burakumin*. However,
the highly developed ability of the Japanese to think themselves
superior leads to disdain for the Okinawans, whose language is
much closer to the ancient Japanese tongue, and hence more
"primitive." Intolerance against Okinawans is of long standing.
During the Meiji Restoration, two Okinawan women were put on
display as curiosities in a Hall of Races at a fair in Osaka. Okinawans were labelled, along with Koreans, as undesirables, and the
island was governed as a colony until 1945. During the war, over
100,000 Okinawans died and the survivors were subsequently
placed under U.S. sovereignty in 1953. Okinawa was returned to
Japan on 15 May 1972. At no time were the native people con-
sulted by the United States or Japan.

It is worth repeating that the Koreans and Okinawans were
both colonial peoples of Japan and suffered not unlike the
subjects of other imperial powers at other times. Certainly no nation is guiltless when it comes to racism and discrimination, but
by the late twentieth century racial inequities have been admitted
by all of the advanced industrial capitalist states save one – Japan. Japan has incorporated human rights rhetoric into its official
documents, and has spent money to alleviate some of the economic problems arising from bigotry, but has done little to
change those attitudes that make its society one of the most racist
and discriminatory. On the contrary, far from attempting to get at
its causes, bigotry is encouraged by the government through the
emphasis on status, group consciousness and "uniqueness." The

LDP's methods are not so very different from those of the Tokugawa Shoguns and Meiji oligarchs, for whom the LDP shows more than passing admiration.

In one foreign state, at least, the Japanese are recognized as unique. In South Africa, they have achieved the status of "honorary whites," the only orientals to so qualify, which perhaps goes to show that racism has more to do with money than mythology.

Yakuza: 'A Lesser Hierarchy'

Mistrust of the police has mounted in recent years, as many people are coming to fear collusion between the police and gangster elements. Examples of collusion are widely publicized. Resentment, too, of the high-handed attitudes of the force is weakening the effectiveness of the man in the police box, or *Koban*. Many citizens were disillusioned by the near-martial law imposed by the police during the summit of heads of state in Tokyo in May 1986. The winners in this breakdown of trust are the gangs.

The *yakuza* emerged from the feudal society of eighteenth century Japan. Like the Italian mafia, the *yakuza* were first organized in families. Today, the powerful gangs incorporate large numbers of young men who see no other future in their society. The senior "godfather," or *oyabun*, provides protection and help, and receives the unswerving loyalty of the others in return. An old adage, still popular among gang members, says: "If the boss says that a passing crow is white, you must agree."[52] It is this relationship that stands at the heart of the Japanese underworld.

In few countries are criminals so readily accepted by those in the highest echelons of power as in Japan. Gangsters comprise one of the lesser hierarchies of this hierarchical society. The degree of acceptance the *yakuza* have achieved is unique, but hardly surprising when it is remembered that Kodama, the Lockheed "fixer," among others, was instrumental in financing the postwar conservative parties. For years it was virtually taboo to write anything about Kodama in the press. Robert Shaplan, writing in *The New Yorker*, reported the rumour that anyone who probed too deeply into his background or his current activities would be murdered by one of his underworld associates, or by his private army, which was said to number 20,000 men, regularly trained on an island near South Korea. Kodama's network of contacts reached into every ministry and into every branch of the police, which kept his whereabouts a secret.[53]

Gangsters find a natural home among the ultranationalists, with whom they share admiration for the legendary crime gangs of medieval Japan. Conservative by nature, they are instinctive allies of the far right. Since the war, gangsters have provided many services to prime ministers. They have been their body-guards, they're widely used to break up worker and student demonstrations, and they serve as strike breakers when uniformed police might cause unwanted publicity. Prime Ministers Kishi, Ohira and Nakasone are among those who have enjoyed the friendship of *yakuza* leaders. Under such circum-stances, there is obviously little pressure from government to control the gangs. While in some Western nations political careers can be made by prosecuting mobsters, in Japan organized crime is as institutionalized as the ruling Liberal Democratic Party itself, which is subsidized in part by gangsters.

In post-war Japan, three well-known ultranationalists served as a bridge between the *yakuza* and the world of business and mainstream politics. They were Yoshio Kodama, Nobosuke Kishi and Ryoichi Sasakawa. All were "Class A" war criminals and former inmates of Sugamo Prison. Ryoichi Sasakawa was a friend and colleague of Kodama, having shared a cell with him for three years following the war. Upon leaving prison in De-cember 1948, Sasakawa set about building an enormous gam-bling empire. His Motor Boat Racing Association, which grosses over 1,000 billion yen annually, controls the whole sport, al-though it is officially under the supervision of the Ministry of Transport. In 1974, *Time* magazine reported that Sasakawa had boasted, "I am the world's wealthiest fascist."[54]

More than half of Japan's mobsters are supporters of the nationalist wing of the LDP, and are indistinguishable from the neofascist cliques which increasingly thrive within the party.

During the 1980s, under the premiership of Yasuhiro Nakasone, the number of such groups increased. It is estimated there are now about 120,000 right-wing conservatives with *yakuza* ties.[55]

Gangsters have been active in LDP election campaigns. The late Rokusuke Tanaka, one time secretary-general of the Liberal Democratic Party, was one of those elected with gangster support. In one case, when a campaign chairman was released from jail after he had been arrested in connection with a manslaughter, Tanaka reportedly welcomed him, arguing, "It is the responsibility of a politician to rehabilitate ex-convicts."[56]

Yakuza influence is so strong that mobsters have virtual free rein in some cities and prefectures. Police, mobster and party relations are close. This is common knowledge and little effort is made to hide it. An editorial in a leading newspaper reads:

> . . . it is not unusual to see men who can be identified at first glance as hoodlums *inside police boxes* in busy entertainment shopping areas at night smoking, laughing, and chatting with policemen.[57]

Philosophically, the interests of politicians and mobsters converge. All are by tradition authoritarian, nationalist, conservative and strongly anti-communist. Policemen, as well, are corrupted by their ties with gangsters. Events in Osaka bear this out.

Osaka is a mob town much like Chicago during the 1920s, and the adjacent port of Kobe is home base for the *Yamaguchi-gumi*. In November 1982, a former Osaka police chief committed suicide in the midst of a widespread corruption scandal. At the time of his death, he was president of the National Police Academy and it was common knowledge that he was slated for the position of deputy minister of justice in the Nakasone cabinet. A further government connection was exposed by the newspaper *Mainichi Shimbun* in December 1983. It reported that Akira Hatano, Justice Minister in the Nakasone cabinet, was linked to defendants in the same Osaka bribery case.[58] Hatano protested his innocence but suspicion lingered.

Exposures of this kind raise no eyebrows in Japan. They are accepted as part of the system. While gang leaders in Western countries go to great lengths to maintain their anonymity, there is little need for them to do so in Japan. When the boss, or *oyabun*, of Japan's largest syndicate died in 1984, the ceremony was broadcast live on national TV. The new gang leader was later interviewed, together with his top aides, by NHK, the national broadcasting company.

The underworld attracts the bottom rungs of society in all countries, the victims of discrimination, poverty and abuse. For some Koreans and *Burakumin*, joining a mob is a path up the ladder of status and glamour. One recruiting ground is the *bosozoku*, or motorcycle gangs. There are some 70 of these in Japan, with 42,000 members. Recruits are easy to come by. Japan's rigid, hierarchical society, with few escape valves, produces an abundance of dropouts. Many are easy pickings for the *bosozoku*. Once accepted in the *yakuza*, many ex-bikers wear the gang's crest not only on their sleeve, but everywhere, in the form of full body tattoos. Their superiors are usually conspicuous patrolling their turf in Mercedes or large American cars.

The police and government go out of their way to downplay the significance and power of gangsters. Officially, the number of *yakuza* has been halved in the last twenty years, from 184,000 in 5,200 gangs in the 1960s to about 2,500 groups with 94,000 members today.[59] The authorities claim that mobsters have an annual business of one trillion yen, of which they say that 44 per cent derives from soft drugs and 25 per cent from hard drugs. Few informed Japanese believe these figures: the real turnover is estimated at seven trillion yen or more, with 70 to 80 per cent generated from more legitimate activities related to political and business corruption. An editorial in *Tokyo Business Today* of 1986 observes that

> The reason why government authorities appear to create the impression that narcotics and gambling are the sole sources of income for the underworld is perhaps because they do not wish to expose the real picture.[60]

The *yakuza* are rapidly becoming the world's largest gangster network. The theft of art treasures is one of the more recent branches of the network's activities. Five works of art were stolen from France in a series of thefts beginning in 1985, including Claude Monet's *Impression: Sunrise* and works by Jean Corot. The British Broadcasting Corporation announced on its Overseas Service on 24 October 1987:

> . . . these paintings have been offered for ransom. The sums demanded are astronomical. The *yakuza* or Japanese gangsters are held responsible for the thefts. The Japanese police are not co-operative.

In France and England it is admitted that the *yakuza* are becoming as dangerous as the Sicilian Mafia in their world-wide scope. They have been behind extortion rackets in London and other European cities, and trading frauds in England and Australia. In November 1987, *yakuza* activities in Britain were the topic of a full-length British TV documentary.

Apart from trafficking in narcotics and stolen works of art, the gangs engage in traditional underworld activities such as loan sharking, running night clubs and Turkish baths, and importing blondes from North America. But the bulk of *yakuza* wealth comes from influence-peddling, political corruption and "business" activities. As with organized crime in other countries, Japanese gangsters have been gravitating toward the profitable world of commerce. Some of their methods of operation, though, are peculiar to Japan.

Soaring land prices are opening up a new area of operations. Real estate agents pay *yakuza* gangs several billion yen to force stubborn owners to agree to sell their houses, apartments or land, a form of intimidation known as *jiage*. A typical offer made by the gangs to reluctant sellers takes the form of arson. In a more moderate approach *yakuza* in Fukoka attempted to drive out the occupants with the noise of pneumatic drills, operated at all hours of the day and night.

Another field of opportunity for the gangsters is found in their role of *sokaiya*, or shareholders' meeting men. After they buy stocks in a corporation, they attend company meetings and work hand-in-glove with the company, acquiring and passing on information, intimidating shareholders and making themselves useful in similar ways. As it is relatively inexpensive to buy stocks in a Japanese corporation, it is easy for the *sokaiya* to operate widely. They need make only a minor investment to obtain the legal rights which form the basis of their livelihood.

Because of the shroud of secrecy under which the *sokaiya* must operate, their numbers are difficult to estimate, but there are probably about 5,000 working in the metropolitan areas of Tokyo and Osaka and perhaps a further 2,300 nationwide. The top ten or twelve are so powerful and influential that they personally attend meetings only rarely, sending instead their representatives. These individuals head so-called "research organizations" with large staffs and expensive suites of offices. Officially, they are called business consultants and confer with members of the *zaikai* when, as we shall see, they are not above a little blackmail. Their primary job, however, is to make sure the stockholders' meetings are brief and critics are silenced. These duties are not arduous, as stockholders' meetings are held only twice a year, usually during May and November. The tactics vary, from physical intimidation of other stockholders to noisy demonstrations aimed at causing an early adjournment.

An excellent example of the value of these short gatherings was the general meeting of the Chisso Corporation in 1970, at the time that the firm had been charged with the 138 deaths resulting from mercury poisoning at Minamata. The *sokaiya* permitted the first stockholders' meeting to last only five minutes: the complainants were assaulted and then thrown out. Harassment of stockholders and violence against demonstrators continued throughout the Minamata scandal. Not until a United States photographer was assaulted did the police show interest, and the Japanese press bring it to public attention.[61]

All major Japanese corporations have close gangster ties. Examples are legion. Whenever corruption is likely to be exposed, the *sokaiya* move in. At a Mitsubishi shareholders' meeting in the 1970s, a stockholder was blocked by hoodlums as he advanced towards the microphone to speak. Using loud applause and other disruptive tactics, the *sokaiya* shareholders terminated the meeting after only 25 minutes. The Marubeni Corporation, and the Itoh Chu, both accused of criminal activities at the time, were able to conclude their meetings within fifteen minutes with the aid of such tactics.

At Nippon Steel, the most modern steel complex in the world, about half of the 500 shareholders who attend the biannual meetings are *sokaiya*. According to its representatives, Nippon Steel contributes huge sums to the *sokaiya* to guarantee that no embarrassing questions be asked of the executives. In June 1973, the corporation announced a record increase in earnings of 46.5 per cent. The *sokaiya* dissuaded those who wanted to know how the money was spent.[62]

As the *Asahi Evening News* admits: ". . . companies treat racketeers who attend stockholders' meetings with deference, as long as murderers are hired by 'honest' citizens."

"The height – or depth – of this sort of business is reached, of course, when gangsters strut over the red carpet of the august Diet [Parliament] Building . . ."[63]

Management sometimes gets its just desserts, becoming the victim of the hoodlums, since the *sokaiya* are not above blackmailing the companies they serve. Such "disclosure" may simply take the form of skilfully questioning company officers at open meetings, or privately blackmailing executives. Senior management is poorly paid by Western standards, so it is a ready target. Because much business is transacted in geisha houses and bars, information is readily come by. Further, the *sokaiya* feel safe because the Japanese are not given to litigation. They would rather pay up, even if innocent, than face the glare of publicity. Gangsters take full advantage of this national idiosyncrasy.

Such practices have persuaded many businessmen that the *sokaiya* are more of a threat than an asset. The *zaikai* therefore pressured the LDP to pass a revised Commercial Law in October 1982 designed to ban the *sokaiya*. Somehow, the law has not worked – the "shareholders' meeting men" are still very much alive.

One incident tells us much about these extortionists. Like other gangsters, they look upon themselves as latter-day *samurai* and are, by implication, extremely patriotic. In February 1985, Norio Oga, Sony's prestigious president, became their victim. During a stockholders' meeting he was submitted to a grilling of thirteen and a half hours. Following this incident, the hoodlums assured Oga that Sony was singled out only for "sentimental" reasons, because their management is too dry for Japanese tastes, too neo-American.

9

PANDORA'S BOX

This is farewell
I shall wait beneath the moss
Until the flowers are fragrant
In this island country of Japan
HIDEKI TOJO, final statement, 23 December 1948[1]

[Japan] ... *going beyond the defence of its*
territories, will make major contributions to the
maintenance of peace and security in Asia.
DEFENCE WHITE PAPER, 1980[2]

'Wholesome Nationalism'

The Liberal Democratic Party has never been happy with
Western-style democracy. Nor are its leaders convinced that the
people want it. Yasuhiro Nakasone expressed this belief in an
interview with Hajime Haraga, an *Asahi Shimbun* reporter, who
quoted him as saying:

> In the press and publication circles, there was probably
> what is called post-war democracy. For the silent majority,
> there were probably such aspects as their [sic] being con-
> soled and saved by it in the period of confusion, but in the
> end, it simply ends in their saying "Oh, I see."[3]

Many politicians of Nakasone's generation view democracy as
foreign to Japan, and alien to its way of doing things. The lip
service paid to democracy, for foreign consumption, is unlikely
to change this.

The party contains influential elements that would prefer to return to traditional ways. Insofar as it has any political platform beyond dismantling the reforms imposed after the war, it favours creating a distinctive corporate-style state, and it has moved some distance in this direction.

As envisaged by the LDP in its proposal of 1982, this state would consist of a rule by a broad coalition of all political parties, save the Communist, supplemented by a single trade union federation and citizens' movements. The ideal is somewhat reminiscent of fascist Italy in 1934, in which, "all parties would have every opportunity to pursue the common good and harmony would ensue more or less spontaneously."

The Japanese conservative proposal is *not* fascism, but some similarities with the Italian fascist philosophy, reflected in the following quotation, are striking:

> The corporate state keeps capital on a light leash whereas labour's freedom is heavily curbed. The corporate state in this way supplies the cloak for ruthless worker exploitation.[4]

Japanese critics see the spectre of such a system gaining power in their own land. As one example, they point to the formation of a "super union" of 5.6 million workers on 20 November 1987, comprising 64 existing private-sector labour unions. The Japanese Private Sector Trade Union Confederation (*Zenminroren*, or "*Rengo*") is openly planned as a catalyst to increase "co-operation" and possibly to "reorganize" opposition political parties.[5]

The new confederation has replaced the generally subservient *Domei*, and is to be joined by *Sohyo* in 1990. A *Rengo* official declares, "Our movement will be more realistic than ideological." As in all right-wing countries, "realistic" is a code word for conservative, and "ideological" for liberal and socialist. Socialist trade union leaders have no doubt about what "realistic" means. A conservative trade unionist barely disguises it when he admits that *Rengo* may very well "lean towards the LDP."[6] This does not mean the union will rubber stamp LDP labour policy on behalf of the employees, but it may well come close. At this point, the LDP's labour strategy appears to be going according to plan. The only fly in the ointment is the Japan Teachers' Union, *Nikkyoso*, many elements of which oppose the merger of Japan's labour movement under a right-wing umbrella.

But the LDP is not united in its vision of the corporate state. The party consists of two general groups: a vocal right wing which demands the revision of the Constitution and expansion of armaments, while the "mainstream" emphasizes economic objectives. Atsushi Odawara, an editorial writer for the *Asahi Shimbun*, contrasts the two.

> I believe we can divide them on the basis of how they evaluate the history of Japanese modernization from the Meiji period onward ... The moderates express regrets and apologies, the ultras mention Japan's noble intentions. In everyday affairs, however, the dividing line between the two is blurred.[7]

Nobody can doubt to which category Yasuhiro Nakasone belongs. In his 1986 address to the annual Liberal Democratic Party Seminar, he peppered his speech with references to "Nakasone-style new nationalism," "wholesome nationalism," and "cherishing Japanese traditions and culture." He credited his party's electoral success of the previous July to the fact the LDP had stressed nationalism.[8]

Supporters of the Nakasone school of "new" nationalism claim that it is just that, and maintain it is wrong to equate it with pre-war ideology. Critics agree that the new nationalism is presented as more urbane, cosmopolitan and middle class than its predecessor, but contend that it is all the more dangerous for that.[9]

Among the critics of new nationalism is Nasaharu Gotoda, the Chief Cabinet Secretary, who observes: "As internationalization progresses in society, nationalism raises its ugly head. Such a tendency is already becoming evident in this country. How to control an evolution of dangerous neo-nationalism from now on is an important task of today's politics."[10] Likewise, Masataka Kosaka, the intellectual spokesman for the LDP mainstream, stresses in a 1985 essay the advantages of avoiding a national ideology and of maintaining a flexible pragmatism.

Also fearful of neonationalism is Naohiro Amaya, who has close connections with the *zaikai*, and is adviser to the Ministry of International Trade and Industry, MITI. Amaya labels the new ideology "Soap Nationalism," a term inspired by the American term "soap opera," and referring to the arrogant Japanese view of their economic power – to wit: "What's wrong with selling goods that are better and cheaper?"[11]

To one Japanese economist, this "soap nationalism" is manifested in a social climate that condones former Minister of Education Masayuki Fujio's statement of September 1986 to the effect that Korea was partly responsible for its annexation by Japan in 1910, or Prime Minister Nakasone's racist comment later that month on the low intellectual level of American society.

To warn their readers of the dangers of nationalism, Japan's newspapers often reprint foreign concerns about Japan's rising nationalism. The *Asahi Evening News* printed an entire article from the London *Observer*, which included the paragraph:

> Japan is becoming more nationalistic and more introverted. All the better, some would argue, remembering what an internally-aggressive nationalistic Japan was like. But looking at the weakness of the United States and the imbalance between its economic muscle and political whisper, jingoistic introversion may well prove to be the worse of all alternatives.[12]

The LDP appears to have some backing for its nationalist campaign. At the level of the common Japanese, nationalist emotion is running high. A foreigner was shaken while attending a Japanese meeting to hear an old, wartime nationalist song followed by an outbreak of chanting by all present: "Japan is great, Japan is the best." The chanting ended quickly when the Japanese realized a foreigner was present. Such expressions appear relatively harmless, but they are taking a nasty turn.

Early in June 1987, an *Asahi* reporter who had criticized the nationalists was murdered in his office, reportedly by the same right-wing fanatical group that bombed the U.S. Consulate in Kobe in 1981. And the big finance houses have started employing body guards for the first time since the violent 1930s. Meanwhile, bestselling author Masami Uno says that "international

Jewish capital is engineering global depression,"[13] and that "the high yen is the first step in the Jewish takeover of Japan." Others point to a revival of the theory of ABCD encirclement, the American-British-Chinese-Dutch plot that supposedly compelled Japan to attack Pearl Harbor.[14]

The "ultras" owe their success more to political than to economic elements. Their fervent nationalism alienates the mainstream supporters within the bureaucracy and business, few of whom would agree with Prime Minister Fukuda's call for a revival of Japan's indigenous religion, Shinto, as the state religion.

> Religion and politics are like two wheels of a cart; only when religion and politics are fused together will a perfect society be created on earth for the first time.[15]

His right-wing vision is reflected by his increasing worship at the Yasukuni Shrine in Tokyo, a symbol of both Shintoism and militarism. It is believed that the souls of all Japanese soldiers killed in battle reside there. Nakasone struck a blow for this militarist side of Shintoism by publicly visiting the shrine while prime minister.

Japan's nationalism and militarism have always been two sides of the same coin. One does not exist without the other. For example, author Jun Nishikawa, editor of a series of textbooks entitled *Contemporary Society* for high school students, was forced by the Ministry of Education to make four changes to his work – changes which reflect the government's protection of the military's interests. First, the ministry did not want children to learn how democracy, imperialism, monopoly and fascism were forged and developed. Second, it wanted to exalt "patriotism," and delete references to the "anti-war ideology and movement in Japan." Third, it deleted all references to the Soviet remarks on co-existence. And fourth, it insisted that any reference to Eisenhower's "military-industrial complex" must be accompanied by a similar reference to the Soviet Union.[16]

Such manifestations of nationalism and militarism are not created in a vacuum; they are caused by the realities of the economic world and by pressure from powerful foreign military-industrial complexes, which we are about to examine. What is galling to the Japanese is that their efforts to respond to foreign complaints about Japanese dominance and protectionism have gained little recognition abroad.

Economic nationalism is thus fuelling the fires of political nationalism, as many Japanese of all political persuasions believe their nation is being made a scapegoat for the ills of others. They do not like it.

Baring the Sword

Anti-American sentiment in Japan has arisen not only because of what the Japanese view as the U.S. attempt to blame Japan for its own economic woes, but also because of U.S. efforts to turn Japan into a military power.

To date, Japan has played the role of America's faithful supporter. It has permitted an increase in U.S. military facilities on Japanese soil, and its "overseas development assistance" has often been deployed to best serve American interests – in the Philippines, to bolster the recent Marcos regime in its rigged elections; in Thailand, after Vietnam found itself involved in Kampuchea; in Iran, to feed information and analysis to the U.S. on the domestic politics of the country following the American break in relations; and in Pakistan, after the Soviets came to the support of the Afghan Marxists in Kabul.

Under continued U.S. pressure, Japan is rearming. It now has the world's ninth highest level of defence spending, a military budget which has increased at an average rate of 6.35 per cent since 1982. Japan already has more than 50 modern destroyers and frigates, fourteen submarines, 430 aircraft and 1,100 tanks – an impressive arsenal for a country whose Constitution renounces war and the possession of "war potential."

Since the days of the Korean War, the U.S. has used every opening to force Japan to become a military power. In 1951, Prime Minister Yoshida was forced to promise U.S. Secretary of State John Foster Dulles that he could establish military bases in Japan in return for a treaty. The threat was clear; no bases, no peace treaty.

Nakasone is on record as observing that a truly sovereign nation needs significant armed forces. In February 1987, a Pentagon spokesman said that by 1990 Japan would equal the United States in the number of advanced fighters defending its own mainland. He also added that the "Land Defence Forces" would comprise thirteen divisions. Japan will soon rank as the fourth military power in the world, preceded only by the two superpowers and China.

The Japanese government formally announced its willingness to participate in research for "Star Wars" – the U.S. Strategic Defense Initiative – on 9 September 1986. One Tokyo professor thinks the time has come to increase military expenditure, to export arms, and to consider dispatching the Self Defence Forces overseas.[17]

The Japanese military has yet to be as outspoken. The official Japanese Defence White Paper of 1987 is vague on the interpretation of self-defence. It goes no further than stating:

> The necessary minimum force to defend Japan employed in the exercise of her right of self-defense is not necessarily confined to the geographic scope of the Japanese territorial land, sea and airspace. However, it is difficult to make a wholesale definition on how extensive this geographic area stretches because it would vary with the separate individual situation.[18]

Nakasone is less reserved. He has hinted that the defence area could stretch as far as the Persian Gulf, from which more than 70 per cent of Japan's oil is supplied.

President Reagan, like political leaders in other countries, used trade as a political carrot in his desire for strategic power. Because Japan is perceived as an obedient ally, his administration opposed restrictions of U.S. imports from Japan despite congressional pressure.

It was ironic to many liberal Americans that a Republican administration dedicated to big business had told American companies that the executive "would consider a finding [by them] of unfair trade practices as the equivalent of branding Japan, America's foremost Pacific ally, as an enemy" and, hence, as unthinkable. Likewise, as part of this Occupation mentality,

American pressure on Japan's economic affairs has traditionally rested on the assumption that U.S. forces stationed in the country are defending Japan from the communists. As Masashi Nishihara, an expert on Japanese defence, puts it: "Japan's rearmament has taken place 'under an American shadow,' and has been influenced if not dictated by Washington."[19]

Captain Doerr, the U.S. officer of a Pacific carrier battle group, put it more delicately in 1983 when he observed the United States needed "to assist the government of Japan to develop a more persuasive justification for changes in Japan Self-Defense Force Missions."[20]

But the Japanese people are unsympathetic to rearmament. Repeated polls have shown that they do not desire any increase in military expenditure. Only 15 per cent of those polled by the *Asahi Shimbun* in March 1987 approved of the removal of the ceiling for arms expenditure of 1 per cent of the GNP, while 61 per cent disapproved.[21] Meanwhile, Japan's 1986 White Paper on Defence notes that citizen protest is stalling the construction both of a training field for carrier aircraft landings on Miyake Island, and of housing for families of U.S. servicemen at Zushi.

To justify military expansion, the LDP has fanned the fear of foreign invasion. Hawks both in Japan and the Pentagon characterize Soviet armaments in East Asia as a threat to Japan. Detailed analysis, however, of the Soviet arms build-up in the area shows it to be "reactive" rather than "leading," and to be part of an effort not to be "encircled by hostile nations."[22]

Hisae Maeda, chief of the first research office, security police of the National Defence College, admitted in 1980 that:

> ... Japan need not fear a military conflict in nearby countries affecting us. It is untrue that U.S. naval forces secure our sea lanes because there is no reason why Japan should become subject to a naval blockade. All that has been said in defense of the fact, e.g. ... Japan has been protected by the U.S. nuclear umbrella, etc., has been hogwash.[23]

Maeda points out that, even if the Soviet Union should harbour dreams of conquering Japan, such a conquest would be of no value. Japan has no natural resources. To suppress it with brute force would require half a million or even a million troops.

It is unlikely, he believes, that Moscow would throw such huge forces into such a venture.

The question, then, asked by some Japanese defence experts, is why the U.S. maintains military bases in Japan. It is a question also asked by most Japanese politicians. Both tend to see the American presence as a way for the U.S. to maintain influence over Japan, to deter the Soviet Union from just beyond its border and, in short, to involve Japan in the Cold War. This view is shared by prominent conservatives within the Liberal Democratic Party.

Masataka Kosaka, one of the party's mainstream spokesmen, argues against the views of Nakasone and other military expansionists on three counts. First, he believes that, because of the stalemate between the two nuclear superpowers, the positive uses of military power are few. Further, since protecting Japan and maintaining peace in the Pacific are in America's own national interest, "it may not be necessary for us to pay a large cost" for that protection. Third, since Japan has become a source of essential credit and exports to the United States, the Japanese-American relationship cannot be easily broken even if Japan draws the line and refuses to contribute any more militarily.[24] This argument is the antithesis of Nakasone's grand design.

Even among the party's hawks there are those who oppose the methods used by the Americans to pressure Japan. Raizo Matsuno, a former defence minister, complains, "It seems that the nation's defence policy is now being formulated without the knowledge of and participation by the ruling party." A leading member of the Suzuki faction agrees, observing, "Recent defense policies are all based on the Japan-U.S. joint strategic plan formulated by the men in uniform on both sides of the Pacific.[25]"

According to Japanese sources, the joint strategic plan is designed primarily to protect the U.S. Pacific naval forces, not the Japanese islands, from Soviet attack. Matsuno states that strong air defence on the high seas does not protect the northern island of Hokkaido, but rather shields the U.S. Seventh Fleet from Soviet air attacks.

A Tanaka faction leader elaborated:

> Prime Minister Nakasone often talks about the impor-
> tance of air defense on the high seas. He, however, does not
> know what he is talking about. He is simply parroting what
> the men in uniform tell him. If the Soviets really decide to
> invade Hokkaido, they can reach the northern island in only
> a few hours by surface vessel. In such a case, air defense on
> the high seas is nothing but nonsense.[26]

The increasing power of Japan's military establishment is not
just an academic footnote; it represents a very real threat to the
position of the politicians. It should be remembered that Japan's
pre-war military build-up started when the power balance between the political and military establishments began favouring
the latter. Despite this lesson of history, the U.S. Pentagon is
apparently disregarding Japan's ruling party and stepping up
pressure on Japan's military to exclude the government from for-
mulating U.S.-Japanese military agreements. Even Japan's Defence Agency Secretariat, as well as the ruling party's defence
council, learn of the detailed military plans only at the very last
minute. They are faced with a *fait accompli.*

Japan's image as a compliant military ally may reassure
Japanese and Western Cold War warriors, but it scares many
Japanese. An executive of Keidanren observes, "If America
thinks Japan's defense efforts are inadequate, the U.S. armed
forces are free to withdraw and we ought to go it alone in our
own way."[27]

But the U.S. has a very different solution. In October 1987,
the U.S. House of Representatives agreed to call upon the U.S.
government to sign an agreement which would oblige Japan to
spend a minimum of 3 per cent of its GNP on defence.

What if Japan refuses? Some congressmen tried to amend the
legislation to force Japan to pay the United States a "defense
tax," the difference between its military expenditure and the 3
per cent of its GNP, as "compensation" for U.S. military support
in case of refusal. This amendment was defeated by the House,
but the attempt annoyed the Japanese.

Despite Japan's escalating rearmament, U.S. criticism of Japan has not been quelled. Some in America's ruling circles have
joined with the protectionist Japan-bashers in a display of anti-

Japanism unrivalled since World War II. The most recent target of this sentiment is Toshiba Corporation.

Television viewers in Japan saw an extraordinary scene on the morning of 2 July 1987: nine members of the U.S. Congress were smashing a small Toshiba radio with sledge hammers at a press conference on Capitol Hill. The scene, largely ignored by the American media, was shown over and over again in Japan, to the point where it is now lodged uneasily in the collective national consciousness.[28]

The reason for the anti-Japan outburst was the revelation that Toshiba had sold computerized machinery to the Soviet Union in violation of a Western embargo of the Socialist bloc organized by the Coordinating Committee for Export Control (COCOM). Outrage in the United States was matched by anger in Japan. Japanese leaders noted that no Norwegian products had been smashed, although a Norwegian state-controlled enterprise had been equally guilty of violating COCOM regulations.

On 23 August 1988, the United States Congress passed the Omnibus Trade Bill. Section 2443 included a ban on all trade with the Toshiba Machinery Company for a period of three years. It should be noted that an identical ban was placed on the products of the Norwegian corporation.

There is a cynical view in Japan, shared in some other countries, that the COCOM regulations were invented by American interests to hinder the high-tech business in Japan and Europe. There is also a tendency to view the U.S. reaction to the violation – a ban on entry of Toshiba goods into the United States – as a reflection of American fear that its ability to compete in high technology is being threatened by competition from Japan.

Typical of American fear was the Pentagon's dismay on learning, early in 1987, that the Japanese were planning to design and build their own jet fighter, the FSX, for the 1990s. No Japanese leader doubted Japan's ability to make a better fighter plane than any produced by American industry, although the unit cost might be higher. It took the Toshiba incident and pending U.S. trade legislation to force Japan to back away from its plan for the fighter. Japan is now developing it together with the Americans.

Two other incidents also affected Japan-U.S. relations in

1987. In one, a Japanese spy stole an F-16 jet fighter manual and sold it to China and the Soviet Union; in the other, Prime Minister Nakasone, in his last days of office, introduced a National Secrecy Act as his "final gift" to the U.S. The United States had long feared that Japanese high-tech was finding its way to the Eastern Bloc. The spy case gave Nakasone the excuse to bring in the Act and at the same time please Washington. Both events occurred at a time when the U.S. was trying to control Japan's technological expertise in areas such as electronics and computers. Some observers found the timing of the two incidents fit the needs of Nakasone and America so adroitly that the spy case had been a setup.[29]

One of the results of these affairs is that Japanese companies are thinking twice about getting involved in Reagan's $26 billion Strategic Defense Initiative (SDI), although an agreement on Japan's participation was signed between the two governments on 22 July 1987. Japanese companies are concerned about working in areas where they might be held responsible for the handling of secret information. The Toshiba affair brought this fear to a head.

Firms also fear that the unpublished regulations governing the agreement will give the Pentagon too much power over the commercial exploitation of the newly discovered technology. The fear is well-founded, as patent rights to the technology will be vested with the U.S. Defense Department.

The Nakasone policy of appeasing the United States continues under Prime Minister Noboru Takeshita, who took office after Nakasone's resignation took effect in November 1987. The new prime minister proposed to increase Japanese support for the American military. Japan now pays about a third of the costs of keeping 49,000 U.S. servicemen stationed in Japan, a figure Takeshita wanted increased to half. But in this he lacked public support.

Most Japanese believe armaments should remain on Japanese soil, but at the present level. By 1987 the opposition Japan Socialist Party had got the message. After its electoral setback in 1987, the JSP recognized the need for some defence forces and moved to the political centre on the issue. It is interesting to note, as *Mainichi Shimbun* reported, that a non-armament position, which had been the basis of the JSP's policies ever since the establishment of the party, has disappeared from its literature, and that such expressions as "Anti-Security Treaty" and "Anti-Self Defence Forces" have also disappeared completely.[30]

There is important agreement between the JSP and the LDP positions on one point – neither is prepared to accept a revival of military control of political parties, the LDP members because they value their own power too much. Yet the actions of the re-armament advocates could result in such control, and the post-war conservative politicians could find themselves in the same role as their wartime counterparts. In that era, it will be recalled, politicians were merged into the Imperial Rule Assistance Association, and parties were left with little influence.

America's Shadow

American accusations against Japan increase Japan's paranoia about U.S. intentions. Reaction was swift, for example, to an article by the late Theodore White in the *New York Times Magazine* of 28 July 1985. White's story began on the deck of the USS *Missouri* in World War II. He then purported to show how the Japanese were destroying American industry sector by sector in the 1980s. "Today, 40 years after the end of the War," said White, "the Japanese are on the move again in one of history's most brilliant commercial offensives."[31]

Japanese businesses' distaste for White's criticism, as expressed in the daily press, was equalled by reaction to views of Lee Iacocca, president of Chrysler Corporation. Kenichi Ohmae, who has been called Japan's "only management guru" by London's *Financial Times*, observed:

> This potential presidential candidate is . . . a man who would strengthen the Yellow Peril psychology that is growing in the United States today. At every chance, he attempts to whip up bad feeling by, for example, calling the United States a Japanese colony. Question: What do you call a country that exports raw materials and imports finished goods? Answer: A colony. His words are chosen to provoke

anger in American listeners, not mature reflection, self-criticism, or reasoning.[32]

Anger there is, in Japan as well as in the U.S., and it provides fertile soil for the new Japanese nationalism. Historically, nationalists thrive on distrust and fear of the outside world. A column in the *Nihon Keizai Shimbun*, Japan's version of the *Wall Street Journal*, reflects the perceived danger: "The world economy is sitting on two time bombs: the increasing drop of the U.S. dollar and rise of the yen, and protectionist measures against Japan."[33] Ominously, the columnist continues:

> If trade figures on both sides of the Pacific Ocean do not show a steady improvement ... the small amount of faith remaining in the method of international cooperation will likely evaporate.[34]

Friendly leadership in Japan can no longer be taken for granted by the U.S. There *has* been a generation of Japanese who have felt a very real obligation to the United States for its generous policies immediately following World War II, but these men are passing from the scene, yielding to a younger group who have no such feelings. U.S. policymakers seem unaware that their bank of post-war credits is now largely exhausted.[35]

A Japanese economist believes there is a danger in the Japanese fear that something will change their comfortable status quo. In particular, he points to the emotional response of many Japanese to what they consider unfair trade practices by foreigners trying to break into Japan's closed rice market. In his view,

> ... the fear of disturbing the status quo combines with a strong reaction against things alien, a belief in the superiority of an ethnically homogeneous society, and a disdain for other ethnic groups to form a volatile brew that could explode, given the right catalyst.[36]

And Japan's racism is manifesting itself once more as anti-Americanism. A Prime Minister's Office poll conducted in 1987 showed that 28.1 per cent of the Japanese people exhibit "no friendliness towards the United States." This nationalist backlash is being fuelled by what is seen as United States protectionism.

A Japanese businessman maintains: "... the Japanese take the view that the raging vitriolic sentiment against Japan in the U.S. Congress in particular is the result of the irritation of a nation which is used to taking its dominant position for granted."[37]

Vitriolic sentiment is in evidence, too, among Japan's business community. Yo Kurosawa, a senior executive at the Industrial Bank of Japan, referring to Japanese institutional investors' massive purchase of U.S. bonds, said:

> Why do we, people who live in rabbit hutches, have to
> finance the U.S. budget deficits to help Americans support
> a style of life with swimming pools and tennis courts?[38]

One example of what the Japanese see as a blatant U.S. trade incursion is the tobacco issue. While the U.S. government is waging a health campaign against smoking at home, it is encouraging the export of tobacco to Third World countries, among which it includes Japan. Washington won an agreement to increase sales to Japan on 1 April 1987. Analysts estimate the U.S. market for tobacco in Japan could reach $1 billion annually, a fact that enrages Japanese businesses hit by U.S. protectionism. The fact that one tobacco shipment was contaminated with herbicide did not help the American exporter's cause, nor the U.S. reputation in Japan.[39]

United States interests have been hard hit by Japanese action. In 1987, the government-owned Japan Tobacco Corporation reacted to U.S. competition by ordering its employees to tear down advertising for foreign brands. Knowing the Americans and other foreigners were about to introduce brands, the government company then applied for the Japanese trademark rights to some 50 brands, using U.S. trade names on Japanese packets. Company officials then feigned surprise at the angry U.S. reaction, describing it as "extraordinary." This is just one example of the irritants which play into the hands of antagonists in each country.

'A Tight-Fisted Market?'

"The Japanese market is as open as any other." This is not Japanese propaganda: the source is a well-known American authority on Japan, James C. Abegglen. He observes:

> In Europe and the United States, descriptions of the Japanese economy as closed and Japanese trade practices as unfair have become mindless cliches in political and business rhetoric. They have a ritual quality, repeated over and over again without critical examination.[40]

He names some of the many Western companies doing well in Japan – companies like Merck and Pfizer, Du Pont and Dow, Warner Lambert and Coca-Cola, Xerox and Kodak, Mobil and Exxon – among many others.

But such companies go about their business profitably and quietly. It is the failures who are vocal. They do not blame the poor quality of their products or their management – instead, they denounce the "system" and the policy of the Japanese government. But the companies that can refute these views are silent, a silence that perpetuates the myth.

The best of the American companies know how critical sound relations with Japan are to the U.S. One reason for not speaking up is fear of the reactions of their United States consumers, who may boycott their products. But as Professor Abegglen points out, "Their gutless failure to speak up is inexcusable as tensions build and political mistakes multiply."[41]

If true, this silence also plays into the hands of American politicians who gain votes by casting blame on Japan and other countries for the economic woes of the United States. The examples are legion. A U.S. cabinet member suggested in late 1987 that Japan change its consumer habits to aid U.S. marketing efforts in Japan; U.S. government officials urged the Japanese to save less and spend more; the Japanese press claimed a Senator even wanted the U.S. government to try Japanese nationals for high treason over the Toshiba affair.

Japanese companies in key industries such as steel and semi-conductors are expected to, and do, open their accounts to U.S. government scrutiny.

As one American scholar of Japan observes:

> A proud and independent people, as the Japanese certainly are, must surely over time find a relationship of subordination and continued critical demands intolerable.[42]

Many Japanese believe the turning point in Japanese-U.S. relations came on 17 April 1987, when the United States imposed a 100 per cent tariff on Japanese-made electronic goods. The U.S. claimed the tariff was in retaliation for Japanese non-compliance with a semi-conductor agreement, which required the Japanese to promote the sales of U.S. semi-conductors in Japan and to monitor the prices of Japanese semi-conductors shipped to third-country markets. On these counts the U.S. believed Japan had failed.

It was the first time that the U.S. had retaliated under the terms of the 1974 Trade Act. The Japanese press reacted emotionally, with headlines such as, "It's America That is to Blame" (*Bungei Shunju*, June 1987), "Japan Isolated" (*Seiron*, July 1987) and "The Age of Japan-U.S. 'Total War'" (*Voice*, April 1987).[43]

Most Japanese responses were not as emotional, characterized rather by puzzlement and some resentment. As economist Naoki Tanaka begins his article, "Many Japanese are beginning to wonder where on earth the United States is going" (*Sekai*, June 1987). Tanaka argues that Japan should realistically examine whether it has the resources to prevent a collapse of the global economic system, and if so, how it should use these resources.[44]

Not all share this view. Osamu Shimomura, a prominent economist and one of the architects of Japan's high-growth period, believes that nothing can or should be done.[45]

This is the "let the Americans stew in their own juices" school of thought. It is based on the belief that the United States domestic policy of tax reduction caused the problem in the first place, by encouraging U.S. consumption and increasing U.S. imports. According to this viewpoint, it is the United States which should act, not Japan.

Many Japanese see themselves as the victims of America's mismanagement, and their relations with the United States as an endless series of capitulations under pressure. And, in fact, Japan has agreed since the 1960s to subordinate its foreign ambitions to America's anti-Soviet policies, in return for developing its economy as it sees fit. Now the United States wants from Japan radical change in its complex distribution system, in which cuts taken by many middlemen keep the price of imported goods high.

The U.S. also wants Japan to reduce its agricultural subsidies, while it and other Western countries oppose all measures which would lead to freer trade in farm produce. Ironically, it is the LDP, under Prime Minister Nakasone, which launched its own attack on the powerful agricultural lobby, a measure which Western governments have hesitated to take against their own farmers. Using the American demands for liberalization as an excuse, the LDP has confronted the Japanese Agricultural Cooperative Federation, *Nokyo*, not because of a moral obligation, but because of growing consumer pressure. The Japanese public is fed up with the soaring cost of food, and the government is aware of this.

Yet the cost-of-food problem is unlikely to go away. Nakasone's successor, Prime Minister Noboru Takeshita, has close ties with the agricultural sector. As the eldest son of a sake (rice wine) brewer, he has strong vested interests. It is no coincidence that his Minister of Agriculture, Mutsuki Kato, is a hardliner, nicknamed "Mr. Rice" by the Americans. He has stated bluntly that Japan should never decontrol the importation of rice.[46]

Asked about the U.S. proposal for eliminating all agricultural subsidies, he was non-committal about domestic price support systems. At the same time, he is aware of the wide differences between domestic and international prices. He is also aware that Japanese consumers are unhappy.

The Japanese believe that Washington wants Japan to give up its lead in key industrial areas. Suspicious of American motives, Japan resisted U.S. pressure to reach a computer-chip agreement in 1987. Under its terms, Japan was to back out of the lucrative field so that less efficient United States firms could move in. Such an incursion does not sit well in Japan.

It is a common view in Japanese business circles, expressed recently by the former editor-in-chief of *Business Japan*, that the U.S. forcefully imposes its view in trade disputes, even when it is clear to all parties that the demands are unreasonable.

The bulk of the *zaikai* characteristically cast the blame for the trade imbalance on U.S. business. In the *Japan Economic Journal*, a Japanese managing director outlined the three causes, as he saw it, for the failure of the U.S. to penetrate the Japanese market. First, he maintained that, if it became widely known that Japan was an easy and lucrative market, U.S. competitors would rush into it – something successful U.S. companies in Japan did not want. From this viewpoint, it is in the interest of these few companies to perpetuate the image of a difficult Japanese market, placing responsibility for the imbalance on the shoulders of American corporations and absolving the Japanese.

The second reason given for the lack of a Japanese market is opposition from the U.S. labour movement. He argued that, by publicly disclosing the facts about their successful Japanese subsidiaries, American firms could expose themselves to valid charges from U.S. trade unions that job opportunities have been exported to Japan. Finally, he argued that the U.S. government courts international popularity by painting the Japanese as the global villains. Some Westerners agree.

Kenichi Ohmae, a senior Japanese business consultant whose clients include the top multinationals in Europe, the United States and Japan, is among those informed persons who claim that the tight-fisted Japanese market is a myth. In fact, he argues, Japanese consumers spend three times as much on foreign brand-name products as do their United States counterparts. In arriving at this conclusion, he claims that the total of U.S. exports, combined with production and sales of U.S. affiliates in Japan, comes to $70 billion, equal to the total Japanese presence in the United States economy. He argues that the gross trade imbalance between the two countries is a fabrication.

Enzio von Pfiel, a London business economist, also questions the current wisdom. He estimates that, for twenty years, Japanese-owned companies ran a trade *deficit* with the rest of the world. It was the Japanese affiliates of *foreign* companies, such as IBM, that ran up the measured *surpluses*. Had the foreign companies stayed at home and exported to Japan, there would have been a 51 per cent increase in Japanese imports.

One key reason for foreigners' common misunderstanding of Japan's economy is the belief that Japan belongs in that loose category known as capitalist free market economies. It is true that Japan emphasizes a strong private sector, but it remains unwilling to rely on free market forces alone for its economic well-being. This economic philosophy has been spelled out by Shinji Jukukawa, MITI's Director General: "The market, in reality, is imperfect, unlike the market depicted by economic theories."

What he might have said is that Japan continues to practice the wartime style economy it has used throughout its entire free enterprise history.

Momentum For Change

Japan has been returning to a highly controlled society throughout much of its post-war history. The gradual erosion of local autonomy and the re-establishment or enhancement of central, bureaucratic authority is particularly evident in matters of justice, education and management-labour relations. Much of the rigidity that runs through Japanese society is a direct legacy from the pre-war past which spawned it. However, the difference in the degree of authoritarianism between the old and new Japan is very great. Any examination of Japanese democracy today must bear the difference in mind, while remaining aware of the continuing pull of old values and habits, especially as they affect Japan's leaders.

What can be said of democracy and state power in present day Japan? The LDP has governed without a break since 1948. Yet, according to a 1987 issue of a conservative business newspaper, only 19 per cent of Japanese strongly support a continuing LDP administration. Sixty-two per cent of Japanese express a reluctant support for the LDP because they have no faith in any of the opposition parties, while a sizeable minority who vote socialist or communist do so out of disgust for the LDP.

Opposition to the LDP is weak: the major opposition parties are divided among themselves, and also suffer from their own internal divisions. The largest, the Japan Socialist Party (JSP), has never gained more than 29 per cent of the popular vote; the Communist Party hovers around the 10 per cent mark, or some five million votes. Because the JSP is strongly anti-communist, there is no immediate hope for a coalition. The Komeito, or Clean Government Party, has little in common with the other two. A party with strong religious origins, it attracts only slightly greater support than the Communists.

While these parties are engaged in attacking each other with as much venom as they attack the LDP, they are overlooking the potential power base of Japan's working class. The Liberal Democratic Party and its allies are not making that mistake. That is why the one super-union, *Rengo*, has been encouraged by every organ of the state.

The LDP wants *Rengo* on its side. Noboru Takeshita was to have been invited to the new federation's inaugural celebration on 20 November 1986. However, the consummate diplomat, he decided rather to send words of welcome in private to union leaders. As one observer wrote: "He knows the value of bringing them within the magic circle of patronage."[47] Akira Iwai, former secretary-general of *Sohyo*, says, "*Rengo* is led by labour unions of the nation's big businesses, which profit at the expense of subcontractor workers."[48]

With mounting unemployment in mining, shipbuilding and steel, the question is, how long can corporate Japan keep the lid on worker discontent? If it ever approaches the level evinced in the early post-war years, Japan will face a serious crisis.

This situation has worried Japan's ruling circles during the entire decade. It was during the Suzuki cabinet, late in 1980, that Nakasone, then minister in charge of the Administrative Management Agency, launched "administrative reform," an innocuous term which, in fact, signifies plans for a conservative restructuring of society. One aspect of reform tackles the fiscal problem of reducing the huge public deficit, by paring the welfare budget, reducing public service spending, and privatizing debt-ridden public corporations. It is the same type of program introduced by President Reagan in the U.S. and by Prime Minister Thatcher in Britain. However, the Japanese program does not stop there, as the report of the Special Committee on Administrative Reform makes clear:

> From now on, it will be necessary to further develop the special character of our own country's society. We will have to implement a welfare [system] in which an appropriate share is met by a highly efficient government, but which is based on the solidarity of home, neighborhood, enterprise, and local society, which is in turn founded on the spirit of self-help and independence of the individual.[49]

In plain words, the government is going to cut its aid to the needy but try to revive the institutions of a supposed traditional Japanese "special character" to meet the gap in social needs.

The goal of administrative reform is sometimes described as the cultivation of a "lean and hungry attitude" (*hangri seishin*) – the kind of voraciousness which many foreign experts believe already characterizes Japan. What Japanese business and bureaucracy have in mind is a revival of the work ethic and of Shintoism and its related values.

The immensity of the program cannot be doubted. It is a movement centred around the shibboleths of "security" and "patriotism," promising a transition from the present business and consumer orientation toward authoritarianism.[50]

Muneyuki Shindo, a political scientist at Senshu University, argues, "the ruling party . . . lacks the policy-formulating capabilities to responsibly meet social needs."[51] He believes the current Japanese system is drifting hopelessly towards authoritarianism.[52]

It is a fear borne out by the apparent victory of the nationalist Nakasone wing in the LDP, which represents political rather than economic elements in the party. The faction stands for right-wing values and the militarization of Japan.

Can Japan's movement toward authoritarianism and its development as a militarist superpower be prevented? Can the collapse of Japan's post-war democracy be avoided?

If Western pressure for trade concessions and militarization continues, the hawks within Japan will continue to gain influence, particularly as concessions lead to a rise in unemployment. Under such circumstances, increased military expenditure and arms exports would strengthen the hand of Japan's right wing; the creation of military jobs can be expected to translate into voter support.[53]

The Japanese establishment can therefore raise the bogey of a militarized Japan in its dealings with the U.S. If market access for Japanese manufacturers is cut off, Japanese businessmen and mainstream LDP politicians argue, it may not be long before Japan develops its own military complex.[54] It takes an optimist to say they are wrong. What is certain is that the Japanese political system has now arrived at a major turning point – and a difficult one.

Political competition appears as far away as ever. When Takeshita became prime minister on 6 November 1987, he immediately set the tone for his administration – a hardline conservatism that continues the Nakasone legacy. In selecting his cabinet members, Takeshita placed top priority on balancing the power of the factions within his ruling party rather than on the quality of appointees' policy-making and execution skills.[55] In other words, Takeshita's regime is more of the same, and the LDP continues to govern less like a political party than an invincible dynasty.

This steady course suits the hierarchies. The last thing the right wing wants is political instability; its aim is to keep the political lid on the 32 per cent of Japanese who are dissatisfied with the LDP. But this task is not going to be easy.

The founders of the post-war factions, the "political bosses," are quickly passing from the scene. Noboru Takeshita was a member of the once all-powerful Tanaka faction – but Takeshita is but a shadow of a Tanaka, or a Sato or a Fukuda. He is a product of the faction system, not a founder.

As the strength of the political movers weakens, it appears that external forces, political and economic, will play a greater, even dominant, role in determining Japan's democratic fate. One Japanese scholar goes so far as to say that Japanese democracy is in the hands of outsiders. He writes:

For the foreseeable future, Japan will continue to be a reactive state whose policies will be largely shaped by external forces, by the play of international events.[56]

As one political scientist notes:

> In the absence of real competition in Japan's domestic politics, however, the only direction to go is toward "politics of self-reform," but the deep-seated political cynicism held by the Japanese people will not provide the impetus for such change. It follows, therefore, that foreign demands on Japan will continue to be a necessary substitute for internal political competition.[57]

The rise of the yen, in particular, has driven home the importance of external pressure. It has also taught the Japanese that, while they work harder, the value of the yen goes up and their jobs are lost to foreign countries.

On the day that Noboru Takeshita was succeeding Yasuhiro Nakasone as prime minister, 6 November 1987, cataclysmic events were taking place on the world's stock exchanges. On 19 October 1987 – Black Monday – the dollar closed at 137.58 yen after hitting a post-war low of 136.85. The stock price crash in New York touched off a major chain reaction. As one newspaper editorialized:

> A continued rise in the yen's value would inevitably injure the Japanese economy, which in turn would make it difficult for Japan to keep its pledge to change its export-oriented economy and would make Japanese people lose confidence . . .[58]

The outlook seems bleak: new conservatism from within Japan and economic pressure from without. But there is cause for hope. The LDP is moving into a new political era, epitomized by two major political issues in the late 1980s. The first is Nakasone's failure in 1987 to push through tax reforms despite the LDP's absolute majority in both houses; the second is the realignment of the LDP factions, with the split in the Tanaka faction.

The government wished to implement a new indirect tax despite strong public feeling that the tax system is unfair. Wage earners are particularly frustrated, feeling they are already shouldering an unfairly heavy tax burden by paying the majority of income taxes, with farmers and independent business operators much less severely taxed.

The failure of tax reform was a victory of sorts – it showed that no one man, however charismatic, can count on unquestioned backing, even from his own supporters. Nakasone at first paid no attention to his opposition, but he was eventually forced to withdraw the tax bill.

In the summer of 1987 the Liberal Democratic Party's largest faction – that of former Prime Minister Kakuei Tanaka – dissolved, bringing to an end its decade-long control of the party. Its members reorganized into two groups, the majority joining a faction newly set up by the LDP secretary-general, Noboru Takeshita. This event marks a change in the nature of the LDP and the arrival of a new political era: an era which marks the passing away of the all-powerful old political bosses.

Popular opposition to the tax bill, combined with a split in the LDP's wealthiest and most corrupt faction, may signal that Japan's post-war democracy is approaching maturity.

There is further cause for optimism. Since World War II, Japan has demonstrated to the world that a determined nation can regain self-respect and influence without military power. Nonalignment has several advantages, which are obvious to some business circles in Japan which are looking to Asia to balance lost trade with the U.S. If there is any further decline in Japan's trade with the U.S., Japan may be able to meet her resource needs in Southeast Asia, in China, and in the Soviet Union, particularly Siberia.

The strain of pacifism remains strong in Japan. Almost half of the Japanese people believe that maintaining a Peace Constitution is the most effective way of ensuring Japan's security. A straw in the wind is the attitude of Japan's scientists. Asked whether they wished to participate in researching "Star Wars," a poll of 3,500 researchers showed that 80 per cent were against participation in SDI and only 4 per cent in favour.[59]

Economist Hiroshi Kato puts it this way:

> Now that Japan has come out the winner in the economic sphere it must make tangible contributions to the world. The

first step would be for the nation to reconfirm its commitment to its "peace constitution" and dispel any fears about it
becoming a military power. Takeshita's task is to inspire a
spirit of national idealism.[60]

Militarism may be one of the easier aspects of authoritarianism
to defuse. As the conservatives take stock, they may well understand that for a resource-poor country like Japan to survive in
international society, military postures are an unaffordable luxury, especially in a world in which the effectiveness of conventional arsenals is in decline.

While the danger from the extreme right may be held in check,
there remains little immediate hope for a loosening of today's
regimented society. Democracy has never taken root within the
Liberal Democratic Party. The party has attacked every opposition. It emasculated the post-war working class movement, it
divided and weakened the Left as a viable political force, and it
attacked virtually all citizens' movements.

As we have seen, cabinet-style democracy has always been
weak. What, in fact, exists is rule by overlapping elites – conservative politicians, big business and a powerful bureaucracy. The
fate of Japan's democracy depends on forces and events yet to
come. It depends on whether Japan's political parties of the
centre and left, trade unions, students, youth, women, intellectuals and unorganized workers can forge a new democracy in
which all share.

Achieving this democracy will not be easy, as evinced by two
events in 1988 – a high-level corruption scandal and the government's reaction to the terminal illness of Emperor Hirohito.

Japan's leaders feinted and dodged for four months in a vain
effort to avoid the repercussions of a trading scandal involving
stock worth US$50 million. The scandal claimed its first victim
when Finance Minister Kiichi Miyazawa was forced to resign on
5 December 1988 amid opposition clamour. But the allegations
of corruption also implicated the prime minister, Noboru
Takeshita, former Prime Minister Yasuhiro Nakasone, and the
secretary-general of the LDP, Shintaro Abe, as well as about
100 politicians and business executives.

All had bought stock in the Recruit Company at a reduced

price in October 1986, before it was publicly listed. When they sold the stock, shortly after it was listed, they netted an average US$515,000 each. And the corruption spread further. The Recruit Company had received favours involving employment recruitment, resort development and telecommunications from the Nakasone government. Its former chairman, Hiromasa Ezoe, was appointed to four government advisory commissions as a reward for the stock sales.[61]

Emperor Hirohito's lengthy illness was seen by some as a blessing in disguise for the scandal-shocked LDP. One media analyst noted:

> I would assume it is beneficial to the government that the Emperor's condition and the cancellation of events are capturing public attention because it would take [the public's] eyes away from ... controversial issues.[62]

Reaction to the illness also brought to the surface the divisions within Japanese society. Many Japanese saw a sinister purpose behind the excessive homage to the dying emperor; the nationalist fervour created around the emperor's death gave the ultraright a chance to advance its agenda. In reaction, the Socialist Party, Christian groups, the Communist Party and unions affiliated with the Socialist Party expressed unease over the massive official attention paid to the illness.

Typical of the right wing is Hideaki Kase, son of a former Japanese ambassador to the UN, who is quoted by the London *Observer* as saying that Hirohito's death will allow Japan "to rise up from under the yoke of the U.S. Occupation, revise the 'Peace Constitution' and further strengthen its military."[63] Kase is backed by a coalition of army veterans and militarist Shinto believers who have many sympathizers in the government.

In the midst of scandal and national mourning, a third event passed almost unnoticed. Former Prime Minister Takeo Miki, "Mr. Clean," died in November 1988, aged 81.

For those who believed that a new order had come to Japanese politics, the events of 1988 underscored how little had changed. As one cynical Japanese advertising executive remarked:

> Corruption among politicians has been part of our lives. It's

something like a *kabuki* play – the actors change over the
years, but the roles they play are always the same.[64]

However, the momentum for change exists. A strong brew of
social ills – political corruption, disproportionate and unchecked
power of the corporations, the high cost of education, the part-
time work system, oppression of women, increasing unemployment, abysmal housing, unfair taxation, an antiquated justice
system and racism – has alienated much of Japanese society and
contributed to the emergence of movements which challenge the
elites' image of the nation.

In the process, we must see the death of a time-honoured myth
– the fiction that Japan is a unique society in which individuals
mechanically show extremely strong loyalty, dedication and
commitment to family, school, corporation, and country. The
reality is that the Japanese as individuals and as a people have
rejected the myth, going along with it only when powerful, external circumstances permitted no other option. But the Japanese
have a great history of fighting for social justice and the betterment of their society. As the yoke of pre-war Japan and Tanaka-
style politics loosens its grip on the nation, the humanistic ideals
of the Japanese people are increasingly likely to find expression
in an emerging and authentic democracy.

NOTES

Preface

1. Halberstam, David. *The Reckoning*. Morrow and Company Inc. New York. 1986, quoted on p. 730.
2. Shiba, Kimpei. *OH, JAPAN! Yesterday, Today and Probably Tomorrow*. Paul Norbury Publications. Tenterden, Kent, U.K. 1979, p. xiii.
3. Van Wolferen, Karel G. "The Japan Problem," *Foreign Affairs*, Winter 1986/87, Vol. 65, No. 2. Council on Foreign Relations Inc. New York. 1986, p. 300.

Chapter 1: Rule by the Few

1. Okuma, Shigenobu. "Okuma Haku Sekijitsu-Tan (Count Okuma's Story of Former Times)," Tokyo. 1895, p. 175; cited in Norman, E.H. *Feudal Background of Japanese Politics*. Institute of Pacific Relations. New York. 1978, p. 3.
2. Kaplan, David E., and Alec Dubro. *YAKUZA: The Explosive Account of Japan's Criminal Underworld*. Addison-Wesley Publishing Company Inc. Reading, Mass. 1986, p. 43.
3. Norman, E.H. *Japan's Emergence as a Modern Japanese State*. I.P.R. Inquiry Series, Greenwood Press, Publishers. Westport, Connecticut. 1973, p. 47.
4. Shibusawa, Keizo, ed. *Japanese Life and Culture in the Meiji Era*, Vol. 5; translated and adapted by Charles S. Terry. Obunsha. Tokyo. 1958, p. 312.
5. *Japan Advertiser (JA)*, editorial. 23 January 1930.
6. Yoshino, Sakuozo. "Fascism in Japan," *Contemporary Japan (CJ)*. September 1932, p. 194.
7. Lockwood, W.W. *The Economic Development of Japan*. Oxford University Press. London. 1955, p. 339.
8. Marshall, Byron K. "The Ideology of the Business Elite, 1868-1941," in *Capitalism and Nationalism in Pre-War Japan*. Stanford University Press. Stanford, California. 1967, p. 50.
9. Busch, Noel F. *The Horizon Concise History of Japan*. American Heritage Publishing Co. Inc. New York. 1972, pp. 200-201.

10. Harada, Shuichi. *Labor Conditions in Japan*. Columbia University Press. New York. 1928, p. 237.

11. Gordon, Andrew. *The Evolution of Labor Relations in Japan, Heavy Industry, 1853-1955*. Council on East Asian Studies, Harvard University, Harvard University Press. Cambridge, Mass. 1985, p. 130.

12. Smethurst, Richard J. "The Creation of the Military Reserve Association in Japan," *Journal of Asian Studies*, Vol. XXX, No. 4. August 1971, pp. 815-828.

13. Baba, Tsunego. "On the Eve of the General Election," *CJ*, Vol. IV, No. 2. September 1935, pp. 187-188.

14. *JA*. 12 October 1935.

15. Shillony, Ben-Ami. *Politics and Culture in Wartime Japan*. Clarendon Press. Oxford. 1981, p. 10.

16. Dower, John W. *Empire and Aftermath: Yoshida Shigeru and the Japanese Experience 1878-1954*. Harvard University Press. Cambridge, Mass. 1979, pp. 312-313.

17. For Kodama's apparent deal with U.S. intelligence see *New York Times (NYT)* 2 April 1976; Tad Szulc, "The Money Changer," *New Republic*, 10 April 1976, pp. 10-13; and *Asahi Evening News*, 23 April 1976. Also Hanzawa Hiroshi. "Two Right Wing Bosses – A Comparison of Sugiyama and Kodama," *Japan Quarterly (JQ)*, Vol. XXIII, No. 3. July-September 1976, pp. 245-246.

18. Wildes, Harry Emerson. "Post-War Politics in Japan: Underground Politics in Post-War Japan," *The American Political Science Review*, Vol. XLII, No. 6. December 1948, pp. 1149-1162. Also see Hanzawa Hiroshi, "Two Right-Wing Bosses – A Comparison of Sugiyama and Kodama," *JQ*, Vol. XXIII. July-September 1976, pp. 245-246.

19. Dower, John W. *op. cit.*, p. 278.

20. Harries, Meiron, and Susan Harries. *Sheathing the Sword: The Remilitarization of Japan*. Hamish Hamilton. London. 1987, pp. 92-93.

21. McNelly, Theodore. "The Japanese Constitution: Child of the Cold War," *Political Science Quarterly*, Vol. LXXIV, No. 2. June 1959, p. 185.

22. Roberts, John G. *Mitsui: Three Centuries of Japanese Business*. Weatherhill. Tokyo. 1973, pp. 458-459.

23. Gayne, Mark. *Japan Diary*. Charles E. Tuttle Company. Tokyo. 1981, p. 339.

24. Dower, John W. *op. cit.*, pp. 363-364.

25. *Ibid.*, pp. 305-306.

26. *Ibid.*, p. 319.

27. *The New Statesman and Nation*. "The Week End Review. MacArthur's Legacy in Japan," Vol. XLI, No. 1050. 21 April 1951, p. 440.

28. Roberts, John G. "The Japan Crowd and the *Zaibatsu* Restoration," *The Japan Interpreter*, Vol. 12, 3-4. Summer 1979, p. 387.

29. *Newsweek*. 23 June 1947, pp. 41-42.

30. Roberts, John G. "The Japan Crowd and *Zaibatsu* Restoration." *op. cit.*, pp. 390-391.

31. *Mainichi Shimbun*. "Junen No Ayumi, 16 August 1945"; cited in Dower, John W. *op. cit.*, p. 294.

32. *Asahi Shimbun*, "Ersatz Democracy in Japan – U.S. Policy Shifts from Passive Tolerance to Active Support of the Old Guard," 19 August 1946; quoted in *Amerasia: A Monthly Analysis of America and Asia*, Vol. X, No. IV. October 1946, pp. 123-124.

33. Kosaka, Masataka. *100 Million Japanese – The Postwar Experience*. Kodansha International. Tokyo. 1972, p. 72.

34. *NYT*. "Japan Will Place Onus on the Poor." 3 November 1947.

35. Manchester, William. *American Caesar: Douglas MacArthur 1880-1946*. Dell Publishing. New York. 1978, p. 302. Also Susan Harries. *op. cit.*, pp. 221-222.

36. Kluckhorn, Frank. "Heidelburg to Madrid – The Story of General Willoughby," *Reporter*. 19 August 1952. Also Susan Harries. *op. cit.*, pp. 221-222.

37. Gayne, Mark. *op. cit.*, p. 342.

38. Harries, Susan. *op. cit.*, pp. 224-225.

39. Kosaka, Masataka. *op. cit.*, p. 85.

40. Davidson, Basil. *Japanese Ally? The Facade and the Facts*. Union of Democratic Control Publication. London. 1951, pp. 66-67.

41. *The Times*. "Roots of Democracy Still Weak," 29 January 1967.

42. Kaplan, David E., and Alec Dubro. *op. cit.*, pp. 73-74.

43. *Ibid.*, p. 71.

44. Dower, John W. *op. cit.*, p. 363.

45. *Constitution of the LDP*, English Language edition. (LDP, Tokyo. 1967), revised version, preamble. Also see Jon Halliday. *A Political History of Japanese Capitalism*. Pantheon Books. New York. 1975, p. 266.

46. Sayle, Murray. "Kakuei Tanaka and his money-making way in politics," *Far Eastern Economic Review (FEER)*. 27 August 1987, p. 34.

47. *Ibid.*, p. 33.

48. Baerwold, Hans H. *The Purge of Japanese Leaders Under the Occupation*. University of California Press. Berkeley. 1959, p. 80.

49. Haga, Yasushi. "Seiron – Sound Opinion, and the Power of Bureaucracy," *Business Japan*. September 1987, p. 7.

50. Shiba, Kimpei. *OH, JAPAN! Yesterday, Today and Probably Tomorrow*. Paul Norbury Publications. Tenterden, Kent, U.K. 1979, pp. 153-154.

51. *Ibid.*

52. *Asahi Shimbun*. 28 July 1970, p. 4, quoted in Tsurutani, Tsaketsugo. "Response to the Post Industrial Challenge," *Political Change in Japan*. David McKay Company Inc. New York. 1977, p. 106.

53. Mitsusada, Hisayuki. "Takeshita power ignites business ardor," *Japan Economic Journal*. 26 December 1987, p. 28.

54. *Ibid*.

Chapter 2: Money Politics

1. Halliday, Jon. *A Political History of Japanese Capitalism*. Pantheon Books. New York. 1975, p. 267.

2. Shiba, Kimpei. *OH, JAPAN! Yesterday, Today and Probably Tomorrow*. Paul Norbury Publications. Tenterden, Kent, U.K. 1979, p. 172. The award is made annually by leading newspapers, news agencies and radio and television companies to a journalist contributing to the advancement of English-language journalism in Japan.

3. Roberts, John G. *Mitsui – Three Centuries of Japanese Business*. Weatherhill. Tokyo. 1973, pp. 458-459.

4. *Ibid*.

5. *Ibid*.

6. Utsumomiya, Tokuma. "On Returning from Santa Barbara: An Attack Against Corruption in Japanese Politics," *Sekai*, April 1969.

7. Kaplan, David E., and Alec Dubro. *YAKUZA, op. cit.*, pp. 78-79.

8. *Ibid*., pp. 79-82.

9. *Asahi Evening News (AEN)*, 3 November 1960.

10. Watanabe, Tsuneo. *Daijin* (Minister) (Tokyo: Kobundo. 1959), pp. 1-2, quoted in Nathaniel B. Thayer, *How the Conservatives Rule Japan*. Studies of the East Asian Institute, Columbia University, Princeton University Press. Princeton, New Jersey. 1969, p. 189.

11. *Asahi Shimbun (AS)*. "Tensei Jingo." 26 May 1960.

12. Kaplan, David E., and Alec Dubro. *op. cit.*, pp. 224-258.

13. Nakamura, Koji, writing in the *Far Eastern Economic Review (FEER)*, quoted in *Ibid*., pp. 85-86.

14. One of Kodama's colleagues who bossed many gangs substantiated these facts. See Hiroshi Inakami, quoted in *Mainichi Daily News (MDN)*, 19 July 1964. Another example of this period appears in the *Daily Yomiuri (DY)*, 9 April 1960.

15. Shiba, *op. cit.*, p. 167.

16. *Ibid*., p. 168.

17. *AEN*. "Vox Populi, Vox Dei." 7 June 1964, p. 4.

18. *AS*. "Vox Populi, Vox Dei." 3 August 1963.

19. *AEN. op cit.*, 11 August 1964.

20. *AS*. 12 December 1966.

21. Maruyama, Masao. "From Carnal Literature to Carnal Politics," translated by Barbara Rusch, *Thought and Behaviour in Modern*

272   JAPAN: The Blighted Blossom

2*Japanese Politics*. Ivan Morris, ed. Oxford University Press. London. 1963, pp. 265-266.

23. *The Times*. "Roots of Democracy Still Weak." 29 January 1967.
24. *Ampo: Japan Asian Quarterly Review*. "Eyes of the Times, Nothing to Offer – Tanaka Kakuei Steps Into Power – Tanaka's Position Precarious." Vol. 13-14. May-July 1972, p. 4.
25. *Japan Times Weekly (JTW)*. 7 August 1976.
26. *Ampo. op. cit.*, p. 4.
27. Johnson, Chalmers. "Tanaka Kakuei, Structural Corruption, and the Advent of Machine Politics in Japan," *Journal of Japanese Studies*, Vol. 12, No. 1. Winter 1986, p. 5.
28. *Ibid.*, p. 6.
29. *Sankei Shimbun*. 9 December 1966.
30. Huddle, Norie. *Island of Dreams*. Autumn Press. New York. 1975, p. 251.
31. *AEN*, editorial, "Big Business and Politics." 10 July 1974.
32. Packard, George R. *Protest in Tokyo: The Security Treaty Crisis of 1960*. Princeton University Press. 1966, p. 129.
33. Van Wolferen, Karel G. "Reflections on the Japanese System," *Survey*, Vol. 21, No. 1. Winter 1982, p. 137.
34. Johnson, Chalmers. *op. cit.*, pp. 10-11.
35. *JTW*. "A Farm Boy's Rise to Fortune." 7 August 1976, p. 10.
36. Ishihara, Shintaro. "A Nation Without Morality," and "Nippon No Dogi," *Japan Interpreter*, Vol. III, No. 9. Winter 1975, p. 286.
37. *JTW*. "Tanaka's Way to Wealth and Power." 2 November 1974, p. 2.
38. Takano, H. "Tokyo Scandal – Media Maneuverings," *Tokyo Business Today (TBT)*. March 1987, p. 26.
39. *Ibid.*
40. Kusaka, Meguma. "Conservative Politics, LDP is being shaken to its foundations," *AEN*. 20 July 1976.
41. *JTW*. "I'm a Born Parliamentarian: Miki." 7 December 1974.
42. Arima, Sumisato. "The Emergence of P.M. Miki Takeo," *Japan Quarterly (JQ)*, Vol. XXII, No. 2. April-June 1975, p. 26.
43. Nakasone was a protegé of Kodama, with whom he had shared a secretary adviser. Also see coverage of Kodama's final days: *Japan Times (JT)*, 24 January 1984; *MDN*, 19 January 1984.
44. *Saturday Review*, cover. Saturday Review Magazine Corporation. New York. 9 July 1977.
45. *Ibid.*, p. 8.
46. Kodama's ouster of the ANA president is described in *AEN*, 23 March 1976.
47. *JTW*. "Tanaka's Arrest Shakes LDP." 27 July 1976.
48. *JTW*. "Vernacular Views." 28 August 1976.
49. *Ibid.*

50. Murobushi, Tetsuro. "Crimes Involving Men in Power and Structural Corruption," translated from *Asahi Journal*, 12 March 1976, in *JE*, Vol. III, No. 2. 1976, pp. 36-37.

51. Szulc, Tad. "Money Changers," *New Republic*. 10 April 1976, pp. 10-13.

52. Ishizuka, Masahiko. "Stepping on tiger's tail," *Japan Economic Journal (JEJ)*. 11 July 1987, p. 6.

53. *JTW*. "Over 200 Tory Dietmen Resolve to Unseat Miki." 30 October 1976.

54. *The Economist (E)*. "Japan: Who's Next?" 21 August 1976, p. 40.

55. *FEER*. "Bribes: Tip of the Iceberg." 23 July 1976, pp. 20-22.

56. Quoting an aide to a former cabinet minister. *Ibid*.

57. *E*. "Very Japanese." 2 December 1978, p. 13.

58. *AEN*. "Vox Populi, Vox Dei." 8 May 1979.

59. *JQ*. "A Paradise Lost: Bureaucracy Shaken by Expense Scandals," Vol. XXVII, No. 2. April-June 1980, *op. cit.*, p. 154.

60. *Ibid*.

61. *AEN*. "Vox Populi, Vox Dei." 10 January 1980.

62. Nakae, Toshitada, Managing Editor. "The Nation, Weather Vane," *AS*, reprinted in *AEN*. 24 June 1982.

63. The nickname was widely used at home and abroad. See Minoru Shimizu. "Unpopular Nakasone Cabinet," *JTW*. 1982; and Murray Sayle. "Kakuei Tanaka and his money-making way in politics," *FEER*, 27 August 1987.

64. *JTW*. "Profiles of New Cabinet Ministers." 4 December 1982.

65. *YAKUZA*, *op. cit.*, p. 160.

66. Hatano's actions are reported in *JT*, 15 December 1982, and *MDN*, 10 December 1982.

67. The younger Ohno's mob connections are detailed in *DY*, 12 December 1982; *JT*, 27 October 1980 and 3 April 1983; and *MDN*, 28 November 1982, 1 January 1983 and 3 April 1983.

68. *Tokyo Shimbun*. "Nakasone Era," quoted in "Press Comments Summarized," *JTW*. 4 December 1982.

69. *JTW*. "LDP Faction Holds Party." 6 July 1985.

70. Tsutsumi, Teruo. "Nakasone bonus to no one in forming new administration," *JEJ*. 2 August 1986, p. 6.

71. *TBT*. "Tokyo Scandal." September 1986, p. 37.

72. Johnson, Chalmers. *op. cit.*, p. 6.

Chapter 3: The Death of Educational Democracy

1. *The Journal of Social and Political Ideas in Japan (JSPIJ)*, Vol. 1, No. 3. Appendix I. "Imperial Rescript on Education." December 1963, p. 122.

2. Yamasumi, Masami. "Educational democracy versus state con-

trol. Part One, Textbook Revision: the evolution of ultranationalistic textbooks," *Democracy in Contemporary Japan*. McCormack, Gavan, and Yoshio Sugimoto, eds. Hale and Iremonger. Sydney, Australia. 1986, p. 95.

3. *Ibid.*, p. 98.

4. Kanda, Kohei. *Five Most Pressing Tasks*. Nihonkoku Tokon Kyumu Gokaio No Koto. Tokyo. 1868.

5. Hearn, Lafcadio. *Japan: An Attempt at Interpretation*. Charles E. Tuttle Company. Tokyo. 1955, p. 420.

6. Karasawa, Tomitaro. "Changes in Japanese Education as Revealed in Textbooks," *Japan Quarterly (JQ)*, Vol. II, No. 3. July-September 1955, pp. 377-378.

7. Halliday, Jon. *A Political History of Japanese Capitalism*. Pantheon Books. New York. 1975, pp. 69-70.

8. Hoshino, Ai. "The Education of Women," in I. Nitobe, *Western Influence in Modern Japan*. University of Chicago Press. Chicago. 1931, p. 215.

9. Karasawa, Tomitaro. *op. cit.*, p. 379.

10. *Japan Advertiser*, editorial. "Students and Dangerous Thoughts." 17 January 1930, p. 4.

11. Araki, Sadao, General. "State and Education," *Contemporary Japan, A Review of Japanese Affairs*, Vol. VIII, No. 8. October 1939, p. 425.

12. *The New York Times*. 11 October 1948.

13. *Nippon Times*. 26 July 1949.

14. Morito, Tatsuo. "What Constitutes a Good Teacher?" Nihon Kyoiku No Kaiko To Tenbo, Kyoiku Shuppan KK. 1959, pp. 95-98, in *JSPIJ*, Vol. 1, No. 3. December 1963, p. 97.

15. Ito, Noboru. "The Reform of Japanese Education," *JQ*, Vol. 3, No. 4. 1956, p. 430.

16. Ball, MacMahon, British Commonwealth Representative on the Allied Council for Japan. "Japan Returns to the Past," *The Nation*. 27 March 1954, pp. 253-256.

17. Tsuji, Kiyaoki. "Toward Understanding the Teachers' Efficiency Rating System," *Seijo O. Kangaeru Shihyo*, Iwanami Shoten. 1960, pp. 156-174, cited in *JSPIJ*, Vol. 1, No. 3. December 1963, p. 51.

18. *Japan Times*. 11 July 1961.

19. Reischauer, Edwin O. *The United States and Japan*. Harvard University Press. Cambridge, Mass. 1957, p. 268.

20. Shigeki, Toyoma. "The Meiji Restoration and the Present Day," *Bulletin of Concerned Asian Scholars*, Vol. 2, No. 1. October 1969, p. 12.

21. *Japan Times Weekly (JTW)*. "Only 50% of High School Students Support Art." 23 May 1987.

22. Whymant, Robert, Tokyo Correspondent. "Japanese Gloss Over the War," *The Guardian*. 11 July 1982.

23. Yamazumi, Masami. *op. cit.*, p. 92.

24. *Ibid.*, p. 94.

25. Awanohara, Susumu. "The Buck Stops Here," *Far Eastern Economic Review (FEER)*. 21 August 1986, pp. 26-27.

26. For one of the first United States articles on the subject, see Robert Gomer, John W. Powell and Bert V.A. Roling. "Japan's biological weapons: 1930-1945," *The Bulletin of the Atomic Scientists*, Vol. 37, No. 8. October 1981, pp. 43-53. Also Tabata Masamuri. "Legacy of Lt. Gen. Ishii lives on – with U.S. help," *JTW*. 18 September 1982. "General Douglas A. MacArthur . . . [promised] . . . General Ishii immunity from prosecution if he would surrender the records of the 731st Unit."

27. *Ibid.*, also Ienaga, Saburo. *The Pacific War, 1931-1945: A Critical Perspective on Japan's Role in World War II*. Pantheon Books. New York. 1978, pp. 188-190. Professor Ienaga added a few new details about Unit 731 and described fatal vivisection experiments on downed American flyers at Kyushu Imperial University. Further reference is found in *JTW*, 10 April 1982, in Masanori Tabata. "Beyond the Nazis: Murder in the Name of War, Medical Science."

28. Yamazumi, Masami. *op. cit.*, p. 112.

29. Ienaga, Saburo. "The Historical Significance of the Japanese Textbook Lawsuit," *Bulletin of Concerned Asian Scholars*, Vol. 2, No. 4. Fall 1970, pp. 3-14.

30. Awanohara, Susumu. "No More Grovelling," *FEER*. 21 August 1986, pp. 26-27.

31. Kaplan, David E., and Alec Dubro. *op. cit.*, p. 82.

32. *Mainichi Shimbun*, Evening Edition. 17 December 1962.

33. *Asahi Evening News (AEN)*. "Sunugawa is Surveyed; Score Hurt – Police Resort to Violence." 13 September 1956.

34. Tsurumi, Kazuko. "Japan Before and After Defeat in World War II," *Social Change and the Individual*. Princeton University Press. Princeton, N.J. 1970, pp. 329-330.

35. *Mainichi Daily News (MDN)*. 26 February 1966.

36. Uno, Hisashi. "Here in Japan – Students Rebelling Against Fee Hike," *MDN*. 23 February 1966.

37. *Ibid.*

38. *MDN*. 26 February 1966.

39. Uno, Hisashi. *op. cit.*

40. *Japan Economic Journal*. 28 February 1987.

41. *AEN*. "Vox Populi, Vox Dei." 12 July 1968.

42. *Ibid.*, 14 July 1968.

43. McCormack, G., and J. Halliday. "The Student Left in Japan,

Mishima's Suicide," *New Left Review*, 65. January-February 1971, pp. 50-51.

44. *JTW*, editorial. 28 June 1970.

45. *Tokyo Business Today*. "Japan's Education." October 1986, p. 10.

Chapter 4: Money First, Merit Second

1. Yamazumi, Masami. "Educational democracy versus state control. Part One. Textbook Revision: the evolution of ultra-nationalistic text books," *Democracy in Contemporary Japan*. McCormack, Gavan, and Yoshio Sugimoto, eds. Hale and Iremonger. Sydney, Australia. 1986, p. 94.

2. *Asahi Evening News (AEN)*, quoting Leo Esaki, Japanese Nobel Prize Winner in Science, 2 July 1982.

3. *AEN*. "Vox Populi, Vox Dei." 4 December 1965.

4. Organization for Economic Co-operation and Development. *Social Sciences Policy – Japan*. Paris. 1977, p. 55.

5. Uchihashi, Katsuto. "Toward Methodology Innovation in Industry," *Japan Quarterly (JQ)*, Vol. XXXIV, No. 1. January-March 1987, p. 6.

6. *Ibid.*

7. Kokusai Tokei Yoran (International Statistics Manual), Prime Minister's Office. 1980; and *Facts and Figures of Japan*. Foreign Press Center. Tokyo. 1982, p. 88.

8. *Ioid.*, p. 94.

9. Cummings, William K. *Education and Equality in Japan*. Princeton University Press. Princeton, N.J. 1980, p. 214.

10. *AEN*. "Vox Populi, Vox Dei." 9 March 1979.

11. *Yomiuri Shimbun*, March 1984, reprinted in *Discussions on Educational Reform in Japan*. Reference Reading Series 15, Foreign Press Center. Japan. 1985, pp. 27-28.

12. Sato, Kinko. "The Schools vs. Juku: Why a Conflict? Children Go to Cram Schools Because Juku Meets Needs Ignored by Too 'Equalitarian' School System," *Japan Times Weekly (JTW)*, 10 March 1979.

13. Orihara, Hiroshi. "'Test Hell' and Alienation, a Study of Tokyo University Freshmen," *Journal of Social and Political Ideas in Japan (JSPIJ)*, Vol. V, No. 2-3. December 1967, p. 247.

14. Interview with author. Tokyo. April 1986.

15. *AEN*. 17 March 1980.

16. Interview with author. Tokyo. April 1986.

17. Iwai, Hiroaki. "Delinquent Groups and Organized Crime," in *Japanese Culture and Behavior, Selected Readings*. The University Press of Hawaii. Honolulu. 1974, p. 386.

18. *Asahi Journal.* 14 May 1982, p. 15, quoted in Yoshio Sugimoto's "The manipulative basis of 'consensus' in Japan," in *Democracy in Contemporary Japan. op. cit.*, p. 72.

19. *JTW*, editorial. "A Disturbing Social Trend." 10 January 1981.

20. *Daily Yomiuri.* 12 January 1981.

21. *Ibid.*, 27 January 1982.

22. *AEN.* "Vox Populi, Vox Dei." 12 March 1980.

23. *Ibid.*

24. *JTW.* "School Violence Becoming Biggest Social Problem – Stabbing at Junior High Sparks Debate." 5 March 1983.

25. Kuroda, Ryoichi. "Exam Hell Symbolizes Tournament Society." *Look Japan.* 10 April 1980.

26. Interview with author. Tokyo. April 1966.

27. Shimizu, Yoshihiro. "Entrance Examinations: A Challenge to Equal Opportunity in Education," *JSPIJ*, Vol. 1, No. 3. December 1963, p. 93.

28. *AEN.* "The High Cost of Education." 1 June 1982.

29. Buckley, Sandra, and Vera Mackie. "Women in the New Japanese State," *Democracy in Contemporary Japan, op. cit.*, p. 182.

30. Fujii, Harve. "In Search of Women's Independence: Education for Women, The Personal and Social Damage of Anachronistic Policy," *JQ*, Vol. XXIX, No. 3. July-September 1982, p. 305.

31. *Far Eastern Economic Review.* 13 March 1971, p. 13.

32. Buckley, Sandra, and Vera Mackie. *op. cit.*, p. 182.

33. Buckley, Sandra, and Vera Mackie. *op. cit.*, p. 182, citing Komano Yoko, *Kyoiku no ba de mirareru seisabetsu* (Sexual Discrimination in Education), Shiso no kagaku, No. 127. Tokyo. 1981, pp. 32-38.

34. *AEN.* "Vox Populi, Vox Dei." 22 January 1982.

35. *AEN*, editorial. "Private Schools," 19 January 1982.

36. *Japan Times (JT).* 8 July 1977.

37. *Ibid.*

38. *JT*, editorial. "The Medical College Scandal." 11 July 1977.

39. *The Yomiuri Shimbun*, editorial. "Training of Doctors." 16 May 1982.

40. Nagai, Michio. "The University and the Intellectual," *JQ*, Vol. XII, No. 1. January-March 1965, p. 49. Also, Organization for Economic Co-operation and Development. *Social Sciences Policy – Japan.* Paris. 1977, p. 50.

41. Tsurumi, Kazuko, "Japan Before and After Defeat in World War II." *Social Change and the Individual.* Princeton University Press. Princeton, N.J. 1970, p. 326.

42. *Ibid.*

43. Fukuda, Kanichi. "A Professor's View on University Education," *JSPIJ*, Vol. 5, No. 2-3. December 1967, p. 119.

44. *AEN.* 2 July 1982.

45. *Review of National Policies on Education.* Paris. 1971, pp. 83-84.

46. Matsushita, Konosuke. *Japan at the Brink.* Kodansha International. Tokyo. 1976, pp. 78-97.

47. Clark, Gregory. "Japan's Education," *Tokyo Business Today.* October 1986, p. 10.

48. Miyasaki, Kazuo. "Coping with a School-Conscious Society," *Japan Echo*, Vol. IX. 1982, *op. cit.*, pp. 63-64.

Chapter 5: Fabricated Traditions

1. Shoda, Heigoro, cited by Andrew Gordon in "Heavy Industry, 1875-1955," *The Evolution of Labor Relations in Japan.* Council on East Asian Studies, Harvard University. Cambridge, Mass. 1985, pp. 66-67.

2. *Ibid.*, p. 310-311.

3. Marshall, Byron K. *op. cit.*, pp. 46-47.

4. Gordon, Andrew. *The Evolution of Labor Relations in Japan, Heavy Industry, 1853-1955.* Council on East Asian Studies, Harvard University. Cambridge, Mass. 1985, pp. 66-67.

5. Sumiya, Mikio. *Kojoho taikei to roshi kankei* (The Factory Law System and Labor Relations in Japan), *Tokyo Daigaku Shuppan Kai.* 1977, p. 26, cited in Andrew Gordon, *ibid.*

6. *The Labor Movement in Japan.* Charles H. Kerr and Company Co-operative. 1918, pp. 36-38.

7. Gordon, Andrew. *op. cit.*, p. 116.

8. Kosaka, Masataka. *100 Million Japanese: The Post War Experience.* Kodansha International. Tokyo. 1972, pp. 68-69.

9. *Ibid.*

10. *Mainichi Shimbun.* 21 December 1945, cited in Kosaka, *Ibid.*

11. Honda, Shugo. *Monogatara Sengo Bungakushi.* Shinchosha. 1960, cited in Masataka Kosaka, *op. cit.*

12. Moore, Joe. "Production Control in Early Post War Japan," *Bulletin of Concerned Asian Scholars*, Vol. XVII, No. 4. 1985, p. 10.

13. Dower, J.W. *Empire and Aftermath: Yoshida Shigeru and the Japanese Experience, 1878-1954.* Harvard University Press. Cambridge, Mass. 1979, p. 333.

14. Kodama, Yoshio. *I Was Defeated.* Translated from the Japanese by Robert Booth and Taro Fukuda. An Asian Publication. 1951, p. 206.

15. Johnson, Chalmers. *Conspiracy at Matsukawa.* University of California Press. Berkeley. 1972, pp. 296-297.

16. *Ibid.*, p. 358. Also Correspondent Mark Gayne, writing 5 October 1946: "Where the Labor Division was talking in pious phrases

to Japanese union leaders, counter intelligence agents were breaking up labor demonstrations . . ." *Japan Diary*, p. 331.

17. *Nippon Times*, 4 April 1949.
18. Gordon, Andrew. "Retaking Control," *The Evolution of Labor Relations in Japan. op. cit.*, pp. 368-374.
19. Gordon. *op. cit.*, pp. 371-372.
20. Gordon. *op. cit.*, pp. 68-69.
21. Halberstam, David. *The Reckoning.* William Morrow and Company, Inc. New York. 1986, p. 163.
22. *Ibid.*, pp. 168-169.
23. *Ibid.*, pp. 183-185.
24. *Ibid.*, pp. 186-187.
25. Rohlen, Thomas P. *For Harmony and Strength: Japanese White Collar Organization in Anthropological Perspective.* University of California Press. Berkeley. 1974, pp. 177-178.
26. Dore, Ronald. *British Factory – Japanese Factory: The Origins of National Diversity in Industrial Relations.* University of California Press. Berkeley and Los Angeles. 1973, p. 163.
27. Muto, Ichiyo. "Class Struggle in Post War Japan," *Democracy in Contemporary Japan.* Gavan McCormack and Yoshio Sugimoto, eds. Hale and Iremonger. Sydney, Australia. 1986, p. 118.
28. Fukui Hoso Company Case. Central Labor Relations Commission. 5 March 1971, cited in Tadashi Hanami, *Labor Relations in Japan Today.* Kodansha International. Tokyo. 1979, pp. 190-191.
29. *Ibid.*
30. *Ibid.*, p. 148.
31. *Ibid.*, pp. 153-154.
32. Reischauer, Edwin O. *The Japanese.* Charles E. Tuttle. 1978, p. 154.
33. Kamata, Satoshi. *Japan in the Passing Lane.* Pantheon Books. New York. 1982, pp. 22-23.
34. Gordon, *op. cit.*, pp. 82-83.
35. Dore, Ronald. *op. cit.*, p. 239.
36. Economic Planning Agency, Japanese Government 1981. *In Search of a Good Quality of Life*, Annual Report on National Life, 1981, pp. 181-182; based on surveys carried out by the Public Relations Office, Prime Minister's Office.
37. Ohmae, Kenichi. *Beyond National Borders: Reflections on Japan and the World.* Dow Jones-Irwin. Homewood, Illinois. 1987, pp. 18-19.
38. National Assembly for Youth Development. *The Rising Generation in Japan '82.* Tokyo. 1982, pp. 10-11.
39. *Ibid.*
40. Tada, Michitaro: "The Glory and Misery of My Home," *Tokyo:*

Yomiuri Shimbunsha. 1971, translated by Robert Wargo in *Japan Interpreter*, Vol. 9, No. 1. Spring 1974, pp. 108-113.

41. Economic Planning Agency. "Public Opinion Survey on Job and Leisure." Prime Minister's Office. 1977, in *In Search of a Good Quality of Life. op. cit.*, pp. 181-184.

42. *Japan Economic Review.* "Overseas Ventures Increasing, Bankruptcies Rising." 15 February 1987, p. 5.

43. *Japan Economic Journal (JEJ).* 15 February 1987.

44. *Tokyo Business Today (TBT).* "Tragedies of an Economic Superpower." June 1987, pp. 27-28.

45. *Ibid.*

46. *Ibid.*, pp. 25-26.

47. *Industrial Safety and Health*, Japan Industrial Relations, Series 9. The Japan Institute of Labor. Tokyo. 1982, p. 31.

48. Halliday, Jon. *A Political History of Japanese Capitalism.* Pantheon Books. New York. 1975, pp. 220-221.

49. Keieishi, Henshushitu, cited in Gordon. *op. cit.*, p. 377.

50. *TBT.* "Business Briefs: Unions – Divided We Fall." July 1987, p. 8. Also see *JEJ.* "The Week." 25 July 1987, p. 2.

51. Muto, Ichiyo. *op. cit.*, pp. 114-119.

Chapter 6: Social Control

1. Orwell, George. *Nineteen Eighty-Four.* Secker and Warburg. London. 1949, p. 4.

2. Kamata, Satoshi. *Japan in the Passing Lane: An Insider's Account of Life in a Japanese Auto Factory.* Pantheon Books. New York. 1982, p. 11.

3. Muto, Ichiyo. *op. cit.*, p. 131; and David Halberstam. *The Reckoning.* William Morrow and Company Inc. New York. 1986, pp. 182 and 408-409.

4. Muto, Ichiyo. *Ibid.*, pp. 132-134.

5. *Facts and Figures of Japan.* Foreign Press Center. Tokyo. 1982, p. 69.

6. *Labor Statistics Manual.* Ministry of Labor. 1981. Notes: 1) Excluding retroactive pay and irregular bonuses; 2) Weighted average of wages for adult men and women, young people and part-time workers; 3) Excluding vacation and year-end bonuses.

7. *Japan Economic Journal (JEJ)*, No. 14. "Yen pushes up average salary but few Japanese feel richer." 1 November 1986, p. 32.

8. *Look Japan.* "Low Work Drive Among Japanese Youth – An Ominous Threat to Society." Tokyo. 10 June 1984, p. 28.

9. Kamata, Satoshi. *op. cit.*, pp. 13-14.

10. Muto, Ichiyo. *op. cit.*, p. 125.

11. *Ibid.*

12. Cited in Wolf, Marvin J. *The Japanese Conspiracy: A Stunning Analysis of the International Trade War*. New English Library. Kent, England. 1983, pp. 221-222.

13. Kamata, Satoshi. *op. cit.*, p. 131.

14. Roscoe, Bruce. "Life Time Employment?" *Far Eastern Economic Review*. 18 December 1986, p. 75.

15. Japan Committee for Economic Development (*Keizai Doyukai*). "Changing Labor Market and Corporate Activity," 1963, quoted by Kenichi Furuya in "Labor-Management Relations in Post War Japan, Their Reality and Change," *Japan Quarterly (JQ)*, Vol. XXVIII, No. 1. January-March 1980, p. 31.

16. Tsuda, Masumi. "The End of a Way of Life?" *JEJ*, Special Survey on Japanese Management. Summer 1988, pp. 10-11.

17. *JEJ*. "Wave of layoffs will greet workers after New Year break." 20 December 1986, pp. 1 and 22.

18. Interview with author. Tokyo. April 1986.

19. Roberts, John G. *Mitsui: Three Centuries of Japanese Business*. Weatherhill. New York and Tokyo. 1973, pp. 472-473.

20. *Ibid.*

21. *Asahi Evening News*. "Vox Populi, Vox Dei." 10 November 1965.

22. *Ibid.*

23. *Japan Times Weekly*. 4 June 1965.

24. Kawabata, Tai. "When 'Money First' is Motto, Mine Disasters No Surprise," *JTW*. 14 November 1981.

25. *Ibid.*

26. *Ibid.*

27. Gordon, Andrew. *The Evolution of Labor Relations in Japan, Heavy Industry, 1853-1955*. *op. cit.*, pp. 368-369.

28. Kamata, Satoshi. *op. cit.*, pp. 142-143.

29. Dore, Ronald. "Introduction" in Kamata, Satoshi. *op. cit.*, pp. xxxvi-xxxvii.

30. *Time*. 18 October 1971, pp. 60-61.

31. Itoh, Eichi. "Labor Control Through Small Groups," quoted in *Radical America*, Vol. 18, No. 2-3. Somerville, Mass. 1984, pp. 34-35.

32. Kurokawa, Nobuyuki. "Intelligent Buildings Rise in Tokyo," *JQ*. April-June 1986, Vol. XXXIII, No. 2. pp 154-158.

33. *Asahi Journal*. 14 May 1982, p. 15.

34. Kamata, Satoshi. *op. cit.*, pp. 80-87.

35. Muto, Ichiyo. *op. cit.*, p. 129.

36. *AMPO: Japan Asia Quarterly Review*. 15 December 1972.

37. *Ibid.*

38. Muto, Ichiyo. *op. cit.*, p. 131.

39. Muto, Ichiyo. *Ibid.*, p. 132.

40. Halberstam, David. *The Reckoning*. William Morrow and Co. Inc. New York. 1986, pp. 316-317.

41. Sekine, S. "The Almighty God – TQC," *Tokyo Business Today*. August 1986, p. 43.

42. Itoh, Eichi. *op. cit.*, p. 34.

43. Sekine, S. *op. cit.*

44. Itoh, Eichi. *op. cit.*, p. 28.

45. Cited in Wolf, Marvin J. *op. cit.*, p. 247.

46. Itoh, Eichi. *op. cit.*, p. 28.

47. *Summary of Actual Labor Market for Women, 1985, Ministry of Labor, August 1985*. Foreign Press Center. Japan. October 1985, pp. 18 and 19.

48. Cook, Alice H., and Hiroko Hagashi. *Working Women in Japan – Discrimination, Resistance and Reform*. Cornell University Press. Ithaca, N.Y. 1980, p. 39.

49. Prime Minister's Office. *Outline of Survey Results Concerning Women's Participation in Decision-Making Process*. Foreign Press Center. Tokyo. 1979, p. 2.

50. *JEJ*. "Statistics from Management and Co-ordination Agency." 13 September 1986, p. 20.

51. Kaji, Etsuko. "'The Invisible Proletariat': Working Women in Japan," *AMPO: Japan Asia Quarterly Review*. Autumn 1973, pp. 50-61.

52. *Japan Times*, editorial. "Looking Behind the Facade." 17 March 1970, p. 16.

53. *Ibid.*

54. *Summary of Actual Labor Market for Women, 1985. op. cit.*

55. de Bary, Brett. "Sanya: Japan's Internal Colony," *The Other Japan*. E. Patricia Tsurumi, ed. M.E. Sharpe, Publishers. London. 1988, p. 115.

56. *Ibid.*

Chapter 7: Rich Country, Poor People

1. Inaba, Hidezo. "Is Good Life Beyond Reach of Japanese?" *Japan Times Weekly (JTW)*. 6 June 1987.

2. Kishida, Hiroshi, company employee, Urawa City, Saitama Prefecture, in "Japan: Hows and Whys," *Japanese Economic Journal (JEJ)*. 8 August 1987, p. 10.

3. *Tokyo Business Today (TBT)*. "Japan: The Top 300." June 1988, p. 25.

4. Namai, Toshishige. *TBT*, editorial. May 1987, p. 5.

5. *TBT*, "Japan's Billionaires." October 1987, pp. 16-17.

6. Organization for Economic Co-operation and Development

(OECD). Statistics cited in Fallows, James. "Japan: Playing by Different Rules," *The Atlantic*, Vol. 260, No. 3. September 1987, pp. 27-28.

7. *Ibid.*

8. Cited in Huddle, Norie, and Michael Reich with Nahum Stiksen. *Island of Dreams: Environmental Crisis in Japan.* Autumn Press. New York. 1975, p. 78.

9. *Asahi Shimbun.* 14 September 1964.

10. Clark, Gregory. "Japanese Agriculture: Who's Fooling Whom?" *TBT.* December 1986, p. 12.

11. Ishizuka, Masahiko. "Disgruntled Taxpayers," *JEJ.* 15 November 1986, p. 16.

12. *Japan Economic Review.* 15 November 1986, p. 4.

13. McCormack, Gavan, and Yoshio Sugimoto, eds. *op. cit.*, p. 15.

14. Ishizuka, Masahiko. "Ohtemachi Diary – Rich Country, Poor People," *JEJ*, 13 June 1987, p. 6.

15. *TBT.* "A New Tokyo in the Making." May 1987, p. 15.

16. *TBT. Ibid.*, p. 17.

17. *JTW*, editorials. "Down-to-Earth Land Prices." 6 June 1987, p. 12.

18. Rudnisky, Howard, Allan Aloan and Peter Fuhrmen. "The Land of the Rising Stocks," *Forbes.* 18 May 1987, p. 141.

19. *Japan Echo.* "A Prescription for Japan's Housing Malady." Vol. XIII, No. 2. In JAPEC Group. 1986, p. 18.

20. Sato, Mikio. "Housing – The Most Backward Aspect of an 'Economic Superpower,'" *Japan Quarterly*, Vol. XXVIII, No. 2. April-June 1981, p. 231.

21. *Asahi Evening News (AEN).* "The Impossible Dream: Vox Populi, Vox Dei." 3 April 1980.

22. Economic Planning Agency. *1981 Public Opinion Poll on Standard of Living.* Foreign Press Center. Tokyo. November 1981, p. 19.

23. Kumindo, Kusako, General Manager, Business Development Division, The Long Term Credit Bank of Japan. "Tokyo Housing Offers a Total Life Style, What Homes Lack in Space More than Compensated by Array of Services, Facilities Available," *JTW.* 25 November 1978.

24. Nakagawa, Yatsuhiro. "Japan, the Welfare Super-Power," *Journal of Japanese Studies (JJS)*, Vol. 5, No. 1. Winter 1979, p. 12.

25. Sekimoto, Tadhiro, President, NEC Corporation, quoted in "Japan: Hows and Whys," *JEJ.* 4 July 1987, p. 8.

26. Jutaku sangyo handobukku (Housing Industry Handbook). Housing Information Service, 1985. *Facts and Figures of Japan.* Foreign Press Center. Tokyo. 1985, p. 110.

27. *AEN.* "Family Day." 1 February 1980.

28. *JEJ*. 13 September 1986.

29. *Ibid.*, 20 December 1986.

30. Plath, David. "Ecstasy Years – Old Age in Japan," *Pacific Affairs*, Vol. 46, No. 3. Fall 1973, p. 422.

31. Pons, Philippe. "Bleak Prospects Face Japan's Aging Population," *Manchester Guardian Weekly*. 8 February 1987, p. 13.

32. Pepper, Anne G. "Silver Columbus: Not Every Cloud Has a Silver Lining." *Business Japan*. March 1987, p. 11.

33. Nakagawa. *op. cit.*

34. *Ibid.*, pp. 20 and 22.

35. *JEJ*, poll by Nikkei Industry Research Institute. 30 August 1986, p. 4.

36. Economic Planning Agency. "New Undercurrents in People's Livelihood," *White Paper on National Life*. Japanese Government. 1976, p. 1.

37. OECD. "Measuring Employment and Unemployment." Paris. 1979, pp. 154-155.

38. *Facts and Figures of Japan*. Foreign Press Center. Tokyo. 1987, p. 74.

39. Niki, Riki (a housewife and clerical worker), Kasuga City, Aichi Prefecture, cited in "Japan: Hows and Whys," *JEJ*. 4 July 1987, pp. 8-9.

40. Inaba, Hidezo. "Is Good Life Beyond Reach of Japanese?" Article translated from the "Seiron" column of the *Sankei Shimbun*. Quoted in *JTW*. 6 June 1987, p. 4.

41. *JEJ*. "Government Public Opinion Poll on Living Conditions Brings Mixed Results, 'Middle Class Feeling' Losing Ground." 15 December 1986, p. 5.

42. Ishizuka, Masahiko. *op. cit.*, 13 June 1987, p. 6.

43. Inoguchi, Kuniko. "Prosperity Without Amenities," *JJS*, Vol. 13, No. 1. Winter 1987, p. 126.

44. Maekawa, Hiroshi. Interviewed in "Japan: Hows and Whys," *JEJ*. 8 August 1987, p. 10.

Chapter 8: Society's Shadows

1. Igarashi, Futaba. "Forced to Confess." Translated and with explanatory notes by Gavan McCormack, in *Democracy in Contemporary Japan*. McCormack, Gavan, and Yoshio Sugimoto, eds. Hale and Iremonger. Sydney, Australia. 1986, p. 95.

2. Huddle, Norie, and Michael Reich with Nahum Striskin. *Island of Dreams: Environmental Crisis in Japan*. Autumn Press. Tokyo. 1975, p. 25.

3. Igarashi, Futaba. *op. cit.*, p. 195-199.

4. Johnson, Chalmers. *Conspiracy at Matsukawa*. University of California Press. Berkeley, Los Angeles, London. 1972, pp. 150-151.

5. Shapiro, Margaret. "Group Psychology Leaves the Japanese Criminal Out on a Limb," *Manchester Guardian Weekly (MGW)*. 11 October 1987, p. 17.

6. Whymant, Robert. "Police in Japan readily use force say lawyers," *Age*. 7 March 1984, quoted in Gavan McCormack, "Crime, confession, and control," *Democracy in Contemporary Japan, op. cit.*, p. 187.

7. Igarashi, Futaba. *op. cit.*, pp. 197-199.

8. *Ibid.*, pp. 201-202.

9. *Japan Advertiser*. 9 April 1930.

10. Johnson, Chalmers. *op. cit.*

11. *Japan Times Weekly (JTW) Overseas Edition*, editorial. "A New Police Reform." 28 November 1987.

12. Buraku Liberation Research Institute. *Long-Suffering Brothers and Sisters, Unite!* Buraku Kaiho Kenkyusho. Osaka. 1981, pp. 39-47.

13. Igarashi, Futaba. *op. cit.*, p. 214.

14. Weatherall, William. "Mentally ill shunted behind locked doors," *Far Eastern Economic Review (FEER)*. 13 August 1987, pp. 36-37.

15. *Ibid.*

16. *Japan Economic Journal*. 19 July 1986.

17. Kelley, Donald R., Kenneth R. Stunkel and Richard R. Westcott. *The Economic Superpowers and the Environment*. W.H. Freeman. San Francisco. 1976, p. 184.

18. Hidaka, Rokuro, *The Price of Affluence: Dilemmas of Contemporary Japan*. Penguin Books. Australia. 1985, p. 160.

19. McKean, Margaret A. *Environmental Protest and Citizen Politics in Japan*. University of California Press. Berkeley. 1981, p. 51.

20. *Japan Times (JT)*. 28 June 1973.

21. Gunnarsson, Bo. Quoted in David E. Kaplan and Alec Dubro. *YAKUZA*. Addison-Wesley Publishing Company Inc. Reading, Mass. 1986, p. 177.

22. Thurston, Donald R. "Aftermath in Minamata," *Japan Interpreter*, Vol. 9, No. 1. Spring 1974, pp. 25-26.

23. Huddle, Norie. *op. cit.*, p. 130.

24. *JT*, editorial. "Not Pollution – But Murder." 20 November 1970.

25. Huddle, Norie. *op. cit.*, pp. 75-76.

26. Kelley, Donald R. *op. cit.*, p. 265.

27. "Resolution adopted at the 31st Regular General Meeting of Keidanren (Federation of Economic Organizations)," released 25 May 1970, in John G. Roberts. *Mitsui: Three Centuries of Japanese Business*. Weatherhill. New York. 1973, p. 496.

28. *Asahi Evening News (AEN)*. "Vox Populi, Vox Dei." 2 March 1966.

29. *JT*, editorial. 9 August 1970.

30. *Japan Quarterly (JQ)*. "Pollution Irresponsibility," Vol. XXIII, No. 1. January-March 1976, p. 3.

31. Halliday, Jon. *A Political History of Japanese Capitalism*. Pantheon Books. New York, 1975, p. 267.

32. *White Paper on the Environment*. Environment Agency. The Japan Institute of International Affairs. Tokyo. 1984.

33. Whymant, Robert. "Japanese Battle Pollution from Politics and Skies," *The Guardian*. 28 March 1983.

34. Martineau, Lisa. "Race Apart," *MGW*. 11 October 1987.

35. *Ibid*.

36. *Ibid*.

37. *JTW*. 18 October 1986.

38. Dower, John W. *War Without Mercy, Peace and Power in the Pacific War*. Pantheon Books. New York. 1986, p. 15.

39. McCormack, Gavan, and Yoshio Sugimoto. "Introduction – Democracy and Japan," *Democracy in Contemporary Japan*, *op. cit.*, p. 15.

40. Wetherall, William. "Japan in the grip of alien finger printing row," *FEER*. 9 July 1987, pp. 48-50.

41. *Ibid.*, p. 50.

42. *Ibid.*, p. 49.

43. Mizuno, Takaaki. "*Ainu*: The Invisible Minority," *JQ*, Vol. XXXIV, No. 2. April-June 1987, p. 146.

44. *Ibid*.

45. *Ibid.*, pp. 143-148.

46. Mizuno, Takaaki. *op. cit.*

47. Murakoshi, Sueo. "A Note on the Law on Special Measures for Dowa Projects," in Buraku Liberation Research Institute. *Long-Suffering Brothers and Sisters, Unite!* Buraku Kaiho Kenkyusho. Osaka. 1981, p. 29.

48. *Ibid.*, pp. 50-59.

49. Murakoshi, Sueo. *op. cit.*, p. 35.

50. *Ibid*.

51. Buraku Liberation Research Institute. *op. cit.*, pp. 52-53.

52. Kaplan, David E., and Alec Dubro. *YAKUZA*. Addison-Wesley Publishing Company Inc. Reading, Mass. 1986, p. 20.

53. Shaplan, Robert. "Annals of Crime (Lockheed in Japan), Part III," *The New Yorker*, 30 January 1978, pp. 84-85.

54. *Time*. 26 August 1974.

55. Kaplan, David E. *op. cit.*, p. 121.

56. *Ibid.*, pp. 117-118.

57. *AEN*, editorial. 27 September 1967.

58. Kaplan, David E., and Alec Dubro. *op. cit.*, pp. 158-159.

59. Tanako, H. "Tokyo Scandal," *Tokyo Business Today*. October 1986, p. 57.

60. *Ibid.*

61. *JT*, 2 and 4 June 1971; *AEN*, 4 June 1971. The assault on a U.S. photographer was reported in *AEN*, 10 April 1947.

62. *JTW*. 9 June 1973, p. 10.

63. *AEN*, editorial. 3 February 1966, p. 4.

Chapter 9: Pandora's Box

1. Butow, R.J.C. *Tojo and the Coming War*. Stanford University Press. Stanford, Calif. 1961, p. 536.

2. *Japan Quarterly (JQ)*, Vol. XXXI, No. 2. April-June 1984, p. 143.

3. *Asahi Shimbun*. 18 June 1980, quoted in Radha Sinha. *Japan's Options for the 1980's*. Croom Helm. London. 1982, pp. 208-209.

4. Cassells, Alan. *Fascism*. Crowell. New York. 1975, p. 60.

5. Shibayama, Shigehisa. "The Union of 5.6M workers brings new labor era," *Japan Economic Journal (JEJ)*. 7 November 1987, p. 28.

6. *Ibid.*

7. Odawara, Atsushi. "The Conservative Dual Mind," *JQ*. April-June 1987, p. 161.

8. Hamada, Takujiro. "Spiritual vs. Material," *Tokyo Business Today (TBT)*. January 1987, p. 64.

9. Pyle, Kenneth B. "In Pursuit of a Grand Design: Nakasone Betwixt the Past and the Future," *Journal of Japanese Studies*, Vol. 13, No. 2. Summer 1987, pp. 264-265.

10. *TBT*. "Anti-American Feeling Germinating," October 1986, p. 13.

11. Miyachi, Soshichi. "The Dangerous Tide of 'Soap Nationalism,'" *Japan Echo*, Vol. XIV, No. 1. Spring 1987, p. 51.

12. Hamilton, Adrian. "Japan: The New Nationalism – 'No Longer in Mood to Apologize for Past,'" *Observer*. London. Reprinted in *Asahi Evening News*. 27 June 1987, p. 7.

13. Sayle, Murray. "The Ballad of Ron and Yasu," *New Republic*. 15 June 1987, p. 21.

14. *Ibid.*

15. McCormack, Gavan. "Beyond Economism: Japan in a State of Transition," *Democracy in Contemporary Japan. op. cit.*, p. 58.

16. Nishikawa, Jun. "Military Growth, Economic Growth and Human Rights," *UNESCO*, 1983. Paris Conference, 28-30 October 1982, pp. 1-9.

17. Masuzoe, Yoichi. "Reassessing Japan's Defense," *Look Japan (LJ)*. 10 November 1986, pp. 2-3.

18. Cited by Nigel Holloway, "Directing shadow plays," *Far Eastern Economic Review (FEER)*. 10 September 1987, p. 36.

19. Nishihara, Masashi. "The Japanese Central Organization of De-

fense," in *Central Organizations of Defense*. Edmonds, M., ed. Francis Pinter. London. 1985, p. 20. Also in Malcolm McIntosh. *Japan Re-Armed*. Francis Pinter. London. 1986, pp. 44-45.

20. Doerr, P.I. "Japan: Keeping the Balance." From U.S. Naval Institute Proceedings. Washington, D.C. August 1985, p. 39.

21. Chuma, Kiyofuka. "What Price the Defense of Japan?" *JQ*, Vol. XXXIV, No. 3. July-September 1987, p. 258.

22. McIntosh, Malcolm, *Japan Re-Armed*. Francis Pinter. London. 1986, p. 73.

23. *Japan Times (JT)*. "Soviet Threat Exaggerated," 15 September 1981. Quoted in McCormack, Gavan, *op. cit.*

24. Pyle, Kenneth B. *op. cit.*, pp. 269-270.

25. Koboniwa, Kaichiro. "Conservative politicians warn of declining civilian control," *JEJ*. 23 November 1985, p. 6.

26. *Ibid.*

27. *TBT*. "Anti-American Feeling Germinating?" October 1986, p. 13.

28. Ishizuka, Masahiko. "Ohtemachi Diary: Stepping on Tiger's Tail," *JEJ*. 11 July 1987, p. 6.

29. Takano H., editor of *Insider*. "Tokyo Scandal," *TBT*. July 1987, p. 44.

30. *Mainichi Shimbun*. 26 July 1980, pp. 1-2, as quoted in Radha Sinha, *op. cit.*, p. 205.

31. Ohmae, Kenichi. *Beyond National Borders – Reflection on Japan and the World*. Dow Jones-Irwin. Homewood, Illinois. 1987, p. 19.

32. *Ibid.*, p. 59.

33. *JEJ*. "Analysis." 4 April 1987, p. 6.

34. *Ibid.*

35. Abegglen, James C. *op. cit.*, p. 6.

36. Miyachi, Soshichi. *op. cit.*, pp. 52-53.

37. Ishizuka, Masahiko. "Danger from America," *JEJ*. 14 September 1985, p. 6.

38. *JEJ*. 13 June 1986, p. 6.

39. *Business Week*. "Tainted Tobacco Could Poison Hot Market." 15 June 1987, pp. 45-46.

40. Abegglen, James C. "Speak up," *TBT*. November 1987, p. 6.

41. *Ibid.*

42. Abegglen, James C. "Alliance," *TBT*. September 1987, p. 6.

43. Tanaka, Okiko. "Reactions to Retaliation," *LJ*. August 1987, p. 15.

44. *Ibid.*

45. *Ibid.*

46. *JEJ*. 24 October 1987, p. 1.

47. *The Economist (E)*. "All that's left." 28 November-4 December 1987, p. 38.

48. *Japan Times Weekly (JTW)*. "*Rengo* assumes top spot in labor group hierarchy," 5 December 1987.

49. From an April 1981 conference on Administrative Reform sponsored by *Domei*, the right-wing labour federation.

50. McCormack, Gavan. "Beyond Economism: Japan in a state of transition," in *Democracy in Contemporary Japan. op. cit.*, pp. 52-55.

51. Shindo, Maneyuki. Cited in Akahiko Tanaka. "A New Political Framework?" *LJ*. September 1987, p. 13.

52. *Ibid*.

53. Radha Sinha. *op. cit.*, pp. 248-249.

54. *Ibid*.

55. Kitamatsu, Katsuro. "Takeshita unlikely to revamp policy," *JEJ*. 14 November 1987, p. 1.

56. Pyle, Kenneth B. *op. cit.*, p. 270.

57. Sasaki, Takeshi. "Foreign pressure needed to reform Japanese politics," *JEJ*. 24 October 1987, p. 26.

58. *JT* (Weekly Overseas Edition), editorial. "Rough Seas Ahead for Mr. Takeshita." 21 November 1987.

59. Holloway, Nigel. "Flying Into the Future," *FEER*. 10 September 1987, p. 37.

60. Nakatani, Iwao. "Takeshita's task is to inspire spirit of national idealism," *JEJ*. 24 October 1987, p. 24.

61. Ito, Shinji. "Nakasone Cabinet at center of Recruit Scandal: JSP paper," *JTW*. 26 November 1988, p. 2.

62. Kusaoi, Akiko. "Cancellation of events tied to fear of standing out," *JTW* (Weekly Overseas Edition). 5 November 1988.

63. McGill, Peter. "God or Man," *The Observer*, 25 September 1988.

64. Simons, Lewis. "Seoul-style democracy," *The Ottawa Citizen*. 3 December 1988.

INDEX

Marshall, Gen. George C. 14
Marubeni Corporation 47-48,
   237
Marunouchi (Tokyo) 182
Masuda, Takashi 122
Masuda, Tatsuo 132-33
Matsuda (Education Minister)
   83
Matsukawa 129, 134, 206
Matsuno, Raizo 54, 248
Matsushita Electric Industrial
   Corporation 119, 164-65,
   169-70, 192
Matsushita, Konosuke 119, 164
Mazda Corporation 42, 139
McCarthy, Sen. Joseph 19
McDonnell-Douglas
   Corporation 54
Meany, George 141
Meiji Centennial (1967) 76
Meiji Constitution 3-4, 80
Meiji Restoration 1-5, 16, 65-
   67, 76, 118-19, 121;
   education system 65
Menda, Sakai 206-7
Mental Health Law 208
mentally ill 207-8
Miike mine 160-61
Miki, Kiyoshi 12
Miki, Takeo 33, 45-46, 48,
   50-51, 56, 74, 266
militarism 12, 20, 62, 66, 69,
   78, 244
military 4-9 *passim*, 18, 23,
   66, 91-92, 246-47, 249
Minamata 211-14, 237
Ministry of Agriculture,
   Forestry and Fisheries 37,
   181, 210, 216
Ministry of Construction 210
Ministry of Education 66, 70,
   76, 80-84 *passim*, 94, 109,
   120
Ministry of Finance 24, 28
Ministry of Health and Welfare

208, 210, 212-14
Ministry of International Trade
   and Industry (MITI) 24-25,
   28, 35, 40, 52, 162, 194,
   210, 212-14, 243
Ministry of Labour 147-48,
   150, 159
Ministry of Posts and
   Communications 134
Ministry of Transport 233
Minobe, Ryokichi 218-19
minorities, treatment of 224;
   see also *Ainu, Burakumin,*
   Chinese, Koreans,
   Taiwanese, discrimination
Minseito 4
Mishima 216-17
Mishima Improvement
   Association 216
Mitsubishi Corporation 4, 42,
   121-22, 146, 182, 189
Mitsui Corporation, 4, 7, 26,
   122, 146, 160-61, 182, 189,
   215-16
Miyake Island 247
Miyazawa, Kiichi 265
Monet, Claude 236
Moral Reform League 51
Motor Boat Racing Association
   233
Mount Fuji 218

Nada High School (Kobe) 103
Nadao, Hirokichi 33
Nagasaki Prefecture 229
Nagoya University 107
Nakagawa, Yatsuhiro 187, 195
Nakasone faction 40, 58-59,
   81, 261
Nakasone, Yasuhiro 32, 40-41,
   46, 53-54, 57-63 *passim*,
   91, 101-2, 120, 208, 223,
   228, 233-34, 241-43, 246,
   248-49, 251, 257, 260, 263-
   65

92, 203-7, 233-36
pollution 45, 179, 209-21
    passim
Pollution Diet 218
Pollution-Related Health
    Damage Compensation Law
    220
Popular Rights Movement
population 209
Portugal 1, 64
press, relations with govern-
    ment 44, 46, 56; see also
    kishi clubs
Prison Act 207
Progressive Party 12
Public Employees' Union 73
Public Offices Election Law 53
Public Peace Preservation Law
    12
Public Safety Investigating
    Agency 76
Purge Program 20

Quality Control Circles 167-68

Reagan, Ronald 58, 60
real estate values 182-83, 236
rearmament 11, 60, 77, 242,
    245-47, 249, 252
Recruit Company 265-66
Reischauer, Dr. Edwin O. 76
Rengo (Japanese Private Sector
    Trade Confederation) 241,
    260
retirement 158-60, 173, 192
Ribbentrop, Joachim von 14
Rokkasho 41
ronin 108
Russia 66
Russian Revolution 124
Russo-Japanese War 5, 66

Saipan 9
Saitama Medical College 112
Sampo 125, 128, 141

samurai 1, 3, 5, 121, 229
Sanbetsu 141
Sanken (Industrial Relations
    Study Council) 27-28
Sanrizuka 209-10
Sanwa 146
Sanyo Electric 169-70
Sasakawa, Ryoichi 233
Sasaki, Kichinosuke 178
Sato, Eisaku 33, 36-38, 90
Sato, Kinko 98
Sawia-Oji District (Izumi City)
    228
SCAP, see Supreme Command
    for Allied Powers
Seclusion 1, 64
Seicho-no-Iye 62
Seiyukai 4
Self-Defence Forces, see
    military
Shiba, Kimpei 30, 34
Shibushi Bay 41
Shidehara, Kijoro 11
Shimada, Kenichi 212-13
Shindo, Muneyuki 261
Shintoism 13, 62, 66, 69, 244,
    261, 266
Shioji, Ichiro 132-33
Shiseido Corporation 42
Shoda, Heigoro 121-22
Showa Denko Company 18,
    40, 213-14
Shukyo Seijo Kenkyukai 62
Shunto 142-43
'Silver Columbus' 194
Sino-Japanese War 78, 81, 125
Smoot-Hawley Tariff 7
Social Democratic Party 17
social programs 195-97, 199
Socialist Party 12, 16-18, 42,
    56, 60, 71, 110, 123, 142,
    144, 172, 218, 251-52, 260,
    266
Sohyo 141-44, 241, 260; see
    also enterprise unions

Other current New Star titles

NUCLEAR EMPIRE by *Robert C. Aldridge* An overview of current Pentagon nuclear war-fighting capabilities and plans, *Nuclear Empire* covers topics from the doctrine of 'Flexible Response' in Europe to the nuclear arms buildup in the Pacific and Indian Oceans, and brings the reader up to date on the latest technological changes in 'Star Wars', military computing, and navigational equipment.
160 pages.   **$11.95 Cdn/$9.95 U.S.**

BUDDY'S Meditations on Desire by *Stan Persky*. A frank and engaging portrayal – part fiction, part autobiography, part social criticism – of gay life and culture in the late eighties. 134 pages, hardcover   **$19.95 Cdn./$16.95 U.S.**

TAXI! A Novel by *Helen Potrebenko* Shannon drives a cab in Vancouver. She drives drunks around Skid Road, takes oil executives out to the airport, and encounters the grinding despair of urban poverty in the midst of upper-class apathy and self-satisfaction. An uncompromising portrait of life in the late twentieth century, spiced with black humour and vivid writing. 160 pages   **$11.95 Cdn./$9.95 U.S.**

SHRINK RESISTANT The Struggle Against Psychiatry in Canada Edited by *Bonnie Burstow and Don Weitz*. Through interviews, journal entries, poetry, graphics, and personal narratives, 40 current and former psychiatric inmates relate their experiences inside the walls of mental hospitals and at the hands of psychiatrists. 360 pages.   **$11.95**

LIBERTIES edited by *John Russell*. 17 pieces that sum up 25 years of activism by the British Columbia Civil Liberties Association in such issues as pornography and censorship, prostitution, drugs, hate literature laws, police powers, capital punishment, and AIDS testing. 240 pages   **$14.95 Cdn/$12.95 U.S.**

A PEOPLE IN ARMS by *Marie Jakober*. A dramatic novel of love and revolution, set in Nicaragua. Continues the story begun in her 1985 novel, *Sandinista*.
303 pages.   **$9.95**

NO WAY TO LIVE Poor Women Speak Out by *Sheila Baxter*. Fifty women talk about their poverty. Includes statistical information on poverty and women, as well as a directory of anti-poverty and women's groups in Canada. 231 pages.   **$9.95**

FREE TRADE AND THE NEW RIGHT AGENDA by *John W. Warnock*. The Free Trade Agreement and how it fits into business's response to the crisis in the world's capitalist economies since the 1970's. 324 pages.   **$11.95**

To order, send cheque or money order to New Star Books Ltd. Price shown includes shipping & handling.

For a free catalogue containing a complete list of New Star titles, write to the address below:

New Star Books Ltd.
2504 York Avenue
Vancouver, B.C.
CANADA V6K 1E3